Who is Jesus?

Studies on Personalities of the New Testament
D. Moody Smith, Series Editor

Who is Jesus?

History in Perfect Tense

LEANDER E. KECK

UNIVERSITY OF SOUTH CAROLINA PRESS

© 2000 University of South Carolina

Published in Columbia, South Carolina, by the
University of South Carolina Press

Manufactured in the United States of America

04   03   02   01   00   5   4   3   2   1

Library of Congress Cataloging-in-Publication Data

Keck, Leander E.
  Who is Jesus? : history in perfect tense / Leander E. Keck
      p. cm. — (Studies on personalities of the New Testament)
    Includes bibliographical references and index.
    ISBN 1-57003-338-2 (alk. paper)
    1. Jesus Christ—Historicity. I. Title. II. Series.
  BT303.2 .K435 2000
  232.9'08—dc21   99-050778

For J. Louis Martyn
In gratitude for fifty years of friendship

Contents

Preface

This book has a history. It began as a response to an invitation from Luther Seminary in Saint Paul to give three lectures on the topic "Who Is Jesus?" at the Midwinter Convocation in January 1995. These lectures—now expanded into chapters 2, 4, and 5—were then modified and presented as the Clark Lectures at Duke Divinity School in March of the same year. Subsequently they were revised again and given in March 1997 as the Nadine Beacham and Carlton F. Hall Sr. Lectures at the University of South Carolina, and at Mepkin Abbey. During preparation of the material for publication the originally brief introduction was expanded into chapter 1; the first lecture was revised and presented as "Jesus the Jew" at the College of Charleston in March 1998 and is now incorporated into chapter 2. Chapter 3 was written for inclusion in the book and adds a necessary dimension to the discussion. Even so, the title's question is answered but partly—though a comprehensive answer is surely without apparent bounds. In any case, these essays represent continuing reflection on the ongoing significance of the historical figure of Jesus.

In one way or other the historical figure of Jesus has been a recurring theme of my work, beginning with my dissertation on the Gnostic use of the life of Jesus submitted at Yale in 1957. Since the historical study of Jesus itself has a fascinating history, I developed the Lives of Jesus series (eight volumes), in which important works were made available again. In *A Future for the Historical Jesus* I proposed, in response to Rudolf Bultmann, that the Jesus of history is important for both preaching and theology. Subsequently I began a study of New Testament Christology (which I still plan to complete). While attending to the letters of Paul, I followed the recent resurgence of interest in the Jesus of history, though I have not participated in the Jesus Seminar. The lectures, here supplemented and amplified, provided a welcome opportunity to resume work on Jesus and the gospels.

The precipitating invitation made it clear that what was desired was not one more answer to the question Who *was* Jesus? Nonetheless, it would be risky indeed to say who he is without reference to who he was. While I have eschewed providing even a sketch of Jesus' life and times, answering the question Who *is* Jesus? requires attending, at least briefly, to what can and cannot be known historically about Jesus of Nazareth. The result is something of a hybrid, neither history nor Christology proper but rather theological reflection on history—on those aspects of the Jesus of history that are central to his continuing significance.

Although a script for a lecture differs markedly from a text to be read silently, I have tried to retain something of the oral style because it requires focusing on the subject matter without engaging and assessing at every point the vast scholarly literature. The notes, which could easily have been expanded, cite mostly works in English that might be accessible to most North American readers.

That such a manuscript would be accepted into a distinguished academic series marked by full documentation is due to the persistence of the series editor, Professor D. Moody Smith; the warm encouragement of Catherine Fry, director of the University of South Carolina Press; and the patience of Barry Blose, acquisitions editor at the press. Each of them elicits my abiding gratitude, as does George Parsenios, without whose help the manuscript might still be lodged in the computer. I am especially grateful to Luther Seminary and its president, David Tiede, for the invitation that generated these essays; to Duke Divinity School and its (then) dean, Dennis Campbell; to the Hall Lectureship, administered by Professor Donald L. Jones, for the opportunity to present the Hall Lectures; and to Professor Richard Bodek's invitation to give two lectures for the Jewish Studies Program at the College of Charleston. Above all, I want to record my gratitude for the gracious hospitality extended on each of these occasions, especially that shown at the University of South Carolina by President John M. Palms, Professor Jones, and Mrs. Carlton F. Hall and her son Carlton F. Hall Jr., and by Abbot Francis Kline at Mepkin Abbey.

Who is Jesus?

CHAPTER ONE

The Presence of the Past

Who is Jesus? The question seems simple and straightforward. But the answer is complex and subtle because it concerns the present identity of a person who lived in the ever more distant past. Whereas the question Who *was* Jesus? requests information that would identify him in his own time and place by referring to his date and place of birth, parents, occupation, social status, and time of death, asking Who *is* Jesus? signals an interest in his current identity. And that question is not as simple and straightforward as it may seem at first.

The subtitle of this book—History in Perfect Tense—serves as a metaphor for what is in view. The ancient Greeks used the perfect tense of a verb to distinguish the ongoing import of completed action from its sheer occurrence in the past, for which they used the aorist tense, usually translated as the simple past tense. There are traces of this distinction even in English usage. "The door was opened" asserts that a past action caused the door to be no longer shut, though it might have been closed later. "The door is opened," on the other hand, asserts that it still remains open as the result of past action. Similarly, then, to speak of history in perfect tense is to consider the ongoingness of something from the past, namely Jesus. In short, the question before us concerns the "isness" of the Jesus who was.

Such an undertaking requires a double focus, for it is precisely the concern for the perfect tense that makes attention to the past necessary. It is the perfect tense of Jesus that precludes transforming him into a timeless symbol, the name for a Christ figure, an imaginary construct. Likewise, it is the clear historical referent that precludes regarding Jesus as the name of an ever-recurring myth, for the gospels narrate what happened only once. Jesus is not born every Christmas; he does not die every Good Friday or rise from the dead every Easter. The past tense of Jesus is not replaced by perpetually recurring meanings but rather is carried forward by them and to some extent is renewed and transfigured by them.

The ongoing meaning—the perfect tense—of Jesus can be pursued in either a broad or a narrow sense. Adopting the former would allow one to trace the continuing influence of Jesus in the religious and cultural history of the West and in other parts of the world as well. Such an effort would set us to answering the question Who is Jesus? by detecting and delineating his ongoing role as the subject celebrated in literature and the arts and as the inspirer of diverse activities in medicine, politics, economics, social reform, and revolution. One could also indicate what role he might have played had circumstances been different or his interpreters more imaginative and his followers more resolute. This would require descriptive historical and cultural work quite like studying the ongoing influence of any other figure in the past, such as Plato or Muhammad. Jaroslav Pelikan's *Jesus through the Centuries* (1985) shows how remarkably diverse the impact of Jesus has been, and continues to be, wherever his name is known.

These essays—especially those in chapters 2 through 4—eschew that broad approach and concentrate instead on certain dimensions of Jesus that made him a distinct, historical person in his own time and that prove to be central to his current and future role as well. And that means that these studies are neither simply another attempt to recover and reconstruct "the historical Jesus" nor an effort to say directly who Jesus now "is" without reference to the slice of history that he once was. Although certain aspects of the history of the quest for Jesus are basic to these discussions, they do not require an overview of the burgeoning literature since there is an ample supply of such surveys and interpretations already.[1]

There have been many quests for the Jesus of history, but there has never been a wholly disinterested one. To the contrary, the whole attempt to recover and portray "the real Jesus of history" was set into motion by the conviction that Jesus deserved to be emancipated from the Jesus Christ of the gospels and from Christian dogma that had obscured and distorted who he "really" was and what he "really" said. Indeed, that view keeps much of the quest going today (see p. 67 below). Inevitably such a stance produced efforts

---

1. See, e.g., Charlesworth, "Jesus Research Expands" (169 notes provide ample bibliography); Telford, "Major Trends and Interpretive Issues" (includes a bibliography of bibliographical surveys); Witherington, *The Jesus Quest*; N. T. Wright, *Jesus and the Victory of God*, chaps. 1–2; and Powell, *Jesus*.

to show, also by historical study, that the Jesus of the gospels is not a gross distortion of the Jesus of history. Thus both the radical dismemberers of the tradition and its stout defenders relied on historical study to validate their conviction that who Jesus was matters today, even if they disagreed almost totally on who he was and what he said.

Although the historical study of Jesus is commonly traced to the seventeenth-century English Deists and the eighteenth-century Enlightenment, the concern for the "isness" of the Jesus who was is characteristic of the Jesus tradition from the start and of the later gospels as well, though only Luke makes a point of saying so (Lk 1:1–4). Much twentieth-century gospel criticism has asserted that the gospels are much more interested in Jesus' presentness to their immediate readers than in narrating the past, but recent studies have argued that the gospels *are* interested in the actual past tense of Jesus as well.[2]

This formally similar bifocal interest in Jesus is manifest in two features that the gospels share with the portrayals of Jesus produced by modern historical criticism. First, the narratives produced by both rely on the past tense, even though both the Evangelists and the modern historians have their eye on the present significance of what they recount. Both clearly narrate the past, reporting that Jesus said, came, went, and did instead of writing that he says, comes, goes, and does, because they assume that the ongoing significance of Jesus does not require them to replace the past with the present tense; in fact, both assume that the ongoing significance of Jesus requires a narrative in past tense. Second, characteristically, neither the historians nor the Evangelists refer to the protagonist by titles given him by the Christian community—Christ, Lord, Master, Son of God—but rely on the personal name that his parents gave him, Jesus. This is remarkable, since the gospels make it clear that their authors do in fact believe Jesus is the messiah (Christ), Lord, Master, Son of God. Yet, apart from a few passages in Luke and John, the narrators in the gospels generally avoid sentences that begin "The Lord said" or "Christ went."[3]

Nonetheless, the content of the gospel narratives differs markedly from the content of the Jesus narratives produced by most critical historians. The first task in this chapter, then, is to outline briefly the differences between the Evangelists' Jesus story and that of the critics. A following section presents the critics' rationale for separating what they think probably happened from what the

2. See, e.g., Lemcio, *The Past of Jesus in the Gospels.*
3. See Lk 7:13, 19; 10:1 ,41; 11:39; and Jn 4:1; 6:23.

gospels report. The last task is to indicate the standpoint from which these essays are written.

Two Portrayals of the Jesus Who Was

Compared with the gospels, the historians' Jesus story is shorter in some respects and longer in others. This implies that two strategies are used to express the perfect tense of the Jesus who was. Moreover, it is the historians' strategy that puts the heavier burden on history.

The reduced scope.   The canons of critical historiography require Jesus to be studied as one would study any other historical figure. Accordingly, historians bracket out of consideration any reference to divine actions or the miraculous associated with them. These canons do, of course, permit one to acknowledge that *believing* that divine action occurred was an event in history and that this belief was a factor, even a decisive one, in subsequent history as well. Thus, critical historians cannot affirm as an attestable historical datum *that* God resurrected Jesus; what they can say is that Jesus' followers *believed* that God had done so and that they acted accordingly. Consequently, a strict historical account of Jesus ends with his death. What the disciples subsequently believed happened (Easter) belongs to the history of beliefs about Jesus but not to the history of Jesus himself.

Likewise, divine action is not included in the critical historians' account of Jesus' birth. The stories in the initial chapters of Matthew and Luke are regarded instead as evidence that by the end of the first century some Christians came to account for Jesus' origin by telling these stories. In other words, historians commonly treat these chapters as factual evidence for early Christian beliefs about Jesus but not as historically reliable information about Jesus himself (though the birth stories may contain reliable information, such as the names of his parents). On this basis, solid historical evidence about Jesus begins with the reports of his baptism by John the Baptist. But these reports too include the miraculous—the coming of the Spirit as a visible event and the Voice (of God) saying, "You are my Son, the Beloved [or, my Beloved Son]; with you I am well pleased" (Mk 1:11). Since Jesus' acceptance of John's baptism is rarely doubted, historians generally grant that somehow Jesus' consciousness of a special vocation began in relation to his baptism, and they regard the dove and the words of the Voice to be legendary details that expressed early Christian conviction about his relation to God.

So too, critical historians delete from their Jesus story the account of the Transfiguration, sometimes regarding it as a story of Jesus' resurrection appearance that, for some reason, has been placed near the center of Mark, where it remained in Matthew and Luke. Likewise, the miracle stories—especially the so-called "nature miracles" such as calming the storm or feeding a crowd with one boy's lunch—have been put aside, while those stories that might report psychological healings and exorcisms have been retained since they have analogies today.

After the "Quest of the historical Jesus" (to borrow the title of Albert Schweitzer's classic study) set aside the references to divine action (i.e., the "supernatural"), attention was then directed to the words of Jesus and to the gospel reports of the nonmiraculous events. What must not be missed here is that by deleting from Jesus' history all references to divine action, critics set aside precisely those parts of the gospels by which the Evangelists expressed most explicitly their understanding of the ongoing significance of Jesus, his perfect tense.

The expanded content.   Having omitted the "supernatural" elements from consideration, critical historians add a great deal to the remaining gospel material in order to make up for what the Jesus tradition had omitted. A closer look at the gospels will expose the significance of these additions.

The canonical gospels rely on an anonymous narrator to provide the story line or plot and sometimes to comment on a story or saying. The story line is created by the way the narrator connects the individual Jesus traditions, usually by reporting a change of scene or time, as in Mark 2: "when he returned to Capernaum," "And as he sat at dinner," or "one sabbath." Scholars assume that the Jesus traditions were handed on orally and that in this process the users gave the material a form that was generally stable but not inflexible. Stories were reduced to essential elements, mentioning specific places more often than specific times. Although the action occurs in real places, there is little interaction between Jesus and these places; apart from Jerusalem, place names are mostly stage settings and are not significant parts of the plot. Mentioning place names, however, anchors the stories in historical and geographical reality, especially for readers living in the general area where the action had occurred. Real historical time is indicated in references to known persons such as Pilate or Herod Antipas, but only Luke carefully sets the story in explicitly datable time (Lk 3:1–2). The Jesus story in the gospels did not occur "once upon a time."

Although Matthew and Luke are expansions and modifications of Mark,[4] they generally retain its overall story line: Jesus' mission (of unstated length) is

---

4. These essays assume that the majority of scholars rightly judge Mark to be the oldest of the gospels and that both Matthew and Luke used it and a collection of Jesus' sayings (which scholars have labeled Q); the material found only in Matthew is labeled M, and that found only in Luke is identified as L.

centered in the villages of Galilee until he resolves to go to Jerusalem, where the account becomes more integrated and occupies, from a chronological perspective, a disproportionately large amount of the text. Although resistance to Jesus is mentioned early (Mk 3:6), the gospels do not present a real development of opposition but simply call attention to it from time to time. Opponents are rarely named; they usually are identified as a group ("the Pharisees"). Nor do the gospels show any interest in Jesus' personality, development of ideas, or motivations. In fact, in each gospel the closest participants and observers—the disciples—did not really understand what was happening or who Jesus really was. Until the resurrection, Jesus was an enigma—even though on several occasions he stated the purpose of his mission quite clearly (e.g., Mt 5:17; Mk 10:45).

Apart from the genealogies in Matthew and Luke, neither the narrators nor the traditions show any significant interest in biographical details about Jesus and his followers. Only Luke reports his age (about thirty years old, Lk 3:23); none describes his upbringing, though the peculiarly Lukan story of the twelve-year-old Jesus in the temple implies that he was precocious (Lk 2:41–51). Matthew and Luke each provide a genealogy, but they do not agree completely. We learn that Jesus was a craftsman,[5] that four of his disciples were fishermen, and that one had been a tax collector; of the other seven we know only their names. Customs are noted but rarely explained.[6] While the narrators occasionally summarize what Jesus did (taught and healed) and report the responses of the crowds, they seldom do more than provide a series of short stories, many of which state briefly the occasion that prompted Jesus to say something provocative and memorable. Everything else has been pruned away, lest it divert attention from the words of Jesus. At the same time the reader is placed in a real place at a real time, where real people—even in parables—do the recognizably real things of real ordinary village life, even though these things are but glimpsed because they are simply taken for granted.

Characteristically, at almost every point, critical historians present Jesus differently, largely because they are persuaded that the Jesus traditions do not pro-

---

5. Jesus is called a *tektōn* in Mk 6:3 and in Mt 13:55 "the son of a *tektōn*." The word apparently means "woodworker," not necessarily "carpenter." See Meier, *A Marginal Jew*, I, 278–85, in which Jesus' socioeconomic status is also discussed.

6. Mk 7:3–4, which explains Jewish concern for ritual purity in relation to meals, is a well-known exception. Unexplained are many other matters, such as the kind of tax that Levi collected (Mk 2:14), the reason for the buying and selling in the temple precinct (Mk 11:15–16), and putting money "into the treasury" of the temple (Mk 12:41–44).

vide sufficient evidence to write a "life" of Jesus and that the Markan story line is the Evangelist's construction. If that is the case, then one cannot rely on either the sequence of the stories and sayings or on the narrator's comments to infer cause and effect in the public life of Jesus. Consequently, apart from a rudimentary overview, historians generally avoid a narrative presentation of Jesus altogether and instead analyze and describe aspects of his mission according to themes, such as the core of his message, his teaching about specific topics (e.g., law, wealth, family), and healings and exorcisms. The events that led swiftly to his execution do, however, require a more connected narrative treatment, though this is often marked by the repeated insistence that an account of what actually occurred can no longer be constructed.

A reader who turns from reading a gospel to reading a modern Jesus book finds that what the Jesus tradition eliminated is amply discussed in the book: all sorts of information about the historical, socioeconomic and religious aspects of Jesus' context. This information may be extensive or rudimentary, but it reflects the conviction that to understand who Jesus was one must know something about the turmoil that led to Rome's imperial presence in the area, the tax system's effects on the populace, the role of the Jerusalem temple and of the synagogues in the towns and villages, and the differences among various religious groups (Sadducees, Pharisees, Essenes [not mentioned in the New Testament], Herodians, Zealots). This adduced information pertains not only to persons, places, and events mentioned in the gospels' Jesus story but also to details in the sayings and stories that Jesus told (e.g., inheritance law, the way farmers plowed and planted, the tenant land system, the fishing business). The irony of this should not be missed: critical historians, having eliminated the birth stories and the resurrection from the scope of the Jesus story, and having set aside those elements of the content of what the gospels report about Jesus as unhistorical, surround the reduced body of material about Jesus with a greatly enlarged body of knowledge in order to do what the Evangelists did: say who Jesus was so that his significance can become clear at a later time (our own). A second irony emerges from the first: the less critical historians claim can be known about Jesus, the more their books discuss his context.

History's burden. To ask, Who is Jesus? is to inquire about his present identity, which, while inseparable from his past identity, is also inseparable from his significance. Significance, like importance and meaning, does not exist in a vacuum but only in relation to specific persons and groups. The significance, importance, and meaning of Christopher Columbus are quite different in the

Italian-American community than among Native Americans. Likewise, the gospels recognize that the identity and significance of Jesus are different in the Christian communities than they are for those who are not members of these groups. Moreover, in these communities Jesus' identity and significance do not pose a problem to be solved because in the gospels God's voice declares who he is, the resurrection confirms it, and Jesus himself formulates his significance from time to time. In addition the narrators call attention to the relation between Jesus and the Old Testament. Furthermore, the transcendent, nonphenomenal context of the Jesus story was undergirded by the inclusion of the miraculous, on the one hand, and by the conviction, on the other hand, that the Jesus event was not yet completed, since he was expected to return as the Son of Man. The power of the gospel narratives is traceable, in part, to the ways in which these transcendent features are woven into their coherent Jesus stories, which also refer to actual people, places, and events.

As noted, the canons of critical historiography have required historians of Jesus to set aside these very parts of the gospels as unhistorical and to work instead with data whose reliability has survived critical assessment (discussed below, pp. 14–17). Moreover, the transcendent theological context that identified Jesus by relating him to God's activity and to scripture was replaced by detailed historical and socioeconomic information and in some cases also by generalizations derived from studies of other ancient societies. The goal, in short, was a chastened but accurate portrayal of the Jesus who once was, set in the context of a society that once was.

It is not the success of the historical enterprise that requires brief comment here but the extent to which reconstructed history can itself yield a sense of Jesus' present significance. Although the next chapter will return to this question, it is appropriate here to ask how historians point to the "isness" of the Jesus they reconstruct without reference to God's action or other sorts of theological language.

Characteristically, the contemporary pertinence of Jesus is expressed in the rhetoric used to present the Jesus who was. This rhetoric is manifest in the vocabulary used, in what is emphasized (and marginalized), and in the angle from which Jesus is viewed as well as in the ways in which the silence of the gospels and their traditions is filled in with historical information. Inevitably Jesus is portrayed in the idiom and perspectives that reflect the values and con--victions that the historian, and his or her social location, finds congenial. Six decades ago Henry Cadbury explored this phenomenon in a book no less pertinent today. He noted, "we so easily assume that our approach is the right one, and therefore that a person of Jesus' insight must have shared it. . . . This widespread appreciation for Jesus . . . contains so often a quite unintentional self-flattery." He faults "the assumption that the Christian movement could have been given its great impetus only by such qualities in its founder as would give impetus to a movement today."[7] He goes on to show how different was Jesus' own thinking from our own. In short, the more the Jesus of history is portrayed in terms that moderns and postmoderns find congenial, the less truly historical the portrait is likely to be.

If today one smiles condescendingly at earlier presentations of Jesus that repeatedly referred to his ethical "ideals," one can be assured that future generations will read with comparable amazement today's confident portrayals of him as the leader of a social movement designed to restructure Galilean society. The point is not that efforts to portray Jesus as a historical figure in his own time and place should be abandoned, but that the transitoriness of all historical reconstruction must be acknowledged and all pretentious claims made on its behalf—such as Now we really know what he said and what he was up to!—must not be taken seriously. Also in the case of the Jesus of history, "the past isn't what it used to be—and never was," because the people studying him are not what they used to be either. Whoever wants to understand the historicity of Jesus (his conditionedness by time and circumstance) must reckon with his or her own historicity as well, perhaps more so. From that maxim, the essays that follow are no exception.

These studies respond to the question Who is Jesus? by concentrating on four facets: that he was a Jew, that his mission was energized by his grasp of the kingdom of God, that he was executed without any visible or audible validation from the God he trusted, and that he is the central figure in the moral life of his followers. Since history, including Jesus as a historical figure, is marked not only by shifting probabilities but also by inherent ambiguities, exploring the ongoing meaning of the Jesus of history inevitably relies on theological engagement in which the historicity of the interpreter comes to expression.

The Jesus of history is not subject to probability because it is only probable that he existed; of that there is no reasonable doubt. Degrees of probability are historical judgments based on the confluence of various considerations, which themselves have a history. Because these essays probe the "isness" of the Jesus who was, it is important to understand at the outset the basis on which critical historians portray a Jesus who differs so markedly from the Jesus of the gospels.

7. Cadbury, *The Peril of Modernizing Jesus*, 37–39, 72–73.

Recovering the Jesus Who Was

To grasp the rationale that governs the Jesus quest—an unsatisfactory but usable phrase—it is essential to see the phenomenon as a whole as well as the biblical phenomena that evoked it, though only salient matters can be mentioned here. The convoluted and controversial history of the quest can easily obscure the fact that, like all historical study, it is rooted in the elemental distinction between event and report, for even a totally accurate report is not a complete account of what happened. Indeed, every report is partial in both senses of the word: by giving only part of what occurred and by expressing a point of view. Consequently, there is a fundamental distinction between the exegesis of a text and the reconstruction of the event it reports.

Moreover, applied to the gospels, moderns did not discover this distinction, for it had been already addressed by second-century Christian interpreters who confronted the fact that the emerging New Testament canon contained four gospels whose accounts of Jesus sometimes agreed and sometimes diverged markedly. Then as now, one could regard the gospels either as portraits or as pieces. Tatian viewed them as pieces and so combined them into one account, the Diatessaron (lost but partly recoverable from other sources). Despite the fact that the church in the West rejected this move, it has been repeated relentlessly down to the present. Its best-known forms appear at Christmas when the Matthean and Lukan birth stories are woven together and on Good Friday when "the seven last words" are compiled from the gospels. There are valid reasons why churches should attend to both birth stories and "the seven last words" on the sacred days of the church year. The point here, however, is that these modern followers of Tatian assume that the gospels are incomplete pieces which, if properly combined, report the whole event. In rejecting Tatian, the church opted instead for viewing the gospels as four portraits, each with its own integrity as an adequate rendering of the event. Since the gospels differ, this decision made the historical question permanent: What did happen, and how does one know it?

It was in the modern era, however, that the historical question became a pivotal issue and scholars sought to account, on the basis of critical historiography, for the gospel phenomenon as a whole and to develop criteria for getting at "the facts of the matter." To bring these developments into focus, we will first look more closely at the historicity of the quest, then note the criteria used to detect reliable information in the gospels, and finally sketch what is entailed in reconstructing the history that Jesus was.

The historicity of the quest.   The Jesus quest is a bequest of the En-lightenment. Beginning with the seventeenth century but accelerating in the eighteenth, English Deists no longer believed much of Christian teaching and expressed their doubts also about the historical reliability of the gospels. And the more they disbelieved their inherited beliefs, the more they believed their doubts about the gospels and began trying to extract the truth about Jesus from them. Their governing assumption—that the Jesus of history differed drastically from the Jesus Christ of the Christian faith and from the gospels on which it was based—has shaped the entire quest and generated endless controversies.

These controversies commonly turned on different stances toward the Christian tradition and the gospels. One can view the gospels as embodying the continuing early Christian interpretation of the Jesus who was, in order to let him deal with the ongoing needs of the community, or one can view them negatively, as the results of repeated Christian distortions of "the facts." Both attitudes have characterized the modern study of Jesus and the gospels. Protestant theology has wrestled with the relation of the gospels' "Christ of faith" to the historians' recovered "Jesus of history" from the beginning of the quest. For some the two are the same, whereas for others the differences are so deep that one must choose one or the other. For both sides the eminence of Jesus was assumed. The quarrel was, and remains, over the content to which the name Jesus refers. Those who saw no irreconcilable disparity between the Jesus Christ of the gospels and the Jesus of the historians sought to claim the latter for Christianity, whereas those who insisted on a choice sought either to reconstruct Christianity on the basis of this Jesus or to rescue Jesus from it.[8]

---

8. For example, Hollenbach admits that he studies and reconstructs the Jesus of history "in order to overthrow, not simply correct 'the mistake called Christianity'"—i.e., the Christological understanding of Jesus. See his "The Historical Jesus Question," 20. Others work from virtually the opposite position. Borg, for instance, not only affirms that he is a "committed Christian" deeply involved in the life of the church as well as being engaged in nonsectarian Jesus study, but also says that its "significance . . . for the life of the church . . . seems most important for me"; see *Jesus in Contemporary Scholarship*, 143. So, too, N. T. Wright writes, "I come to this work as a practising historian and as a practising Christian, and . . . my experience of both worlds suggests . . . that neither of these need feel compromised by intimate association with the other"; see *Jesus and the Victory of God*, xiv.

It is hardly accidental that the quest got under way when traditional Christianity was facing its most serious internal challenge in fifteen centuries. Although first limited to the European intelligentsia who read the English Deists, denials of the truth of the Christian understanding of Jesus soon became part of the growing alienation from the church, increasingly viewed as the outmoded bulwark of resistance to progress in science as well as to political freedom. In Germany from the start the symbiotic relation of "throne and altar" inevitably gave a political cast to the differentiation of the Jesus of history from the Christ of church doctrine. For left-wing Hegelians, for example, showing that the real Jesus was not the Christ of the church was a way of hastening the church's demise.[9] But one did not have to be on the team of the Hegelian Left in order to play the game or to rewrite the life of Jesus by combining bits and pieces of the gospels with an imaginative use of nonbiblical materials, especially reports about the Essenes (then known mostly from references in Philo and Josephus). Some claimed that Jesus had secretly been one of the Essenes, who later stage-managed the crucifixion and a fake resurrection.[10] After D. F. Strauss had contended that the gospels are not history in the first place but myth (narrative expressions of early Christian beliefs),[11] others soon went beyond Strauss and claimed that there never had been a Jesus

9. For the political impact of life-of-Jesus research, see Massey, *Christ Unmasked*. Brazill points out that the Young Hegelians "judged criticism was a necessary philosophical weapon in their struggle to show that Christianity was outmoded and that humanism must be accepted as the new spiritual basis for civilization"; he also quotes Bruno Bauer: "religion will be absolutely destroyed by criticism" (*The Young Hegelians*, 61, 199).

10. The "Essene Jesus," apparently fathered by K. F. Bahrdt in the eighteenth century and baptized by K. H. Venturini at the beginning of the nineteenth (see Schweitzer, *The Quest*, chap. 4), has died and come to life repeatedly. Currently Barbara Thiering raids the Dead Sea Scrolls and other texts to rewrite the Jesus story completely, claiming that he was married, divorced, and remarried and that the crucifixion and a feigned resurrection occurred at Qumran. For a summary and critique, see N. T. Wright, *Who Was Jesus?*, chap. 2.

11. George Eliot's translation of the fourth edition (1840) of Strauss's *The Life of Jesus* was included in the Lives of Jesus series and published by Fortress Press in 1972 together with an extensive introduction by Peter C. Hodgson. In 1994 this was republished by Sigler Press. In 1864 Strauss published *The Life of Jesus for the German People*, and a year later appeared a book-length review of Schleiermacher's *Life of Jesus*, which had appeared recently though based on lectures given three decades before. The title of Strauss's review formulates the issue as it long dominated the discussion: *The Christ of Faith and the Jesus of History*. My translation, and introduction, of this is part of the Lives of Jesus series.

in the first place.[12] This prompted other scholars to weigh in with books denying the denials.[13] Today only an eccentric would claim that Jesus never existed.

Much more important were the critics who, while agreeing that many of the teachings of classical Christianity were no longer tenable in the modern scientific era, were nonetheless convinced that the real truth of Christianity was still viable if rethought and placed on a more solid foundation, namely the Jesus of history. One could then be loyal to Jesus without having to accept the Christian theology that had been woven around him, implying that such allegiance is neither irrational nor unwarranted once the historical truth about him came to light. Such, in general, was the outlook of liberal Protestants who until recently produced most of the critical studies of the gospels and Jesus' life, especially of his teachings. Indeed, this outlook is resurgent today.

This way of refurbishing Christianity for the modern era makes strenuous demands on both history and Christianity. Of the former it demands a historically solid reconstruction of Jesus that is sufficiently convincing to elicit a positive religious commitment to him. The next chapter will show that it was at just this point that the Jewishness of Jesus became a problem, because showing that Jesus is indeed worthy of religious commitment entailed showing that he was superior to Judaism. Schweitzer's interpretation of Jesus made matters worse, because by linking him closely to Jewish apocalyptic expectations he tied Jesus to what was sometimes regarded as inferior even to alleged Jewish "legalism"—the failed fantasies about the end of the world. A heavy demand was made also of Christianity, for it was required to surrender or drastically reinterpret the core doctrines about Christ. In other words, whereas the deniers of Christian doctrine used history to call in the loan in order to push Christianity into bankruptcy, the liberal affirmers of Jesus used history to downsize and refinance it.

The historicity of the quest, then, refers to the ways in which it was embedded in larger questions agitating the religious and cultural history of the West. Understandably, the debates produced increased clarification about the cri-

---

12. For example, the American mathematician William Benjamin Smith, of Tulane, in 1906 published *Der Vorchristliche Jesus*, which was taken up by Drews, *Die Christusmythe* (1910–1911). In 1927 Smith completed *The Birth of the Gospel*, which publishers refused until 1957 when the Philosophical Library in New York published it. Smith declared the gospels to be allegorical narratives personifying an ancient Semitic cult god, Yahweh, in terms of Greco-Roman religion. The truth of the gospels endures, however, though their Hero *"as a material physical fact vanishes forever"* (ibid., 132, his italics).

13. See especially Goguel, *Jesus the Nazarene*, which discusses the issues fully.

teria by which one could recover the Jesus of history from the Jesus of the gospels.

The quest and its criterion.   Since virtually all sources of information about Jesus are Christian texts, primarily the New Testament gospels,[14] the overarching, persistent question is, on what basis can one judge the extent to which a reported act or saying of Jesus was really done or said by him? Scholars produce different answers partly because they do not agree on who bears the burden of proof. Those defending the historical reliability of the gospels place the burden on the critic: they trust the text and require the critic to provide convincing evidence for not continuing to do so. Others place the burden on the text: as a matter of principle they approach all texts with skepticism and require each item in it to establish its degree of credibility through vigorous interrogation. The latter has determined the course of the discussion.

To find solid historical information about Jesus—i.e., that which is not attributable to early Christianity—the quest relied largely on the criterion of dissimilarity, also called the negative criterion. Other criteria, such as consistency and coherence, attestation in more than one independent source, and a "fit" with Galilean circumstances of the time, were used to confirm the results of using the negative criterion which has controlled the quest.[15] It is therefore important to understand the negative criterion's rationale and the consequences of using it consistently.

At the beginning the Jesus people (called Christians only later) had a gospel message about Jesus before they had a gospel text about him. Neither the gospels we have nor earlier texts they may incorporate are records of Jesus' teachings made during his ministry. The gospels rest on traditions transmitted orally by Christians and for Christians. The gospels, which contain no sen-

14. Especially important in recent discussions has been the *Gospel of Thomas* (found in 1947), partly because its form resembles the collection of Jesus' sayings in Q and partly because the wording of some of its sayings is sometimes thought to be closer to what Jesus actually said than their parallels in the Synoptic gospels. The Jesus Seminar, for instance, judged 39 of its 114 sayings to be "probably" genuine and 3 to be certainly so—more than it found in the Gospel of Mark (1 certainly genuine, 17 probably so). For a comprehensive discussion of the *Gospel of Thomas*, see Koester, *Ancient Christian Gospels*, 76–128. Much more controversial is Crossan's view that embedded in the *Gospel of Peter* (found in 1892) is the oldest passion narrative (which he calls the Cross Gospel), which was used by all four canonical gospels and then given its present form in the *Gospel of Peter* (see Crossan, *The Cross that Spoke*).

15. The best-known defense of the negative criterion is that of Perrin, *Rediscovering the Teaching of Jesus*, 39–43. For an assessment, see Keck, *Future*, chap. 1.

tences that begin with *we* or refer to *us*, focus on the words and deeds of Jesus as God's way of acting redemptively for the human condition—the theme of the gospel message as well. In other words, the Jesus of the earlier message is congruent with the Jesus of the later text. Those who, for whatever reason, assume that the Jesus of history differed significantly from the Jesus of the gospels therefore also assume that these texts attribute to Jesus what the Christians believed about him. Indeed, it is assumed that the more the gospels' Jesus explicitly teaches what the church also taught, the less likely it is that Jesus actually expressed those thoughts. The Gospel of John therefore was bracketed out of the discussion of the Jesus of history because, apart from certain details, its Jesus expresses the theology of a particular Christian community. In other words, according to the negative criterion, one should subtract from the gospels all sayings of Jesus that coincide with Christian teaching about him, especially those in which he formulates the purpose of his mission.[16] As a result, getting to the real Jesus of history entails a consistent de-Christianizing of the Jesus in the gospels. And the more he is de-Christianized, the more Jewish he becomes.

But this is only part of the story, the easy part, because the first Jesus people, and many Christians later, were themselves Jews with a rich heritage of practices, beliefs, and hopes. Critics therefore also assumed that Jewish believers in Jesus were as likely to have added traditional Jewish beliefs and perspectives to the Jesus tradition as to have added distinctly Christian ones shaped by the resurrection faith. So the negative criterion was applied also to the Jesus tradition after the distinctly Christian elements were removed (a logical sequence, not necessarily an actual sequence of procedure). As a result, only those teachings of Jesus that do not express typical Jewish views as well—such as "till heaven and earth pass away, not an iota, not a dot, will pass away from the law until all is accomplished" (Mt 5:18)—came to be regarded as genuinely from Jesus himself. Consequently, consistent use of the negative criterion produced a Jesus who differed, on the one hand, from his Christian followers and, on the other, from his Jewish forebears. In short, we can be most confident that we are in touch with the real Jesus of history when we find what is original, distinctive,

---

16. For example, "Do not think that I have come to abolish the law or the prophets; I have not come to abolish but to fulfill" (Mt 5:17); "For I have come to call not the righteous but sinners" (Mt 9:13); "Everyone therefore who acknowledges me before others, I also will acknowledge before my Father in heaven, but whoever denies me . . . I also will deny before my Father in heaven" (Mt 10:32–33); "For the Son of Man came not to be served but to serve, and to give his life as a ransom for many" (Mk 10:45).

and unexpected. It is not surprising that through use of this method few sayings have survived the critics' scrutiny.

But some of Jesus' sayings also express hostility toward certain aspects of Judaism and especially of the Pharisees (e.g., Matthew 23). Critics have deleted these polemical sayings also, claiming that while they do not express Christian doctrine about Christ, they do coincide too much with the later church's antipathy toward the synagogue to be authentic words of Jesus. Thereby the Jesus of history has been purged of both characteristic Christian theology and typical Jewish beliefs, on the one hand, and of negative attitudes toward Judaism, on the other. The result is ironic: the real Jesus of history is distanced from the Christianity that emerged in his name and embedded in the Judaism that largely refused the message about him.

Although criticism of a thoroughgoing use of the negative criterion has grown more common recently, it must not be forgotten that using this criterion is the inevitable result of assuming that Jesus "as he really was" differed significantly from what the gospels say he was.[17] Without this criterion one could not identify what can be viewed as undoubtedly from Jesus.

If using the negative criterion controlled the quest for reliable data, the criterion of coherence controlled the reconstruction of Jesus. Here too a powerful assumption has exacted its toll—that Jesus had a mission and a message that were logically so coherent and consistent that they were also free of inner tensions. The critics' judgment that a given saying is genuine is used to assess the genuineness of similar sayings. Inevitably, coherence and consistency have been fundamental in the efforts to reconstruct the mission and message as a whole.

At the same time one should be aware that logical consistency and coherence, prized especially by ideologues and academics, can be problematic when used to recover any ancient figure. For one thing, it is a priori likely that the early Christian communities were more concerned to hand on stories and sayings that they deemed useful in changed circumstances than they were to transmit them as parts of a previous coherent structure of thought. As a result the linkages that scholars make between sayings or between sayings and deeds are not necessarily those that the early church would have seen or that Jesus would have made, had he worried about consistency in the first place. Besides, Jesus' sense of what was consistent and coherent may well have differed from that of Western academics who are trained to make a tight case in a seminar. More-

---

17. For suggestive observations about the role of "difference," including the differences among the gospels, see Watson, *Text and Truth*, 38–41.

over, one can allow for the possibility that Jesus did say things that do not fit together logically when *printed* side by side, especially if one grants that he was a multifaceted person given to ad hoc teachings delivered orally from place to place.[18] Indeed, Jack T. Sanders has proposed that it is characteristic of charismatic leaders of "New Religious Movements" to be logically inconsistent, since such randomness actually increases the charisma to which people respond. Accordingly, "if Jesus had sought such coherence [as scholars seek] he would not have been the leader he was."[19] In any case, some of the diversity of early Christianity may reflect the diverse elements in Jesus' own sayings.

The reconstructive task.   The more apparent it became that it was the Evangelists, beginning with Mark, who assembled and ordered the Jesus traditions into their respective narratives, the more inevitable it became that the search for reliable historical information about Jesus would reverse the gospel-making process so that each piece of tradition could be analyzed and assessed apart from its present setting in the texts. This is only the first step, of course, for now the disjoined and diverse pieces of information, with their varying degrees of probability, must be reassembled in order to reconstruct a credible historical figure in a credible history. In addition, it is not enough to locate Jesus' sayings that are probably authentic and the deeds that he probably did; one must also provide a credible historical account of those traditions that are deemed to be unhistorical, produced by the early church. Both E. P. Sanders and J. D. Crossan have seen that the historical Jesus requires a historical early Christianity as well.[20]

The central task, however, is concentrated on Jesus, and its core is the need to account for the one indubitable fact of his life—that he was crucified on Pilate's orders. It is possible, of course, that he was simply caught up in a web

18. Cadbury's discussion of "Purpose, Aim and Motive in Jesus" is still worth pondering, even if he reacted too strongly to the confident portrayals of Jesus' aim when he proposed "that Jesus probably had no definite, unified, conscious purpose, that an absence of such a program is *a priori* likely and that it suits well the historical evidence" (*The Peril of Modernizing Jesus*, chap. 6).

19. Jack T. Sanders, "The Criterion of Coherence," 24. Sanders's argument, while a useful reminder, is weakened by the fact that his modern example, Bhagwan Shree Rajneesh, who headed a community in eastern Oregon, relied *deliberately* on randomness and contradictions to enhance his power. Thinking that Jesus did so as well puts too much strain on the imagination.

20. It is a strength of E. P. Sanders's *Jesus and Judaism* that it insists on this repeatedly. Crossan asserts that his *The Birth of Christianity* "is the closest possible sequel" he can imagine to his *The Historical Jesus* (*The Birth of Christianity*, 17).

of unexpected and uncontrollable events, similar to people today finding themselves suddenly drawn into controversies and legal battles not of their own making. However, the question does not concern what was possible but what was probable. One must, in other words, provide a historically probable explanation for why a Galilean teacher and healer ended up on a cross, the heinous Roman way of dealing with those deemed dangerous to the *Pax* Romana. There is no evidence that Jesus' crucifixion climaxed a series of his clashes with Roman authority or ideology. In fact, apart from the story of the Roman centurion who asked Jesus to heal his son (Mt 8:5–13), the question put to Jesus concerning payment of tribute (Mk 12:13–17 par.), and the role of Pilate in the passion story, one would hardly know from the gospels that Palestine was under Roman domination. Given the impression made by the gospels, Rome is more on the mind of the current quest than it was on that of Jesus. That does not, however, detract from the central question: why was Jesus crucified?

Pursuing the reconstructive task successfully requires also that Jesus be situated as clearly and as credibly as possible in the historical situation of the Jewish people in the decades between the death of Herod in 4 B.C.E. and the outbreak of the first revolt in 66 C.E. The next chapter will show that this has proven to be a more complex task than the pioneers of the quest surmised, partly because so many sources of information must be considered.

The opposite problem—a dearth of sources—frustrates the effort to reconstruct the probable history of the early Christian movement in which the Jesus traditions were formed and transmitted. To be sure, the Book of Acts does continue the Jesus story, but Acts says little about the earliest community in Jerusalem and nothing at all about Jesus' followers in Galilee. Paul's letters, written before the gospels, deal with questions that arose in his mission to Gentiles in the cities around the Aegean Sea; his few references to Jerusalem and Antioch are more tantalizing than descriptive. It is likely inevitable, then, that scholars turned to the gospels themselves, and to their traditions, for evidence about the communities that produced them, even though this meant moving in a circle. However difficult, one needs to reconstruct earliest Christianity in order to produce a credible portrayal of Jesus in history. This necessity arises from using the negative criterion, for the greater the alleged difference between the Jesus of history and the Jesus of the gospels, the greater the need to account for that difference in a way that is historically credible. Just as one must provide a historically probable bridge between Jesus in Galilee and Jesus before Pilate, so one must provide an analogous bridge between who Jesus was and the communities that emerged in his name and eventually produced the gospels. Oth-

erwise there is no plausible historical reconstruction but only a history that
might have been.

Beyond Reconstruction

Responding to the question Who is Jesus? by referring to history in perfect tense
indicates that the studies that follow take seriously the efforts to reconstruct the
Jesus of history from the gospels, even though neither the assumptions that
underlie the methods used nor the results are beyond question. In fact, each
essay gives considerable attention to historical matters before turning to the reason for doing so—to take up the question So what?

At certain points a somewhat different stance toward the gospels will be evident, one that reflects a growing conviction that the Enlightenment's assumptions and aims, continuing to shape the quest, have skewed the results. This is
the appropriate juncture to identify that stance, which appears occasionally
here, and its basis.

When viewed as a whole, the quest has produced variations on one theme—
difference, clearly manifest in the negative criterion and its rationale. Even
though this criterion was not spelled out at the outset (Reimarus being an
exception; see p. 23, note 3), it was operative from the beginning. It is no exaggeration to say that apart from this preoccupation with difference there would
not have been a quest, for there would have been no reason to develop one.
That the Jesus of history differed from the Jesus of the gospels is not to be
doubted, though for reasons other than those that the Enlightenment cher-
ished. Among them is this consideration: Were there no difference, Jesus' followers—both those who transmitted the traditions orally and the Evangelists
who used them to create a running narrative—would not have believed that
the resurrection disclosed anything about him that they had not known before.
Actually, they were convinced that after the resurrection they understood Jesus
better than those who had been with him at the time of his ministry, for they
did not regard the resurrection as marking a mere resumption. But it is one
thing to affirm (and not merely concede) that the Jesus of history differed from
the Jesus of the gospels and another to think that the discerned difference
reveals a distortion, for one can identify a distortion only when one knows
already what was actually the case —precisely what the quest seeks to learn.[21]

21. Chilton made much the same point with regard to Jesus' relation to Judaism: "The
starting point in understanding Jesus must not be that we know what sort of Jew he was.
That is precisely the information we do not have" (*Pure Kingdom*, 55).

The role of difference has been especially clear in the efforts to distinguish the authentic words of Jesus in the sayings recorded in the gospels. The essays that follow assume that these sayings include words that Jesus did not speak, though distinguishing the genuine from the attributed sayings is complicated by the fact that they are recorded in Greek while Jesus probably used Aramaic. But the real problem lies elsewhere; it arises from the fact that critics customarily set aside as inauthentic precisely those sayings in which Jesus formulates the character and purpose of his mission (see above). The decision to do so is probably correct. But the problem centers in the illusion that thereby the historical question of authenticity has been settled, when actually two closely related questions remain: First, if Jesus did not, for example, say "I have come to call not the righteous but sinners" (Mt 9:13), on what basis did the tradition claim (successfully until critics challenged it) that he did?; second, is it true even if he did not say it? Both questions are answered by reckoning with the same thing: for the early Christians the saying is so true to Jesus as a whole that it did not matter whether he had actually uttered it or not. In other words, for the task of portraying the Jesus of history, answering the question Is it true to Jesus? is as important and as useful as deciding whether a saying came from his mouth or not. Distinguishing the genuine from the nongenuine does not necessarily entail the judgment that the latter distorts Jesus. It does, however, imply that the perception of Jesus that he catalyzed is part of who Jesus was. This stance toward the gospels proves to be especially important in chapter 4, where the word of dereliction is used to probe the significance of Jesus' death for the understanding of God. To anticipate, theologically it does not matter whether Jesus actually uttered this word or not because its question "My God, my God, why have you forsaken me?" is built into the event itself.

Finally, since these essays look into the ongoing significance of certain aspects of the Jesus of history from a Christian standpoint, it is fitting to point out that they are not studies in the Christian doctrine of Christ, though they pertain to it. They assume that it is within the broad stream of Christian tradition and sensibility that it makes sense to think theologically about Jesus' continuing significance and that this is intelligible not only to enrolled Christians but also to Christian alumni who have ceased to be part of the Christian community and to others, whether or not they are applicants for admission to it. The essays are therefore deliberately descriptive rather than prescriptive. They try to penetrate the rationale built into some of the early Christian expressions of the continuing significance of Jesus, not in order to persuade but to understand.

If significance is not somewhere there waiting to be exposed like a vein of coal but rather a discernment that occurs through engagement with the subject matter, as is surely the case, then precisely the stubborn factuality of Jesus elicits the question, So what? What difference does it make who Jesus was? Anyone can ask that question; many have, this writer among them. The essays are not final answers but responses reached on the road toward understanding; they are an invitation to join the journey.

CHAPTER TWO

The Permanent Particular
Jesus the Jew

The fact that Jesus was a Jew cannot be treated as an afterthought (and by the way, he was a Jew), for that would distort fundamentally his ongoing significance. Whatever else one may say about him cannot be severed from this elemental, historical fact.[1] To speak of Jesus in perfect tense is to reckon with the continuing import of the indissoluble datum that from his first breath to his last he was a Jew and that it never occurred to him to become anything else. That datum, however, only marks off the field within which the matter must be pursued farther, for he was not a generic Jew, a Jew for all seasons, but a particular Jew who occupied, for a particular time, a particular place on the map of Jewish religion and culture.

This particularity is important also for the sort of theological reflections undertaken here, which mirror the persistent preoccupation with Jesus that is the hallmark of the Christian tradition, namely "the scandal of particularity"[2] — the offense to reason of the claim that God's self-disclosure was granted to a

---

1. In the heyday of the Third Reich, Walter Grundmann argued that Jesus was not a Jew but the son of Mary (of uncertain ancestry since the area had long been populated by various non-Jews) and Panthera (a surname used by Roman soldiers at the time); see *Jesus der Galiläer*, 200. The book was published by the Institute for the Study of Jewish Influence on German Church Life (which Grundmann helped found in 1939). After the war he lost his Jena professorship but continued to publish. His *Geschichte Jesu Christi* (1956) is largely exegetical and makes no mention of Jesus' parentage. The reference to Panthera relies on Origen, who in the middle of the third century refuted what the anti-Christian Celsus had written seven decades before: Mary "was turned out by a carpenter who was betrothed to her, as she had been convicted of adultery and had a child by a certain soldier named Panthera" (*C. Cels.* 1:32). For a succinct discussion, see Brown, *The Birth of the Messiah*, 534–37.

2. This once-popular phrase may have been coined by Kittel, who used it to begin his essay "The Jesus of History."

particular people, Israel, chosen to be the light to the nations by which they could see the truth of God. These assertions, stated rather apodictically to be sure, point to the horizons of this chapter. Its aim, however, is more modest: to state the continuing significance, primarily for Gentiles related to the Christian tradition, of the kind of Jew Jesus probably was. His significance for Jews is for Jews to decide.

But what kind of Jew was he? Although the Jesus quest has dealt with this question from the start,[3] until recently most results produced by gentile Christian scholars have separated him from his heritage and environment, whereas Jewish scholars have often sought to absorb him into what they regarded as mainstream Judaism. Taking note of these efforts, which usually ran on parallel tracks,[4] will be this chapter's first task, though the discussion must be illustrative rather than comprehensive. The second task will be to note some of the factors that made Jesus the Jew he was and was not.[5] Finally, the chapter will propose for Christian Gentiles the perfect tense of the particular character of Jesus' Jewishness.

The Jesus Quest and the Jewish Jesus

As noted in the foregoing chapter, in order to find information in the gospels about Jesus that is historically trustworthy, critics have relied especially on the negative criterion, which separated him from the Christianity that followed him and from the ordinary Judaism that surrounded him. Although the quest

3. H. S. Reimarus, the eighteenth-century Hamburg Semitist commonly credited with inaugurating the modern scholarly Quest, sought to undermine orthodox Christianity by showing "that Jesus in no way intended to abolish this Jewish religion and introduce a new one in its place. From this it follows incontrovertibly that the apostles taught and acted exactly the reverse of what their master had intended, taught, and commanded, since they released not only the heathen from this law but also those who had converted from Judaism. . . . Soon, therefore, circumcision, sacrifice, purification, Sabbath, new moon, feast days, and the like were abolished completely and Judaism was laid in its grave" (Talbert, *Reimarus: Fragments*, 101). Jesus' aim was not to die to redeem the world from sin but "to build up a worldly kingdom, and to deliver the Israelites from bondage. It was in this that God had forsaken him" (Ibid., 150). Talbert's introduction (Ibid., 1–43) places Reimarus in his context.

4. Schweitzer's *Quest* ignores Jewish studies; subsequent accounts of the Quest have done little to remedy the situation. For references to surveys of Jewish scholarship about Jesus, see below, note 19. The Jewish scholars' participation in Jesus research since World War II (and the Holocaust!) marks a major turning point in the Quest.

5. Vermes notes that "Jesus the Jew" is an "emotionally charged synonym for the Jesus of history" ("Jesus the Jew," 108).

was undertaken mostly by specialists, its attitude toward Jesus' Jewishness—especially in nineteenth-century Germany—reflected two factors in the intellectual climate of the time. One was an antipathy toward Judaism that resulted from a combination of stereotype and ignorance. The other was German idealist thought with its lofty, somewhat ethereal, view of religion as a spiritual state of the soul, an inner sense of kinship with the divine. The essence of religion is what matters, not its external trappings in church order, creeds, and observances. The externals, being historically conditioned, change, but the essence of real religion, after emerging from its more primitive forms, endures. In an era when rapid industrialization and urbanization disturbed the inherited patterns of church life and secularization made Christianity appear ever more superfluous, liberal Protestants put in a good word for real religion, the religion of Jesus as the (alleged) demonstrable alternative to the traditional Christian religion about him, and to Judaism as well. The combination of these two outlooks, the worst and the best of German thought of the time, determined how certain critics, not only in Germany, would view Jesus' Jewishness. The whole history of this phenomenon and its influence on the study of Christian origins remains to be written.[6] The needs of this discussion, however, require only a few samples of how, in the name of history, the Jewishness of Jesus has been marginalized or distorted because the view of the Jewish religion was distorted.

Jesus the Jew in the Christian Gentile quest.   We begin with Adolf von Harnack, the great historian of Christianity. Though reared in the home of an orthodox Lutheran professor of theology, he became one of the best-known exponents of liberal Protestantism. At the University of Berlin in the winter semester of 1899–1900 he gave a series of immensely popular, and subsequently influential, public lectures titled The Essence of Christianity. They were swiftly published and soon translated into English under a quite different title, *What Is Christianity?*

Right off he declared, "The Christian religion is something simple and sublime; it means one thing and one thing only: Eternal life in the midst of time, by the strength and under the eyes of God."[7] Given this view of religion, Harnack excoriated Eastern Orthodoxy, Roman Catholicism, and even aspects of

---

6. An important beginning was made by Moore, "Christian Writers on Judaism."

7. He also declared, "Religion subordinates to itself the whole motley world of phenomena, and defies that world if it claims to be the only real one. Religion gives us only a single experience, but one which presents the world in a new light: the Eternal appears; time becomes means to an end; man is seen to be on the side of the Eternal. This was certainly Jesus' meaning, and to take anything from it is to destroy it" (Harnack, *What Is Christianity?*, 69–70).

Protestantism for obscuring the essence. For him, the key metaphor was the kernel (essence) and the husk (externals). The ideas that Jesus shared with his contemporaries were the husk. Indeed, "'husk' were the whole of the Jewish limitations attaching to his message; husk were also such definite statements as, 'I am not sent but unto the lost sheep of the house of Israel'" (180). Whereas today's scholars emphasize Jesus' relation to the circumstances of the day, Harnack asserted that the threads connecting his teaching to current history "become of no importance at all" (14) because he addressed the "inner man" (115); Jesus' Gospel concerns "God and the soul, the soul and its God" (142).

Harnack, who was vigorously opposed by the church conservatives in the kaiser's Reich, saw in Jesus' opponents, the Pharisees, a parallel to his own time. The passage deserves to be quoted at length:

> What the political church wants . . . is to rule; to get hold of men's souls and bodies, consciences and worldly goods. What political parties want is the same; and when the heads of these parties set themselves up as popular leaders, a terrorism is developed which is often worse than the fear of royal despots. It was not otherwise in . . . Jesus' day. The priests and the Pharisees held the nation in bondage and murdered its soul. For this unconstituted "authority" Jesus showed a really emancipating and refreshing disrespect. He never tired of attacking it—nay, in his struggle with it he roused himself to a state of holy indignation—of exposing its wolfish nature and hypocrisy, and of declaring that its day of judgment was at hand. In whatever domain it had any warrant to act, he accepted it: "Go and show yourselves unto the priests.". . . Towards these spiritual "authorities," then, he filled his disciples with a holy want of respect." (103–4)

Wilhelm Bousset, a charter member of the History of Religion School,[8] expressed similar views, relying on his study of Judaism from the Maccabean era to the second revolt against Rome (132–35 C.E.); only to a limited extent did he use the later rabbinic literature's traditions allegedly going back to this period.[9] Bousset saw the Jewish religion gradually distancing itself from the

8. For a theological biography, see Verheule, *Wilhelm Bousset.*
9. Moore, who was to base his understanding of "normative Judaism" primarily on rabbinic material, criticized Bousset severely for giving insufficient attention to these texts that had acknowledged standing in the Jewish community and for emphasizing instead those individuals whose roles were uncertain, thereby distorting the whole picture. He also faulted

nation and moving toward the sensibility and piety of the individual. Already in Jesus' time, then, the temple had begun to lose its centrality, giving way to the growing significance of the local synagogues as the center of religious life—a view of the temple no longer held.

In an early work he claimed that while externally Jesus remained entirely within the framework of Judaism, internally he was free of it.[10] Compared with Paul, for whom humanity remained divided between Jew and Gentile, Jesus had a truly universal outlook (82–87). Judaism cannot account for Jesus because there are "complete contradictions" between them (130).

After publishing his major study of the Jewish religion in the New Testament era (*Die Religion des Judentums im späthellenistischen Zeitalter,* 1903), he produced a brief book on Jesus in which he modified somewhat his view of Jesus' relation to Judaism.[11] Not only did he flatly reject all speculation about an Essene Jesus but he also insisted that Jesus' mode of teaching was that of the rabbis (29–31, 43). Nonetheless, since Jesus was concerned with the inner disposition of the individual and not with "the mass of casuistic, soul-fettering commandments" and "the superficial, the external, and the purposeless, . . . under the mask of earnestness," he had "no choice but to contend with fervor against a system which had unnerved its votaries and deprived them of the sense of reality." In his "war against the Scribes and Pharisees Jesus appears as the great champion of truth and reality" (138–40). Bousset grants that they wanted "the moral side" of the law yet adds, "but only in addition to a great deal else. And naturally the moral side came off the loser." By contrast, "Jesus' soul . . . was filled only with the majesty of the moral law; the rest he passed by with indifference. He did not attack it; he left it where it was. Only when these non-essentials threatened to hamper the essentials, he rose and struck down the rotten trash" (134–36). In a footnote Bousset grants that a few figures such as Hillel and Gamaliel were exceptions (68). Nonetheless, in keeping with religion's growing concern with the individual, "Jesus adopted the more advanced ideas of later Judaism" (21) and so "freed religion at the critical point from the nation, so far at least as the nation

---

Bousset for "incompetence" in rabbinica, adding that thereby "he only made a bad case worse by arguing it" ("Christian Writers on Judaism," 244–46).

10. Bousset, *Jesu Predigt.*

11. Bousset's *Jesus* was part of a series of popular works, Religionsgeschichtliche Volksbücher für den deutschen christlichen Gegenwart, designed to educate the Christian public about the work of the History of Religion School. The English translation also appeared in a popularizing series, Crown Theological Library. Page numbers in parentheses refer to this English edition.

constituted a danger and a limitation to religion" (95). Thus, while Judaism's individualistic piety does appear from time to time in the view that God is the Father of each person, Jesus made this central and so became "the consummator of what already existed" (113). Still, the ethos of Pharisaism remained essentially negative, "embodied in prohibition and in exact limitations of the moral law," whereas "Jesus' tone is positive" (144–45).

Ernest Renan's *The Life of Jesus*[12] was even more disparaging. Renan, having left the priesthood, mastered Semitic languages and in 1860 began to excavate ancient Byblos, near modern Beirut. While there, he visited Palestine, which to him became "a fifth Gospel" when he returned to write the book in Lebanon.

According to Renan, Jesus was surrounded by Judaism but never was really part of it, "for he was ignorant of the strange scholasticism which was taught in Jerusalem and which would soon [!] constitute the Talmud. If some Pharisees had already brought it into Galilee, he did not associate with them . . . and when later he encountered this silly casuistry, it only inspired him with disgust" (92). After a visit to Jerusalem (Renan follows John in having Jesus go several times) he saw "that there was no union possible between him and the ancient Jewish religion. The abrogation of the sacrifices which had caused him so much disgust, the suppression of an impious and haughty priesthood, and in a general sense, the abrogation of the law, appeared to him as absolute necessity. From this time he appears no more as a Jewish reformer but as a destroyer of Judaism. . . . In other words, Jesus was no longer a Jew. . . . He proclaimed the rights of man, not the rights of the Jew; the deliverance of man, not the deliverance of the Jew" (224–26).

12. *Vie de Jesus* (1863) was the first of several volumes presenting the history of Christianity; but none could match the fame of the first, an immediate best-seller. Editions of five thousand one after another were exhausted in days; in five months sixty thousand had been sold. It was soon translated into German, Dutch, Italian, and English. A cheap French edition appeared in 1864 and sold for Fr 1.25. John Haynes Holmes, who provided the introduction to the Modern Library edition, *The Life of Jesus*, claimed that it ranks with Darwin's *Origin of Species* and Marx's *Das Kapital* as "a work which changed forever the currents of the world's thought and life" ("Introduction," 15)—surely an exaggeration. Despite its popularity, the book had a negligible influence on the scholarship of the Quest. Allen notes that Renan's Jesus was the center of adoring women, especially Mary Magdalene, and that "there is a direct line of descent from Renan's *Life of Jesus* to de Mille's *King of Kings*." She places Renan's entire study of Christian origins in the context of the new interest in the exotic and the (presumed) erotic in the ancient Near East. See Allen, *The Human Christ*, 187. For British responses to Renan, see Pals, *The Victorian "Lives" of Jesus*, 34–39.

Even though Rudolf Bultmann's Jesus book does not separate him from Judaism but instead begins each chapter by anchoring his teaching in the Jewish context, it too follows the common pattern: Jesus is portrayed as superior to Judaism in whatever the scholar takes to be decisive for his view of Christian faith.[13] Thus Bultmann can agree with the view, advocated earlier by his teacher Johannes Weiss and especially by Albert Schweitzer, that Jesus too expected God to bring his kingdom by a dramatic intervention. What matters is that Jesus actually had no interest in describing the event or the result; he used this expectation to call for what was central (for Bultmann as for Jesus) — an existential decision of faith (38–42, 47). Likewise, since for Bultmann faith is obedience to the preached Word, he can point out that the rabbis too saw obedience to God's will as the heart of morality and religion, though for them obedience was formal and "blind," whereas Jesus called for radical obedience of the whole person (50–73). "Radical obedience exists only when a man inwardly assents to what is required of him, when the thing commanded is seen intrinsically as God's command; when the whole man is *in* what he does, when he is not *doing something obediently* but *is* essentially obedient" (77, his italics). Thus "the divergence of Jesus from Judaism is in thinking out the idea of obedience radically to the end, not in setting it aside" (83) — clearly a reformulation of Bousset's "consummator." It is the news of the kingdom's coming that places one in the crisis situation that requires the either/or decision to be obedient or not.

The vitality of this pattern can be seen three decades later when one of Bultmann's students, Günther Bornkamm, published his *Jesus of Nazareth*, a product of the then "new quest of the historical Jesus."[14] For Bornkamm, the superiority of Jesus lies in the directness, the immediacy, the lack of an observer's point of view.

Bornkamm sets the stage carefully, claiming that "without a doubt the religion of ancient Israel underwent in Judaism after the Exile a tremendous narrowing

13. Bultmann's *Jesus* was written for the general reader and published as vol. 17 of the Siebenstern Taschenbuch series. With the author's approval, the English translation was titled *Jesus and the Word*. The page numbers refer to this edition. Throughout, Bultmann assumes the results of his earlier "form critical" analysis of the Jesus traditions first published in 1921 as *Die Geschichte der synoptischen Tradition*. The English translation of the third revised edition (1958), *The History of the Synoptic Tradition*, contains his supplementary notes.

14. Bornkamm's *Jesus von Nazareth* appeared first as a paperback in the Urban-Bücher series aimed at the literate reader. The English translation, *Jesus of Nazareth*, was made from the third edition of 1957. The page numbers refer to this edition. A tenth edition, revised and expanded, appeared in 1975 but was not translated into English.

down and hardening," so that "worship and sacrifice . . . are seen as a ritual obligation. But even in its perversion, the original understanding of God's power and law . . . is recognizable" (37). He writes of a "formalistic legalizing of the law, and a corresponding detailed technique of piety, to which Jesus' message of the divine will stands in sharp contrast" (40). Claiming to "focus those facts which are prior to any pious interpretation and which manifest themselves as undistorted and primary" (53), he places Jesus in a world "between past and future" because "according to the Jewish faith, the immediate present is practically non-existent. . . . All time is in between, . . . founded in God's decision of the past and looking forward to God's decisions in the future." Jesus' milieu "is comparable to a soil hardened and barren through its age-long history and tradition, yet a volcanic, eruptive ground, out of whose cracks and crevices breaks forth again and again the fire of a burning expectation. However, both torpidity and convulsion, petrifaction and blazing eruption [namely, Pharisaism and apocalyptic] have, at bottom, the same origin: they are the outcome and expression of a faith in God who is beyond the world and history" (55–56). Although Jesus "belongs to this world . . . he is of unmistakable otherness. . . . The reality of God and the authority of his will are always directly present, and are fulfilled in him. There is nothing in contemporary Judaism which corresponds to the immediacy with which he teaches" (56–57). Bornkamm continues: "The immediate presence is the hallmark of all the words of Jesus, of his appearance and his actions, in a world which . . . had lost the present" (58). According to Bornkamm, "the Gospels call this patent immediacy of Jesus's sovereign power his 'authority'" (60).

Bornkamm does not err in calling attention to the sense of authority that marks Jesus' teaching, as will be noted in chapter 3. The problem lies elsewhere: in so distorting and denigrating Judaism that, in the name of "facts prior to any pious interpretation," the authority of Jesus becomes historical evidence of his manifest superiority.[15]

The current quest has not abandoned the pattern either, though it is given a somewhat different shape. Thus John Dominic Crossan, for whom the unconventional and the egalitarian appear to be specially prized countercultural values, seems unable to find Jesus affirming anything in his environment or heritage.[16] By ignoring ritual food laws, Jesus subverted them (263). "Jesus'

---

15. For a fuller criticism of Bornkamm's treatment of Judaism, see Keck, "Bornkamm's *Jesus of Nazareth* Revisited." In the tenth edition Bornkamm responded with an epilogue; it was not included in subsequent English editions. For an analysis see Lührmann, "Bornkamm's Response to Keck Revisited."

16. Crossan, *The Historical Jesus*.

Kingdom of nobodies and undesirables in the here and now of this world was surely a radical egalitarian one, and, as such, it rendered sexual and social, political and religious distinctions completely irrelevant and anachronistic" (298). Moreover, by drawing on cross-cultural studies of "possession," he concludes that Jesus' exorcisms are really symbolic individual revolutions (318) and that when Jesus touched the leper he "challenged . . . the religious monopoly of the priests" (324) because he himself was a "purifying alternative to the Temple" (322), the central authority of Judaism. As an itinerant, Jesus represented unbrokered (unmediated) egalitarianism, which was "an even more radical challenge to the localized univocity of Jerusalem's Temple" than John the Baptist's rite of forgiveness. Indeed, "no matter . . . what Jesus thought, said, or did about the Temple, he was its functional opponent, alternative, and substitute" (355). His later action there, symbolizing its destruction, was "but the logical extension" of what he had been doing and saying all along" (360).

Crossan does not need to denigrate Judaism; indeed, his tome is markedly free of disparaging remarks about it. Instead he absorbs Jewish life and religion into a portrayal of Mediterranean culture and simply analyzes the patterns of wealth, privilege, and power in Roman-occupied Palestine; against this he interprets Jesus' words as "a religious and economic egalitarianism that negated alike and at once the hierarchical and patronal normalcies of Jewish religion and Roman power" (422). His Jesus "had both an ideal vision and a social program" (349), for his commensality (shared eating) was "a strategy for building or rebuilding peasant community on radically different principles from those of honor and shame, patronage and clientele. It was based on an egalitarian sharing of spiritual and material power at the most grass-roots level" (344). Crossan also declares, "I emphasize most strongly . . . that such egalitarianism stems not only from peasant Judaism but, even more deeply, from peasant society as such" (263). In short, Crossan's Jesus too has been isolated from his heritage, especially as a religion, and turned against it in the name of peasant resentments.

It is useful to end this brief sampling of Christian Gentile attempts to portray Jesus the Jew by remembering that the gospels too are committed to stating and showing his relation to his Jewish inheritance and context, though from a quite different perspective as well as for different reasons. Because the gospels were written for various uses in Christian communities, their treatment of Jesus' relation to Jewish faith and practice reflects the growing rift between the early churches and the Jewish communities. Consequently the gospels not only claim that in Jesus biblical promises to Israel were actualized but they also present him to be at odds with certain elements of his world, because the Evangelists understood their communities' tensions with current Jewish life to be grounded in, and legitimated by, what Jesus had said and done. In such circumstances Jesus traditions that expressed criticism were more useful than those which evidenced his continuities. Moreover, since the earliest Jesus traditions were formed and transmitted by Jewish believers who, we may assume, used them to persuade fellow Jews to become Jesus people too, they probably valued precisely those traditions that expressed something special about him, including those sayings in which he gave commonly held convictions a new twist. The shared convictions and practices that had nothing special about them, but which may also have characterized Jesus as an observant Galilean Jew, would have been taken for granted and so not mentioned because everybody knows *that*. Modern historians, on the other hand, have a quite different task—to so situate Jesus in his context that those characteristic traits that made him distinctive (and critical) are balanced convincingly with what Nils Dahl aptly formulated as "historical considerations of synchronic similarity and diachronic continuity."[17] Although current Jesus studies produce widely different portraits of Jesus the Jew,[18] these still bear some of the features given him by Harnack and Bousset—perhaps because the whole quest has placed an inordinate emphasis on his teachings and ideas, as if *they* made him what he has been, and is, for Christians. But that is getting ahead of the story.

17. Dahl, "The Early Church and Jesus," 172.

18. For example, E. P. Sanders concludes, "Jesus expected the kingdom in the near future, he awaited the rebuilding of the temple, he called 'twelve' to symbolize the restoration of Israel, and his disciples thought about the kingdom concretely enough to ask about their place in it. Thus we cannot shift the normal expectations of Jewish restoration theology to the periphery" (*Jesus and Judaism*, 156). Precisely the opposite conclusion is reached by Breech, who concludes his study of undoubtedly genuine parables by saying, "Judging from the core sayings and parables, there is absolutely no basis for assuming that Jesus shared the cosmological, mythological, or religious ideas of his contemporaries. . . . Far from *proclaiming* the kingdom of God, . . . a God who acts in history on behalf of his people Israel, Jesus totally reinterprets the 'kingdom of God.' None of his sayings or parables points to history as the *locus* for its activity" (*The Silence of Jesus*, 218). This Jesus is not only a true "original" as he claims but a lone figure, unrelated to what preceded or followed him, if indeed he used kingdom language "in a way that differs explicitly from the usage of his contemporaries, predecessors, and successors" (ibid., 37).

Jesus the Jew in Jewish critical scholarship.[19]   Jewish scholarship has had a triple task: to provide Jewish readers with basic historical information about Jesus;[20] to show them that Jesus can and should be integrated into Jewish history as one of its own and not be regarded as a renegade; and to demonstrate to Christian Gentiles that the Judaism of which he was a part was not a legalistic, sterile, futureless religion but one no less worthy of respect than Christianity. Understandably those who first undertook this complex task were recently emancipated and partly assimilated Jews in Germany, as well as liberal or Reform Jews in Britain and America.[21] Today Jewish participants in the study of Jesus are as diverse as their Christian colleagues. Before looking at some examples, five observations may be useful.

First, because the Jesus quest has assumed that the Jesus of history differed significantly from the Jesus Christ of the Christian faith found in the gospels, Christian scholars have deemed it necessary to address, in one way or other, the issue of how the reconstructed Jesus is to be related to the Christ of faith, worship, and proclamation. No Jewish historian of Jesus has had to worry about that issue—unless considering conversion. All Jewish historians have assumed that Jesus was a human being like any other. Frequently, in fact, past Jews have regarded the

19. The first comprehensive analysis of Jewish scholarship's treatment of Jesus was Lindeskog's *Die Jesusfrage in neuzeitlichen Judentum*. Lindeskog wrote the foreword to Hagner, *The Jewish Reclamation of Jesus*. Hagner claims that this reclamation "has been possible only by being unfair to the Gospels" (ibid., 14)—i.e., the Jewish scholars assume that Jesus was a remarkable man, but no more. A brief survey is provided by Ben-Chorin, "The Image of Jesus in Modern Judaism"; a fuller discussion is offered by Lapide, *Israelis, Jews and Jesus*. Although the book summarizes "Jesus in Hebrew Literature" and "Jesus in Israeli Schoolbooks," half of it provides concise overview and quotations of rabbinic treatments of Jesus from Tannaitic times onward.

20. Lapide reminds Christian readers of the long custom among Jews not even to mention the name of Jesus (*Israelis, Jews and Jesus*, 39). He also quotes, for example, the assembled elders in Poland who in 1631 forbade "under penalty of the great anathema the publishing of anything in the new editions of the Mishnah or the Gemara which refers to Jesus of Nazareth" (ibid., 79).

21. Lapide (*Israelis, Jews, and Jesus*, 109–28) provides useful quotations from liberal rabbis such as Samuel Hirsch, Isaac M. Wise, and Stephen S. Wise, the first rabbi to preach in his synagogue on "Jesus and the Jews," evoking thereby considerable consternation. Berlin sees the writings about Jesus produced by American Reform Jews as part of their responses to anti-Semitism and to efforts to evangelize Jews. Religious freedom did not make American Jews more receptive to Christianity but had the opposite effect: it freed them for new and sharp polemic against it. Accordingly, he claims that by portraying Jesus as a loyal Jew, the Reformers "denied the liberal Protestant claim of spiritual uniqueness of Jesus"; indeed, the superiority of the Jewish Jesus implied the superiority of Judaism (Berlin, *Defending the Faith*, 45–48, 57).

notion that Jesus was "divine" or the "Son" of God as a blasphemous result of the Gentile deification of a man. Given this outlook, it was easy for Jewish scholars to use the negative criterion to delete from consideration those elements that appeared to be Christian additions. On the other hand, they have generally refrained from applying it to the Jewish-sounding materials, for they could hardly integrate Jesus into Jewish history if they called into question the sayings in which he sounded "typically Jewish."

Second, since classical Judaism has been shaped by the Talmuds and the Midrashim produced by the rabbis after the second revolt, it was natural for Jewish scholars to reclaim Jesus by relating him positively to the rabbis' predecessors, presumably the Pharisees. Moreover, since the Jewish study of Jesus was pioneered by liberal or Reformed Jews for whom the moral preachments of the prophets were more important than the rituals and regulations of the Pentateuch, it was also natural that these scholars regarded the Pharisees—especially the more liberal ones such as Hillel—as teachers who combined piety and ethics in ways they found congenial. Indeed, for over a century scholars —Christian as well as Jewish—found it useful, for apologetic reasons, to compare Hillel (circa 60 B.C.E. to 20 C.E.) and Jesus.[22] And since the Jesus tradition also emphasizes one's relation to God and neighbor, it was relatively easy for these scholars to integrate Jesus into a simplified view of first-century Pharisaism, noting that his criticisms were aimed at distortions, not at Pharisaism itself,[23] and in fact were similar to the criticisms leveled by the Pharisees themselves.

22. In 1992 Charlesworth convened a symposium in Jerusalem to probe the possibility and problems of comparison; he, with L. L. Johns, also edited the papers as *Hillel and Jesus: Comparative Studies of Two Major Religious Leaders*. One of the participants, A. Gottstein, argues that Hillel and Jesus cannot be compared because comparison is possible only if they belong to the same class or group; since they do not, comparisons inevitably distort historical reality. See Gottstein, "Hillel and Jesus: Are Comparisons Possible?" This view did not prevent Charlesworth from compiling similarities and differences in the introduction, "Hillel and Jesus: 'Why Comparisons Are Important," or Flusser from writing "Hillel and Jesus: Two Ways of Self-Awareness," chap. 4.

23. Falk has argued, unconvincingly, that "Jesus's debates with the Pharisees were actually disputes recorded in the Talmud between Bet Shammai and Bet Hillel, with Jesus adopting the views of Bet Hillel"; that "Bet Shammai were in control of Jewish life and institutions during most of the first century, and that the murderous Zealots, often represented in the priesthood in Jerusalem, were followers of Bet Shammai"; and that "the Shammaites were responsible for handing Jesus over to the Romans . . . and their decision was in violation of Jewish law" (*Jesus the Pharisee*, 8). Thereby Jesus is integrated into a grossly simplified history, as in a western movie, in which the good Pharisees wear the white hats, the bad wear the black hats, and no one wears gray ones.

Third, the quest of the historical Pharisee is even more complex and controversial than the quest of the historical Jesus. Whereas the latter seeks to recover a single individual, the former seeks to portray a group with a history spanning two centuries during which various internal tensions and differences surely appeared. Between the reexamination of second-temple Jewish culture precipitated by the discovery of the Dead Sea Scrolls, on the one hand, and the more deliberate use of historical critical modes of analysis of rabbinic texts, on the other, the nature of first-century Pharisaism has become ever more problematic and controversial, not less. Saldarini observes that the Pharisees have been pictured "as a sect within Judaism, a powerful religious leadership group, a political leadership group, a learned scholarly group, a lay movement in competition with the priesthood, a group of middle class artisans, or some combination of these." Moreover, many studies "have been marred by an uncritical acceptance of some or all of the sources." In addition, "lack of evidence about the Pharisees and great discord over related issues such as the nature of Second Temple Judaism, its thought, laws, practices, and social structure, have joined to produce a welter of unproven theories concerning every aspect of the Pharisees' thought and history."[24] Two facts suffice to suggest how formidable the problems of the sources are. (a) Although a vast amount of literature produced by Jews during the second-temple period has come down to us, only two of the authors identify themselves as Pharisees—actually, as having been Pharisees: Josephus and Paul.[25] Consequently, we have no text that identifies itself as from a pre-70 Pharisee. (b) Because rabbinic texts assembled and ordered traditions for the purpose of furthering the rabbis' purposes and perspectives in reshaping Jewish life after the temple had been destroyed and two wars lost, it is nearly as precarious to quote a second-century rabbi to document what a pre-70 Pharisee thought as it is to quote a contemporary Presbyterian to explain an English Puritan. Indeed, Alan Segal notes that since the New Testament was written by the beginning of the second century but rabbinic literature was produced two and more centuries later, "The New Testament is . . . much better evidence for the history of Judaism [in the first century]

---

24. Saldarini, "Pharisees." Saldarini provides a concise survey of the issues and the history of scholarship. See also the more recent essay by Sievers, "Who Were the Pharisees?"

25. Sievers ("Who Were the Parisees?," 139) points out that "Rabbinic literature never identifies any named individual as a Pharisee" and that even Hillel and Shammai are first explicitly connected with Pharisees by Jewish-Christian sectarians cited by Jerome (fifth century C.E.). Whether Josephus had actually been a member of a group of Pharisees for a time depends on how one takes his phrase "following the school of the Pharisees" (*Life*, 12), as Sievers points out (ibid., 147).

than is rabbinic Judaism for the origins of Christianity."[26] Rabbinic evidence, including the Targums, cannot be ignored, of course, but must be used carefully, not only because of the problems of dating it but also because it is a quite different type of literature for a quite different kind of community.

Fourth, relating Jesus accurately to Jewish life has become much more complex because the Dead Sea Scrolls, the library of a "monastic" community of Essenes at Qumran that did not survive the first revolt, precipitated a thorough reconsideration of virtually every aspect of Jewish history. This exposed so much diversity in the way faithfulness to the Torah and to the God who gave it was understood at the time that scholars now speak of Judaisms in Jesus' day. As well, Jesus' relation to Essene Judaism has been probed repeatedly, some using the "Scrolls" (and scraps) to prop up the previous centuries' speculation that Jesus had been an Essene (see p. 12). Sober scholars, however, are content to note similarities and differences and to reckon with the possibility that Essenes may well have influenced both Jesus[27] and the earliest Christian group in Jerusalem.[28] One need not infer that he, or John the Baptist, had actually gone to Qumran, for apparently most Essenes lived in the villages where they pursued a less rigorous lifestyle than those at the settlement. Essene "influence," of course, includes the possibility that Jesus had them in mind when he said such things as "You have heard that it was said, 'You shall love your neighbor and hate your enemy'" (Mt 5:43), since they are the only known group that cursed its enemies (outsiders).[29] In any case, Essenism—a complex phenomenon with a far from

26. Segal, "Conversion and Messianism," 299.

27. See, e.g., Charlesworth, "The Dead Sea Scrolls and the Historical Jesus," in which commonalities and differences are noted.

28. Using both archaeological and literary evidence, Pixner has claimed that the early Christian community lived adjacent to the Essene quarter. See his "Jesus and His Community"; see also the earlier study by Riesner, "Jesus, the Primitive Community and the Essene Quarter of Jerusalem."

29. The Community Rule prescribes both liturgical blessing on the community and curse on its enemies: "And the Levites shall curse all the men of the lot of Satan, saying: 'Be cursed because of all your guilty wickedness. May He deliver you up for torture at the hands of the vengeful Avengers! . . . Be cursed without mercy because of the darkness of your deeds. . . . May God not heed you when you call on Him, nor pardon you by blotting out your sin. . . .' And after the blessing and the cursing, all those entering the Covenant shall say, 'Amen, Amen!'" (IQSii, 5–10); see also the fragments of the comparable curses found in Cave 4 (4Q, 286–87; 4Q, 280). The quotation is from Vermes, *The Dead Sea Scrolls in English*, 71; see also ibid., 185–86.

clear history—was a significant and probably unavoidable element in Jesus' var-iegated and somewhat contentious context.

Fifth, efforts to place Jesus accurately in his context have led to an intense study of Galilee—its populace, social and economic conditions, distinct habits of thought and practice, and power relations under Herod Antipas, in whose domain Jesus' mission occurred.[30] These efforts have required a fresh reading of Josephus as well as attending to the archaeological evidence produced recently; information gleaned from Josephus is being read in light of sociological and anthropological studies of matters such as peasant societies, the relation of vil-lages to towns and cities, social unrest, and resistance movements.[31] Although Galilee has fascinated students of Jesus and the gospels since Renan, today's sense of the task is no longer that of locating second-temple-era materials that illumine aspects of Jesus but rather that of first reconstructing as fully as possible the Galilee he knew and then detecting where Jesus should be placed *in* it so that he becomes an integral part *of* it. The success of such an undertaking clearly depends not only on countless critical judgments about the sources of information and the usefulness of cross-disciplinary studies, but also on a disci-plined use of historical imagination, lest the result be imagined history.

"The Jewishness of Jesus" has become a major theme.[32] Ironically, probing this theme is exceedingly difficult, not because there is scant evidence but because there is much of it. In addition to correlating archaeological, sociolog-ical, and literary material one must also assess the reliability of data in five bodies of texts: the heterogeneous writings called "Apocrypha and Pseud-epigrapha," the "Dead Sea Scrolls," traditions embedded in rabbinic literature produced more than a century after Jesus, the writings of Josephus, and the New Testament—each of which bristles with problems for the historian who wishes to reconstruct Jesus' world.[33] The task is far more complicated today

30. See Freyne, *Galilee, Jesus and the Gospels*, and his summary, "The Geography, Pol-itics and Economics."

31. See especially Horsley's recent *Galilee, History, Politics, People*.

32. See the survey article by Chilton, "Jesus Within Judaism."

33. Vermes, aware of these difficulties, has chosen not to be intimidated by them but to view all the Jewish materials—including the Synoptics—as "a common *source*, written or oral, . . . firm in substance but variable in shape, on which both the evangelists and the later writers depended." When all the materials are viewed as "parts of a continuously evolving Jewish religious and literary activity," Jesus will be viewed "as one particular sec-tor on the general map of Jewish cultural history" (*The Religion of Jesus the Jew*, 9, his ital-ics). Where Vermes locates Jesus is noted below. Chilton finds this "simply uncritical," for

than the first modern Jewish scholars who attempted it foresaw. They were quite confident that they knew what being truly "Jewish" entailed in Jesus' day. Recent debates in Israel and elsewhere about Jewish identity alert one to suspect that the question was no less complex and controversial in the first century. In any case, the brief sampling that follows shows that "the Jewishness of Jesus" has a history also in Jewish scholarship.

Harnack's lectures were barely off the press when a young rabbi in Berlin, Leo Baeck, responded with a brief review in which he admired Harnack's style (he lectured from notes) but castigated his treatment of Jesus' relation to Judaism.[34] Right away he saw that Harnack's appeal to history was really apologetics, liberal Protestantism's effort to show by its reconstructed history of Jesus that he clearly merited the devotion of moderns. Moreover, he objected to Harnack's portrayal of Jesus as untouched by rabbinical instruction, insisting instead that "every one of his utterances . . . shows him to be a disciple of the rabbis." He also traced Harnack's error to "woeful ignorance of *halakah* and *haggadah*," saying that "whoever reaches judgments like those of Mr. Harnack knows nothing of a vast area of Jewish life . . . and the time of Jesus and the early church; or he compels himself to know nothing of it" (25). Whereas Harnack had regarded Jesus' Jewishness as husk, Baeck saw it as the kernel, as Martyn points out (26). Baeck insisted "that Jesus, in every one of his traits, was a *thoroughly Jewish character*, that a man such as he could arise only from the soil of Judaism, only there and nowhere else. Jesus is a genuinely Jewish personality, all his striving and doing, his bearing and feeling, his speech and his silence . . . mark him as of the Jewish kind, the kind of Jewish idealism, the best that could and can be found in Judaism, but at that time could be found only in Judaism. . . . Such a man could not have emerged out of any other people, and among no other people could he have been active" (44).

---

it has the effect of portraying Jesus as a figure of later rabbinic Judaism instead of early Judaism (*Pure Kingdom*, 55 n.17).

34. Baeck, "Harnacks Vorlesungen über das Wesen des Christentums"; a somewhat enlarged version was published in Breslau by W. Koebner in 1902. A translated excerpt is included in *Jewish Perspectives on Christianity*, edited by F. A. Rothschild, for which J. L. Martyn provides an excellent introduction by treating Baeck's overall views of Christianity (21–41); he also translates the passages from the review of Harnack that are not included in the excerpt. The page numbers in parentheses here refer to the Rothschild volume. Martyn's piece, retitled "Baeck's Reading of Paul," is included in his collected essays, *Theological Issues in the Letters of Paul*, 47–69.

In 1938 Baeck published a long essay, "The Gospel as a Document of the History of the Jewish Faith."[35] He first explained that Jewish tradition elaborated and modified what it transmitted because it was a living stream; he then outlined the history of the gospel tradition to the second century, ending with his version of the negative criterion. This was followed by a characterization of Jesus and his disciples as thoroughly Jewish, climaxed by a call to fellow Jews: "Judaism should comprehend and take note of what is its own," for Jesus manifested "in every particular what is pure and good in Judaism" (101–2). Given the time and place of its publication, this was a remarkable declaration. The Jewish reclamation of Jesus could hardly have been expressed more strongly—or provocatively.

Whereas Bousset had insisted that Judaism does not account for Jesus, Joseph Klausner's *Jesus of Nazareth*, the first scholarly life of Jesus in Hebrew, anticipated Baeck by asserting that Jesus "is wholly explainable by the scriptural and Pharisaic Judaism of his time" (363) because "throughout the Gospels there is not one item of ethical teaching which cannot be paralleled either in the Old Testament, the Apocrypha, or in the Talmudic and Midrashic literature of the period near to the time of Jesus" (384, italicized). What is different about Jesus is that he "condensed and concentrated" his ethical teachings, whereas in the rabbinic collections "they are interspersed among more commonplace and worthless matter" (389). In fact, "Jesus surpasses Hillel in his ethical ideals," but "his teaching has not proven possible in practice" (397). In the end Klausner faults Jesus for not being sufficiently concerned for culture and the national state, claiming that Jesus ignored "anything concerned with material civilization" (375)—matters important for Klausner, who had moved to Jerusalem as a Zionist.

A quarter-century later Paul Winter, who in England worked in the post office by day to support himself and at night studied Jesus' trial, declared flatly, "in historical reality Jesus was a Pharisee. . . . In the whole of the New Testament we are unable to find a single historically reliable instance of a religious difference between Jesus and the Pharisaic guild" (italicized).[36] No one went further in integrating Jesus into liberal Judaism's understanding of the Pharisees than Kaufmann

---

35. "Das Evangelium als Urkunde der jüdischen Glaubensgeschichte" was to be published in a collection of essays. Although printed, it was never actually published because the Gestapo destroyed nearly all copies. It was published separately nonetheless as a small book in 1938. The English translation, "The Gospel as a Document of the History of the Jewish People," is available in Baeck's *Judaism and Christianity*, 41–136. Baeck himself survived Theresienstadt.

36. Winter, *On the Trial of Jesus*, 133.

Kohler, the eminent German-born leader of American Reform Judaism. After citing Jesus' use of the Shema' he observed, "Jesus was a perfect Jew."[37]

As noted, this smooth integration of Jesus into Pharisaism as seen by liberal Jews has become less and less tenable as "the Pharisees" became more and more elusive. Jacob Neusner, who pioneered the application of sophisticated analyses of form and structure to rabbinic texts and their traditions, also noted that there is a fundamental difference between Pharisaism and the gospels. He claimed that Pharisaism's "central metaphor is the cult"—the concern, originally limited to the temple, for what is ritually clean and unclean; this became the hallmark of the Pharisees. This cultic metaphor implies a distinct ontology, one that emphasizes "regularity, permanence, recurrence." But for the gospels the central ontological affirmation is "very disruptive and disintegrative, profoundly historical and even world denying."[38] Although he refers to the gospels and not to Jesus himself, his observation implies that if Jesus understood the kingdom of God as a God-given irruption into history, then he too would have operated with a disruptive ontology closer to that of the gospels than to the Pharisees—unless at least some of them too had an apocalyptic, disjunctive ontology. Or, despite Crossan's assertions to the contrary, was Jesus also concerned with purity, as Chilton claims (see below), and so in this regard at least was close to the Pharisees? And were the Pharisees as nonpolitical as Neusner has insisted, or were at least a significant number of them also intensely political, deeply committed to the expulsion of the Romans? This aspect of pre-70 Pharisaism could have been edited out of the traditions when the later rabbis codified them for use in a noninsurrectionist Judaism after the second revolt in 132–35 C.E. Should that have been the case, integrating Jesus into Pharisaism could have quite different results.

Some recent Jewish interpretations of Jesus have moved in just this direction, claiming to have found in him what Klausner missed: robust concern for culture and the nation. Even if some Pharisees were more quietist than activist, Jesus is said to have been closer to those who sought the liberation of both people and land from Roman hegemony so that Israel could actualize its God-given destiny. A few non-Jewish scholars have, to be sure, insisted from time to time that Jesus was virtually a Zealot, but such revisionist views remained marginal until recently

37. Kohler, *The Origins of the Synagogue*, 218. Kohler, it should be noted, thought that both John the Baptist and Jesus were "members of the Essene party" (ibid., 205, 227–28), though he also said that "the line between the Essenes, the Hasidim, and the Pharisees was probably never sharply drawn" (ibid., 133).

38. Neusner, "The Use of the Later Rabbinic Evidence," 223–25.

when a distinction began to be made between revolution as insurrection and revolution as radical social and political change that did not require armed rebellion.[39] Some Jewish scholars, however, do not hesitate to see Jesus as an intensely religious patriot, as the following quotation from Pinchas Lapide shows:

> If Jesus was really the pious, Torah-faithful Jew that the Synoptic gospels unanimously portray, he can neither have been indifferent politically nor have collaborated treasonably. Only an active anti-Roman attitude is harmonizable with his intense love for Israel. Also his fiery temperament, that often flashes in his controversy speeches, and his dynamism contradict every passivity in the face of the brutal pagan hegemony of Roman power and its intrusive blasphemous idolatry.
>
> For most of today's [Jewish] authors, this patriotic militancy does not preclude a hyper-Jewish deepening of the biblical ethic. To the contrary! If the impatient assailant of heaven, following the steps of the Maccabees, wanted to liberate Israel from the heathen yoke, he nonetheless knew that only a national return to the basic values of the Torah could bring the "kingdom of the heavens" to a liberated Israel.
>
> Struggle against Rome and return to God were, from the modern Jewish standpoint, the two reciprocally enhancing demands of Jesus.[40]

Like Kohler's Jesus, Lapide's too might be called "a perfect Jew" but of a quite different sort.

The same can be said of Geza Vermes's Jesus, whom he locates not among the Pharisees, Essenes, or Zealots but in the stream of "the holy miracle-workers

39. For a "Zealot Jesus," see Brandon, *Jesus and the Zealots*, esp. chap. 7. He said that Jesus' action in the temple was probably "achieved by the aid of an excited crowd of his supporters and was attended by violence and pillage"—which he later calls a "Zealot uprising" (ibid., 356)—and that by attacking the system that the temple represented "Jesus anticipated what the Zealots achieved in a.d. 66" (ibid., 333, 335), though Jesus himself probably was not a Zealot (ibid., 355). See also Bammel, "The Revolutionary Theory from Reimarus to Brandon." Bammel and Moule, eds., *Jesus and the Politics of His Day* contains essays that respond, at some point or other, to Brandon. Horsley, on the other hand, thinks the whole idea of a Zealot movement from the time of Jesus to 66 c.e. is a modern invention; he emphasizes the socioeconomic aspects of Jesus and concludes that he "was apparently a revolutionary, but not a violent political revolutionary" (*Jesus and the Spiral of Violence*, 326).

40. Lapide, *Der Rabbi von Nazaret*, 132; my translation.

of Galilee," who represent "charismatic Judaism,"[41] going back to the Hasidim whose "prayer was believed to be all-powerful, capable of performing miracles" (69). For Vermes, two figures are especially important instances — Honi the Circle-Drawer (first century B.C.E.) and the Galilean Hanina ben-Dosa (first century C.E.), both of whom, according to rabbinic traditions, were renowned for their miracle-working prayers.[42] Vermes finds the traits of the latter to be quite similar to what is reported about Jesus: both are said to have performed cures at a distance, and "both Jesus and Hanina, and no doubt the Hasidim in general, showed a complete lack of interest in legal and ritual affairs and a corresponding exclusive concentration on moral questions" (77). The independence of these charismatics, for whom "both laxity and severity . . . were peripheral," led inevitably to tensions with those concerned to preserve the correct order (81).

As for Jesus, "no objective and enlightened student of the gospels can help but be struck by the incomparable superiority of Jesus," for not only was he "an unsurpassed master of the art of laying bare the inmost core of spiritual truth and of bringing every issue back to the essence of religion, the existential relationship of man and man, and man and God," but he also went beyond the prophets: they spoke on behalf of the poor, but Jesus "actually took his stand among the pariahs of this world, those despised by the respectable" (224). Despite locating Jesus among the charismatic miracle workers, this way of talking is remarkably anachronistic; not only does it sound like Harnack, but it also reveals the persistent legacy of early-nineteenth-century romanticism, which was fascinated by the heroic individual who stands out from his environment.

Why, then, was Jesus crucified? In Vermes's subsequent volume, *The Religion of Jesus the Jew*, he succinctly summarizes his conclusion: "The arrest and execution of Jesus were due, not directly to his words and deeds, but to their possible insurrectionary consequences feared by the nervous authorities in charge of law and order in that powder-keg of first-century Jerusalem. . . . He died on the cross for having done the wrong thing (caused a commotion) in the wrong place (the Temple) at the wrong time (just before Passover)" (x). Why a superlative charismatic holy man who could bring every issue "back to the essence of religion" should have aroused suspicions of insurrection is not clear, despite the precedent in the case of John the Baptist. That, of course, is the central historical problem.

41. Vermes, *Jesus the Jew*, 223.
42. For a perceptive critique of this reliance on Honi and Hanina, see Chilton, "Jesus Within Judaism," 181–184.

What has become evident is that even if one regards "the Jewish reclamation of Jesus" as the return of the prodigal son from nineteen centuries among Christian Gentiles, it is not easy to describe either the home he had left or the son before he left it, because the historical problems are much more complex than often realized. Nonetheless, the obvious is often overlooked: probably more can be known historically about Jesus than about any other single second-temple-era Jew except Paul.

Jesus the committed Jew.   One animating factor in the current efforts to reconstruct as fully as possible the world in which Jesus lived is the desire to discern how he interacted with it as a participant. This does not imply, however, that he responded to everything in it; some aspects of his world mattered more deeply to him than others, and it is the historians' task to identify those to which he was most committed. It is appropriate, then, that this discussion of Jesus the Jew in critical scholarship conclude by noting briefly three examples of current gentile scholars who portray Jesus as a passionately committed Jew, deeply involved in the issues of the day.

Whereas some have portrayed Jesus as rupturing the prevailing Jewish understanding of purity, Bruce Chilton sees "a Jesus whose passionate concern was for pure offering by forgiven people in Jerusalem. His own program of the purity and personnel of sacrifice was both cognate with Essene, Pharisaic, Sadducean, and Josephan programs, and scandalously distinctive, as events proved." He neither sought to displace the temple nor dramatically symbolized its destruction; rather, "what was in Jerusalem from his perspective *was* his Temple, and his attempt to possess it with his program of purity is what resulted in his crucifixion."[43]

According to Chilton, Jesus' action becomes intelligible only when seen in light of a controversy generated by Caiaphas's decision to sell sacrificial animals in the temple precincts instead of outside the city. This violated the Hillelite construal of the Torah because Hillel had insisted that the sacrifice must be demonstrably one's own, evidenced by the imposition of one's hands on the beast as it was handed over to the priest; simply buying one that had been certified as clean—as if sacrifice "was a matter of offering pure, unblemished animals *simpliciter*"—not only introduced commerce into the sacred area but above all ruptured the link between the worshiper and the sacrifice (109). Jesus therefore "occupied" the temple "to prevent the sacrifice of animals acquired on the site" because they "were to be fully the property of Israel (as distinct from the priesthood or Temple)" (111), and mere

43. Chilton, *The Temple of Jesus*, xi, xii; also Chilton, *Pure Kingdom*, 118–23.

"financial transaction was not sufficient to establish ownership" (128). Jesus, then, was "keenly concerned with purity as such," as were the Pharisees (122).

At the same time Jesus' understanding of forgiveness reverses that of Leviticus, in which forgiveness follows sacrifice, because for him forgiveness "is the condition in which sacrifice is rightly offered." Just as Jesus pronounced the leper "clean" before sending him to the priest (Mk 1:40–45), so he "takes it that Israelites are to be prepared immediately [by forgiveness] to offer pure sacrifice" (133). Ritual action does not make one pure; rather purity was "a condition that Israelites could be assumed to enjoy, and out of which they should act" (125).[44] Jesus' mission as a whole enacted Zechariah 13–14, where forgiveness and purity are mentioned apart from sacrifice (135–36). His "distinctiveness" was in the way he linked that eschatological expectation "with inclusive definitions of purity and forgiveness, with the issue of how sacrifices were to be offered, and with his own ministry. . . . Jesus understood the essential affect of sacrifice to derive from a purity and a forgiveness that God extended to all Israel in anticipation of the climax of worship" (136). In short, "the purity defined by Jesus throughout his ministry focused upon the acts of forgiveness and offering as themselves purifying, assuming the ordinarily pure practice of all Israel. To eat forgivingly and to offer one's own [sacrificial animal] in the Temple was to anticipate the ultimate banquet with the patriarchs within the kingdom of God" (150).

If this is even an approximately accurate portrayal of Jesus, then indeed "a previously obscured Jesus has emerged" (137). The reconstruction, however, is more boldly original than historically persuasive. Apart from the questionable interpretation of gospel texts, it is hardly likely that a village Galilean would have become embroiled in the subtleties of sacrifice in Jerusalem—especially if that were his first visit during his ministry (or must we assume that his negative reactions on previous visits triggered his ministry?). Above all, had Jesus reversed the relation of sacrifice and forgiveness in Leviticus, one would surely expect clearer evidence of it and of controversies generated by it.

---

44. In *The Temple of Jesus* Chilton advances some rather remarkable interpretations of the gospels; e.g., Jesus' directive to his emissaries to eat what is served in whatever town they enter (Lk 10:7–8) means that they are to "treat every village . . . as clean, as pure territory" where sacrifice might be offered; they are to enter the villages "exactly as pilgrims were to enter the Temple" (ibid., 126); in giving Peter the keys (Mt 16:19), Jesus authorized him to determine what might and might not be acceptable in the Temple (ibid., 131).

Richard A. Horsley puts Jesus in the context of various forms of resistance to foreign domination.[45] Accordingly, he outlines the four stages of violence that led to the first revolt: "institutionalized violence" (repressive structures), protest and resistance ("social bandits" in the countryside [reminding one of Robin Hood] and terrorists operating secretly in Jerusalem), repression, and finally revolt (28–58). Horsley notes that between the rebellion following Herod's death in 4 B.C.E. and that against Rome, "the only occurrence of violent resistance was the terrorism of the sicarii (assassins) directed against their own high priests" and "spontaneous demonstrations" in response to specific acts of Roman provocation (117).

Apocalyptic texts manifest "an intensified concern for the survival of 'Israel' and for the realization of God's purposes in history in situations that make that dream appear virtually impossible" and so are opposed to "the dominant Jewish ruling groups and the alien imperial regime" (133). Because "apocalypticism was the distinctive cultural form taken by imagination in late second temple society," it "evoked hope and motivation for resistance . . . because God was about to effect a decisive 'revolution'" (143, 145). This sets the stage for Horsley's portrayal of Jesus as "a revolutionary, but not a violent revolutionary" (326). Jesus does not avoid current social conflicts, however, but "enters into them and even exacerbates or escalates them" (156). Moreover, he believed that "God was now driving Satan from control over personal and historical life [shown by his exorcisms, 184–90], making possible the renewal of the people Israel" (160); he "presupposed as his cultural context what is usually called the Jewish 'apocalyptic' lore and worldview" (172; contrast Breech, note 18). Jesus "declares in no uncertain terms that the kingdom of God has come upon and is among the people, available to be recognized, received, and entered" (178). That he was concerned for "the restoration of Israel" is shown by the appointment of the Twelve (199–206); the impact of Jesus' words and deeds on conditions among the common people in the Galilean villages shows that he was energizing a social revolution "in anticipation of the political revolution being effected by God" (325).

Even if Horsley's understanding of the import of Jesus on specific social structures such as family or on conditions such as peasant poverty is more vivid and detailed than the evidence warrants, this presentation of Jesus does put him plausibly into his society and helps one visualize his impact on it. Moreover, Horsley puts the social-political dimension of Jesus' mission into the context of his apocalyptic eschatology and its concern for the nation.

45. Horsley, *Jesus and the Spiral of Violence.* Horsley insists that there were no Zealots until 67–68 C.E.; see ibid., x–xi, 77–85, 121.

N. T. Wright, who celebrates "the third quest" (from which he appears to exclude the Jesus Seminar) because "there is now a real attempt to do history seriously,"[46] rightly points out that the historians' task is to "produce a coherent synthesis" in which Jesus is understood as "a comprehensible and yet . . . crucifiable first-century Jew" (88, 86). Recognizing that the overarching subject matter is what used to be called "Christian origins," he identifies five subquestions: "How does Jesus fit into the Judaism of his day? What were his aims? Why did he die? How did the early church come into being and why did it take the shape that it did? And Why are the gospels what they are?" (90). If one corrects the errors of Albert Schweitzer, the result will be "a very Jewish Jesus who was nevertheless opposed to some high-profile features of first-century Judaism" (93). Schweitzer's chief error was reading apocalyptic texts so literally that he, and others, inferred that Jesus (and many of his contemporaries) expected the "imminent end of the present space-time order altogether," whereas what they expected was "the end of the present *world order,* i.e., the end of the period when the Gentiles were lording it over the people of the true god [*sic*] and the inauguration of the time when this god [*sic*] would take his power and reign and, in the process, restore the fortunes of his suffering people" (95). In other words, "first-century Judaism, and Jesus firmly within it, can be understood only within a climate of intense eschatological expectation" (96).

Basic for Wright is the view that "in Jesus' day many, if not most, Jews regarded the exile as still continuing" (126) because the great prophecies of Israel's restoration had not been actualized (argued at length in his earlier book, *The New Testament and the People of God*). Distinctive about Jesus is that he "believed that he was the agent" through whom the exile is ended and that "he lived and acted accordingly" (128). This hypothesis allows Jesus to be both similar and dissimilar with respect to his Jewish context (i.e., he affirmed basic theological ideas such as election and eschatology but not "the key symbols of zealous Israel" [395]) as well as with respect to his Christian followers (132). Jesus was a distinctive prophet because "he envisioned his own work as bringing Israel's history to its fateful climax. He believed that he was inaugurating the kingdom" (197) by word and deed. Thus "*Jesus was claiming in some sense to represent Israel in himself*" (537, his italics)—i.e., that he was the Messiah who "applied to himself the three central aspects of his own prophetic kingdom-announcement: the return from exile, the defeat of evil, and the return of YHWH to Zion" (477). Wright agrees with Sanders that Jesus' action in the tem-

---

46. N. T. Wright, *Jesus and the Victory of God*, 84; unless otherwise noted, all page numbers refer to this book.

ple symbolized its destruction (417) but adds that he also was "forming a counter-Temple movement around himself" (437).

By the time Wright is finished, virtually the entire early Christian "Christ of faith" is traced to the mind of Jesus. Still, his Jesus book is surely a major achievement, rhetorically as well as historically, for by refurbishing Schweitzer's understanding of Jewish apocalyptic thought he situates Jesus as a pre-70 Jew who recast and criticized his contemporaries' hopes because he shared them. Rejecting "end of the world" eschatology, moreover, allows Wright to portray Jesus' eschatology as oriented to change that is both this-worldly and God-given, in accord with biblical eschatology. In fact, by showing that Jesus understood himself to be the agent of the impending transformation of Israel's situation, Wright actually tells the Jesus story as one of prophecy and fulfillment; thus the perspective of the gospels is grounded in the aims of Jesus himself. Calling the disparity between the prophets' promises and the actualities of Jewish life under Seleucids, Hasmoneans, and Romans "exile" is, of course, a rhetorical device by which the Jewish experience becomes an umbrella image under which all sorts of things can be given the appearance of a coherent frustration and hope, despite the repeated emphasis on the diversity of Jewish thought and practice. Whether Wright avoids imposing a coherence more than Schweitzer did in positing a coherent apocalyptic schema out of quite diverse texts is a question that can be raised but not answered here. What must be noted, however, is the compatibility between Horsley's Jesus and that of Wright, despite differences in detail and the latter's more explicit theological interests.

The many-sided effort to depict as correctly as possible Jesus' place in second-temple Jewish thought and practice, while at the same time disclosing how the early Christian communities emerged in his name, is being pursued more assiduously than ever. The results will surely continue to vary greatly— inevitably, given both the nature of all the sources being investigated and the ethos of critical historiography. The next step here, however, is to take note of those aspects of the Jew that Jesus probably was that are foundational for reflecting on his ongoing significance for Christian Gentiles.

The particular kind of Jew Jesus was matters more to Christians (who for centuries have been predominantly Gentiles) than it does to Jews. For Jews, what is at stake in a historically reliable profile of Jesus is fairness to a man whose role among Christians has made him persona non grata among his own people. At the same time, since Judaism does not pivot on any single historical person, Jewish scholars can locate him in whatever kind of second-temple

Judaism the evidence supports without affecting Judaism itself. The Jewish religion has nothing at stake in the particular kind of Jew he was, for it has a long habit of including a great variety of figures, ranging from the military Hasmoneans to the mystical Hasidim. This is not so for Christians. Because Christian faith and religion are oriented to Jesus as the defining figure, much of their Christian identity is at stake in the particular kind of Jew he was and was not— more concretely, the kind of Jew his mission suggests he was.

The Jew Jesus Was (and Was Not)

In order to bring into focus the particular aspects of Jesus' Jewishness that are of continuing significance for Christian Gentiles, it is useful first to look briefly at the phenomenon of his mission as a whole, then to speculate on what the alternatives might have been, and finally to explore in more detail Jesus' attitude toward Gentiles. These considerations should set the stage for the next section, The Gentiles' Stake in Jesus' Jewishness.

The Jesus phenomenon. It is the character and scope of Jesus' mission that matters here, for what he did and what he did not do disclose the particular kind of Jew he was and what he sought to achieve as a Jew. However universal the appeal of his teachings—at least some of them—the indissoluble fact is that they were addressed to his fellow Jews as part of his mission to Jews, a mission that fused teaching, healing and exorcism (both discussed in chapter 3), and behavior into what Meier aptly called an "atypical configuration."[47] It is precisely the Jewishness of the whole, of course, that makes the atypicality noteworthy and significant, for it takes shape in a mission so thoroughly Jewish that the gospels report not a single word of criticism of constitutive elements of the religion he inherited and shared, such as the holy days Passover or Day of Atonement. His action in the temple, however one construes its character and purpose, shows that, far from being indifferent to the temple, he cared about it enough to risk doing something to signal his concern. But not one word has been transmitted in which Jesus rejects the sacrificial system itself. Chilton saw this, even though he also claimed to see much else besides. As Jewish scholars have insisted repeatedly, Jesus' criticisms were directed at what he regarded as abuses, not at the "system" itself. Not even the Gospel of Mark, which infers from Jesus' word about what does and does not defile that "he declared all foods clean" (7:15), implies that Jesus ate pork to demonstrate his view. Nor does the fact that occasionally he healed on the Sabbath imply that he generally disre-

47. Meier, *A Marginal Jew*, I, 276.

garded it. Since people tend to remember the unusual more than the routine, the fact that on occasion he ate with "sinners" and others deemed unworthy by the scrupulous does not imply that he deliberately offended common sensibilities at every meal in order to express in-your-face rectitude.

Even if the references to the crowds he attracted are editorial comments, they are not thereby unreliable. To the contrary, it is altogether likely that it was his healing and exorcism that caught people's eye and attracted crowds. But it is equally unlikely that they would have been attracted to one who had abandoned the religious customs—unless they too had ignored them, although there is no evidence to support this.

Since Jesus' teaching style relied on aphorisms and brief, tart replies as he moved from place to place, recently some savants have characterized him as a Jewish edition of the Greco-Roman Cynics—itinerants using terse sayings to puncture pretensions and subvert patterns of loyalty to family and community, and who demonstrated their contempt by obnoxious behavior.[48] This portrayal of Jesus has been challenged vigorously and rightly for reasons that need not be tabulated here (see preceding note). It is enough to recall that more than two decades ago Yoder pointed out that "there is in the New Testament no Franciscan glorification of barefoot itinerancy."[49] Indeed, there is no evidence that Jesus was deliberately unkempt, obnoxious, and contemptuous of Jewish ways and values. Such a Jew probably would have been regarded more as a nuisance than as a threat.

The currently common characterization of Jesus' activity as starting a movement, whether of reform or renewal, is also less than appropriate. In an era of significant social changes energized by intentional groups in various places and guided by several leaders, it has become appropriate to speak of movements. But when applied to the "Jesus phenomenon" this disfigures the picture of historical reality. For one thing, movements catch on as groups of people in one place after another take up the cause. The evidence for that having occurred during Jesus' mission, whether as a spontaneous result of his activ-

---

48. The claim that Jesus is to be understood as a Cynic continues to be debated. Both sides of the argument, as well as the evidence to which the participants appeal, can be found summarized and evaluated in Betz, "Jesus and the Cynics"; Horsley, "Jesus, Itinerant Cynic or Israelite Prophet?"; Eddy, "Jesus as Diogenes?"; and in Seeley's response to Eddy, "Jesus and the Cynics Revisited." Cynicism was a complex phenomenon with a long history that preceded the time of Jesus and extended well beyond it. For a useful overview of the Cynic phenomenon, see Hock, "Cynics."

49. Yoder, *The Politics of Jesus*, 96.

ities or by design, is nil. There is no evidence whatever that groups were formed in his name after he moved to the next village or that they stayed in touch with each other in his absence. Moreover, Jesus' teaching appears not to have been programmatic but rather was given to ad hoc formulations evoked by particular circumstances (even if some of the situations were provided by the Evangelists). A series of such teachings, reported as critiques of the Pharisees for the most part, does not point to a movement, since movements are aimed at changing institutions and social structures and result in reform, not simply pungent protest. Sanders is surely right in saying that Jesus did not ask people "to build an alternative society that would be the kingdom of God."[50] A band of men, plus hangers-on, wandering around the countryside cannot be regarded as the beachhead of a new society any more than the mission on which Jesus sent his disciples could be construed as generating a movement unless there is evidence beyond what Luke (alone) says they reported on their return: "Lord, even the demons are subject to us in your name" (10:17). This hardly sounds like the beginning of a social movement. It is probable that some who heard Jesus, and the disciples on their mission, remembered what had been said, subsequently debated its meaning, and later became the core of communities formed in Jesus' name. But that does not mean that there was a "Jesus movement" during his lifetime. That is an anachronistic modern invention, the "secular" alternative to the idea that Jesus founded the church.

Although Jesus did not form a movement during his lifetime, he evidently did invite some people to "follow" him; in addition, there are good reasons for thinking that he also had a circle of special persons who came to be known simply as "the Twelve." Both phenomena require comment.

The gospels report that Jesus taught large groups of people, but they never say that he invited all of them to "follow" him as did Mattathias in summoning people to revolt (1 Mc 2:27ff.) or as did "messianic" figures such as Judas the Galilean or Theudas, as Hengel rightly notes.[51] Jesus called only specific individuals. The sages, often called "rabbi" in the sense of "my master" as distinguished from the later technical use, too had "disciples," but not because they invited them to their circles; rather, the student sought the teacher. Moreover, both the stories of Jesus' calling disciples (Mk 1:16–20; 2:14; Lk 5:1–11) and his sayings about "following" him express an amazing conviction that he had the right to call persons away from their daily rounds and from families; startling indeed is the terse story in which Jesus tacitly asserts his authority to override

50. E. P. Sanders, *The Historical Figure of Jesus,* 178.
51. Hengel, *The Charismatic Leader,* 59.

even an unquestioned family obligation, burial of the dead (Mt 8:21–22; Lk 9:59–60 [Q]).[52] Evidently he expected those called to let this commitment supersede even family duties, perhaps because he too had left home and family. According to Lk 8:1–3, Jesus' entourage included "some women who had been cured of evil spirits and infirmities . . . and many others, who provided for them out of their resources."[53] To conclude, he specifically called some to share his vocation, though all were invited to accept what he taught and to live by his teachings.

More significant is the fact that according to the gospels there was a special group of twelve around Jesus (Mt 10:1; Mk 3:14; Lk 6:13; Jn 6:70), clearly a symbol of the twelve tribes of Israel, though it had been centuries since they had existed as tribes. That, of course, was probably just the point: somehow Jesus' vocation imaged reconstituting "Israel." Interestingly, the Synoptics list the names of the twelve, even though only a few have any roles in the story; apparently their number was what mattered most in the tradition.[54] Two considerations make it difficult to argue that "the Twelve" is a church creation. First, in 1 Corinthians 15 Paul quotes a tradition that he had "received"—i.e., when he joined the Jesus people, generally thought to be no later than 35 C.E. According to this tradition, the risen Jesus appeared to "the twelve" (v. 5), which some manuscripts correct to "eleven" in view of Judas's suicide (Mt

52. Each Evangelist provided his own setting. In Matthew a disciple requests permission to bury his father before joining Jesus; in Luke, Jesus invites the person who, however, must first bury his father. The core saying, however, is the same: "Let the dead bury their own dead." Luke adds, "but as for you, go and proclaim the kingdom of God." Luke probably preserved better the beginning of the story, though not its ending. See also Fitzmyer, *The Gospel According to Luke* (herein cited as *Luke*), 833–37. Apart from Dt 21:23, which requires prompt burial of executed criminals, the Torah has no burial legislation, though later rabbis included the obligation to bury parents in the meaning of the fourth commandment. Hengel's inference, therefore, is unwarranted: "Jesus did not stand under the authority of the Torah—as all his Jewish contemporaries did—but above it" (*The Charismatic Leader*, 70).

53. See Witherington, *Women in the Ministry of Jesus*, chap. 4.

54. See also E. P. Sanders, *Jesus and Judaism*, 98–102. For a thorough discussion of the evidence and the arguments, see Meier, "The Circle of the Twelve." He concludes that, given the "multiple attestation of sources and forms (Mark, L, John, Q, and the pre-Pauline tradition), the argument from embarrassment, and the argument for the general flow of the NT traditions about the Twelve, and the . . . grave difficulties under which alternative hypotheses labor, one position emerges as clearly the more probable: the circle of the Twelve did exist during Jesus's public ministry" (ibid., 672).

27:3–10). Second, according to the Q tradition used in Mt 19:28 and Lk 22:28–30, Jesus promised that the Twelve would "sit on twelve thrones, judging [i.e., dispensing justice] the twelve tribes of Israel."[55] Since this promise was not actualized by the time Matthew and Luke were written, and since the disciples themselves (presumably) were no longer alive to insist that it would be actualized shortly, both Evangelists could easily have omitted the saying, had it not been embedded too deeply in the tradition to do so. Instead, each gospel interprets it in relation to the Parousia— Matthew by correlating it with the enthronement of the Son of Man, Luke by associating it with Jesus' coming reign ("in my kingdom"). It is precisely the fragmentary character of the evidence for the Twelve as a group during Jesus' lifetime, as well as the fact that it does not dovetail with early Christian history,[56] that argues for the reliability of the tradition, even though it is not clear exactly what Jesus had in mind for them beyond symbolizing "Israel." But that is important, for one does not envision a twelve-tribe "Israel" without the conviction that something stupendous is imminent, God's kingship, nor does one make such a promise apart from the conviction that he is central to it. The fact that no known saying of Jesus explicitly links a reference to Israel with the impending kingdom would be a decisive consideration against these inferences only if we had a full record of what Jesus had said.

Since "Israel" had not existed as twelve tribes for centuries, one is tempted to say that Jesus saw his vocation as the "restoration" of Israel. But this temptation should be resisted because there is no evidence that he expected a return to the past; he did not drive into the future by looking at the rearview mirror. Because "Israel" was a sacral, evocative symbol, he could use "twelve" to suggest the God-given future without describing it or organizing a movement to speed its coming or administer it when it arrived.

It must be admitted, of course, that even if these distinctions and inferences make sense today, we lack adequate evidence to demonstrate that they made the same sense to him then. What we find necessary to analyze for its rationale may well have seemed intuitively so self-evident to him that it never occurred

55. Horbury, "The Twelve and the Phylarchs," having traced the tradition of twelve "rulers" from the Pentateuch to the rabbis, concludes that Jesus did choose twelve, but more for mission than for governance; he also notes that observers would have inferred that Jesus had messianic pretensions.

56. Acts 1:15–26 does, of course, report that Judas was replaced by Matthias, not so that there would be twelve judges but so that there would be twelve "apostles" as witnesses to the resurrection.

to him to explain it. In any case, whoever is grasped by the eschatological, king-dom-linked "Israel" has moved beyond merely reforming one or all of the frag-mented Judaisms of the present, for when God's rule is actualized, they will all be replaced by "Israel," presumably a true, flawless theocratic society. Jesus had not, then, somehow given up on his people; to the contrary, his indestructible loyalty is shown precisely in the fact that he simply assumed that when God's kingdom was actualized, his people would be precisely "Israel."

Because "Israel," like "kingdom of God," is an evocative, "tensive" symbol (see chap. 3), both were available for diverse construals in Jesus' day. Moreover, each of the Judaisms appealed, in one way or other, to scripture. So it is not at all surprising that historians discern similarities between Jesus and the various Judaisms and attempt to link him more closely to one of them than to the others. Some have classified him as a prophet, an apocalyptist, a charismatic wonder-worker, or a rabbi. None is completely arbitrary, yet none is fully con-vincing either, because he appears to fit none of them—partly because these modern categories are created to differentiate for the sake of precision in schol-arly discourse. In any case, what must not be overlooked is the likelihood that Jesus himself is responsible for the scholars' failure to classify him precisely.

That what emerged in the years immediately following his execution was in effect another "Judaism" in his name is one of history's ironies. Subsequently this "Christianized Judaism"[57] (this phrase is more precise than "Jewish Chris-tianity") was first paralleled and then displaced by gentile Christianity—so much so, in fact, that *gentile* became redundant and was simply dropped. Though Gentiles were converted into "Christianized Judaism" in the decades immediately after Jesus, the fact that centuries later Jews were occasionally con-verted by force into gentile Christianity is one of history's tragedies.

The Jew Jesus might have been.   The particularity of Jesus might have had a different shape. Determining what might have been is, of course, a well-known game that historians play occasionally, speculative though it is, because it helps one appreciate better what in fact happened. For instance, what might have happened had the South won the Civil War? or had Gorbachev been a different kind of communist, an old-style Stalinist? The various scenarios one can imagine are useful heuristic exercises because they can check the tendency to take the actual course of history for granted. For similar reasons it is instruc-

57. Crossan insists that in the title of his *The Birth of Christianity*, which deals with the first two decades after Jesus' death, *Christianity* means "Christian Judaism"—one of the "divergent, competing and mutually hostile options *within* the Jewish homeland" (xi, his italics).

tive to speculate briefly about the kind of Jew Jesus might have been, and, given his pivotal significance for Christianity, the difference it might have made for the community of faith that emerged in his name.[58]

Had Jesus been a village Essene[59] (not in the sense that he had formerly been one but later abandoned the group) he might have expected the coming apocalyptic war with the hosts of Belial, whose earthly agents were the Kittim (the Romans; 1QM i 10). He would have regarded the community's founder, never named but known as the Teacher of Righteousness (or, Righteous Teacher), as the one "to whom God made known all the mysteries of His servants the prophets" (1QpHab vii 1–5) and as the one who would "guide them in the way of His heart" (CD i 11); consequently he would have given his energies to expounding a revelation given to someone else. His teaching would not have been public but restricted to fellow members of the Essene community, and it would have been focused on the true but veiled meaning of scripture. The community's hymns suggest that he would have emphasized people's utter sinfulness, while being profoundly grateful that his own had been forgiven. But he would not have gotten the reputation for being "a friend of tax collectors and sinners" (Mt 11:19).[60] His followers would have formed another hierarchical, priest-oriented form of Judaism marked by strict observance of the Torah, by severe discipline for those who violated the community's rules (especially those pertaining to ritual purity and the ablutions associated with it), and by a strong sense that it alone was the true Israel, "the remnant which held fast to the commandments of God" (CD iii 13). And they would have been taught to curse the sons of darkness. Since this community too would have been destroyed in the first revolt, Gentiles would probably never have learned about

58. For heuristic purposes here the imagined scenarios concern only known groups; matters of outlook (e.g., apocalyptic or national emancipation) are not as useful since they were found in various groups.

59. Vermes notes that the Damascus Document, the Temple Scroll, and the Messianic Rule "are concerned with a style of religious existence quite at variance from that at Qumran" because they assume that the members of the group lived in villages, were married and raised children, engaged in commerce, accepted the Jerusalem temple; conversely, these texts show no interest in intensive Torah study or in the doctrine of the two spirits (*The Dead Sea Scrolls in English*, 9). Kee uses sociological factors (e.g., boundaries, status, authority, ritual) to compare Jesus and the community at Qumran. "Membership in the Covenant People at Qumran and in the Teaching of Jesus."

60. Horsley, while granting that the accusation was made, denies that it was true and concludes that "there is simply little or no evidence that Jesus associated with toll collectors, let alone that he regularly banqueted with them" (*Jesus and the Spiral of Violence*, 216).

Jesus—unless, perchance, Josephus had mentioned the group and its founder when he described the Essenes.

Despite the uncertainties surrounding the Pharisees, it is useful to imagine what Jesus might have been like had he been a member of one of their groups, the *haberim*, who were particularly concerned with the laws of purity pertaining to food that defined the circle with whom one ate. Had Jesus been a *haber*, he would have been a student or disciple of a sage, whom he would have cited as an authoritative interpreter of Torah. He too would have valued the oral Torah as an expression of its written form, and, as is the case in much jurisprudence, he would have cited precedents in its interpretation. Whether his *halakah* was lenient or severe would have depended on his choice of following Hillel or Shammai. His haggadic teaching would have emphasized piety and deeds of loving kindness, and he would have understood acknowledging God's kingdom as taking upon oneself "the yoke of the Torah," conscientious obedience to its prescriptions and precepts in every aspect of life. His students would have come to him, but he would not have recruited them. He might well have stayed in Nazareth where he continued to support himself, perhaps minimally, by plying his craft instead of leading his group from village to village and teaching publically wherever the occasion presented the opportunity. If a community of his disciples survived his death, it would have been sufficiently Torah-observant that the Pharisee from Tarsus, Paul, would not have tried to stamp it out, and subsequent Christianity might well have remained closer to Jesus' brother James than to his apostle Paul.

Had Jesus continued the mission of John the Baptist instead of striking out on his own after the baptizer had been murdered, he would not have taken his message to the villages but would have remained in the Jordan valley, where he would have baptized those who, as he had done, responded to John's stern word about the imminent Judgment by accepting his baptism as a sign of their repentance and/or a means of cleansing from sin so they would survive the fiery future.[61] While he might not have imitated John's austere diet and dress (Mt 3:4; Mk 1:6), he would have been an ascetic, not one who was accused—perhaps wrongly— of being "a glutton and a drunkard" (Mt 11:19; Lk 7:34), nor would it have occurred to him to use the image of a wedding celebration to characterize his mission (Mk 2:19). As a continuator of John, he would have expected the "stronger one" to carry out God's eschatological sifting of the Jews into the wheat and the chaff. Like John, he would

---

61. For a discussion of the many problems connected with the reconstruction of John's message, see Meier, *A Marginal Jew*, II, chap. 2.

have denied that being a descendant of Abraham—i.e., being a member of the elect people of God—was a birthright sufficient to preserve one in the Judgment (Mt 3:9; Lk 3:3 [Q]), and he would have left healing and exorcism for others. In short, had Jesus continued the work of the Baptist, his mission would have been one of warning to all and of survival for few, and he would not have focused on the coming kingdom of God.[62] Jesus the Baptizer would probably have attracted followers who, upon returning to their homes, would have repeated his stern message of impending judgment and urged their neighbors to go to Jesus for baptism. After his death they might have repeated his message, and a few might have returned to the Jordan valley to pick up the baton and to baptize those who responded to the repeated message, but there is no reason to think that they would have banded together as a structured community.

These hypothetical scenarios will have served their heuristic purpose if they indicate that Jesus was a particular kind of figure *within* first-century Jewish life. All of them are visualizable only in that context. Jesus, in calling people to respond to his message centered in the kingdom of God, was not asking them to abandon their heritage for some universal "humanity" à la Renan, but to actualize it his way. There is, however, one corollary of his irradicable Jewish outlook that can offend Gentiles, but it does not flow from a distorted view of Jesus' religion as in the examples adduced earlier; instead, it is the obverse of the intense Jewishness of Jesus—namely his disdain for Gentiles. This must be seen before thinking seriously about the permanent meaning of Jesus' Jewishness for Christian Gentiles.

Jesus' view of Gentiles.   Jesus' attitude toward the Gentiles in Galilee was probably rather straightforward, but the evidence for his attitude is more complex and indirect, and some evidence one expects does not exist. Still, silence can be an important clue, as in Arthur Conan Doyle's detective story that turned on the fact that the dog did not bark. The starting point, then, is the silence of the gospels about Jesus' relation to the cities whose populations apparently consisted of both Jews who were at least minimally comfortable with Hellenistic (i.e., gentile) culture and various non-Jews.

Since Jesus was a teacher who traveled from place to place, often named in the gospels, it is remarkable that there is not even a hint that he ever set foot in either of the two cities that were the centers of government—Sepphoris, rebuilt

---

62. Mt 4:2 does, of course, say that John preached the coming of the kingdom as did Jesus; but most critics regard this summary of his message to be the work of the Evangelist; no other gospel has it or its equal.

when Jesus was growing up nearby,[63] and Tiberias, built when he was a young man and to which Herod Antipas later moved his capital from Sepphoris. Whether Jesus avoided these new cities "in light of a conscious decision not to become directly embroiled in a confrontation with political power," as Freyne suggests,[64] or did so because as a villager he had a natural resentment of cities, or for some other reason is hard to decide on the basis of silence. In any case, although he could easily have included these cities in his travels, the gospels' silence suggests that he made no effort to do so, thereby implying that he was deliberately indifferent, at best, to the Gentiles that lived there—and to the Jews who lived among them and perhaps worked for them.

The nature of the gospels, and of the Jesus traditions on which they are based, makes their silence about Sepphoris and Tiberias significant. For one thing, the gospels were written in Greek for Christian communities, probably not in Palestine (though this is far from certain), that increasingly consisted of Gentiles as well as Hellenized Jews. The former would have been the very people who, one may assume, would have remembered and prized any sayings in which Jesus spoke well of them or stories of his mission to people like themselves—if there were any to remember. That they did not invent such traditions is clear. The few stories that report Jesus' positive response to Gentiles who sought his help as healer[65] probably were remembered and treasured precisely because they were exceptional.

63. Since Sepphoris was less than five miles from Nazareth, Case ("Jesus and Sepphoris") speculated that Jesus, being the oldest in a family with a widowed mother, might have gotten a job in the reconstruction of the city, where he would have met a great variety of people; this would have disposed him toward a "spirit of toleration" that marked his ministry later. Moreover, working there might have shaped his attitude toward Rome, since people in the area would have recalled that the Romans had destroyed it in 4 B.C.E. Apparently it did not occur to Case, writing in Chicago, that a villager's experience in such a place might have turned him against all that it represented. More recently Batey ("Jesus and the Theatre") has suggested that Jesus' use of "hypocrite" ("an actor") may reflect his knowledge of the theater in Sepphoris. For a critical assessment of such speculations, see Miller, "Sepphoris, the Well Remembered City" (an allusion to Batey's book, *Jesus and the Forgotten City*). See also Meyers, "The Challenge of Hellenism" (esp. 87–90). For a concise overview of the history of the city, see Strange, "Sepphoris."

64. Freyne, *Galilee, Jesus, and the Gospels*, 140.

65. Mt 8:5–13/Lk 7:1–10; Jn 4:46–53 may be a variant tradition of the same incident; the demon-possessed man healed near Gadara, on the eastern shore of the Sea of Galilee, *might* have been a Gentile (Mk 5:1–20).

From Jesus' travel to the largely gentile Syrian coast (Tyre and Sidon, Mk 7:24–31; Mt 15:21–31 has significant differences) only one story has been preserved—that concerning the gentile woman whose request that Jesus heal her demon-possessed daughter was rudely rebuffed: "Let the children be fed first, for it is not fair to take the children's food and throw it to the dogs." But despite this put-down, she persisted, "Sir, even the dogs under the table eat the children's crumbs." Only then did he relent, although even so, he did not go to her house. It is understandable that Luke, who wrote both the gospel and Acts with the gentile mission in mind, omitted this story. On the other hand, the author of Matthew not only heightens the story's drama by saying that Jesus first refused to answer her and that the disciples urged him to send her away, but also inserts a now-famous saying, "I was sent only to the lost sheep of the house of Israel." One should be wary of using the criterion of multiple attestation to claim that since only Matthew reports the saying it probably is not authentic, for its perspective is supported also by this gospel's report of Jesus' instructions to his disciples, "Go nowhere among the Gentiles, and enter no town of the Samaritans, but go rather to the lost sheep of the house of Israel" (Mt 10:5–6). Since this gospel ends with the "Great Commission" in which the risen Jesus sends the disciples to "all nations" (or all Gentiles), it is clear that Matthew is convinced that Jesus' mission had been to Israel alone and that reaching out to Gentiles began only after Easter. Nor should it be overlooked that every story that reports Jesus healing a Gentile (always a child) also indicates that the action took place at a distance—i.e., he never *goes to* a Gentile. Even in exceptional circumstances they were off-limits.

Moreover, every time Jesus is reported to have mentioned Gentiles, he expresses a negative judgment about their ways. They strive for material things (Mt 6:22); they are a closed group, greeting only one another (Mt 5:47); their prayers are heaps of empty phrases because they think that effectiveness requires many words (Mt 6:7). Gentiles are cited as an example of authoritarian leadership to be avoided (Mk 10:42–43), thus conveniently overlooking the tyranny of the Hasmoneans. According to Jesus' instructions for community discipline, the banned person is to be treated like a Gentile or (despised Jewish) toll collector (Mt 18:7). And as already noted, when rebuffing the Syro-Phoenician woman he implied that she was a dog. Even if one argues that these disparaging references to Gentiles were coined by Christian Jews, it is doubtful that the increasingly gentile churches preserved them simply to appease the prejudices of their fellow believing Jews or that they reflect Matthew's alleged anti-Jewish bias. It is much more likely that they were retained because it was agreed that Jesus might well have said such things and probably did. Evidently there was no contrary memory strong enough to censor such words out of the text. In short, it is altogether likely that Jesus had not one good thing to say about Gentiles as a group. Although Gentiles later were attracted to him through the gospel, he was not attracted to them, nor was he the least interested in attracting them to him.[66]

Distressing though this "underside" of Jesus' particular Jewishness may be, it must be taken on board by any serious consideration of the perfect tense of the Jew Jesus was.[67] At the same time, since historical reconstruction requires balance and proportion, it should not be overlooked that the gospels do not report that Jesus' message was marked by a polemic against Gentiles either,[68] as if their non-Jewishness were the problem. Whatever may have been the cultural or psychological roots of his disparaging remarks about Gentiles, they appear as the obverse of his passionate commitment to recovering his people's true identity as Israel.

The Gentiles' Stake in Jesus' Jewishness

Until this point the chapter has concentrated in one way or other on the aorist (past) tense of Jesus the Jew. Part 1 illustrated various efforts by Christian Gentiles to put distance between him and his Jewish heritage by distorting it, then cited examples of Jewish scholars' attempts to dissolve the alleged distance and to reclaim him for "mainstream" Jewish history, and finally pointed to current Christian Gentiles' efforts to integrate him fully into late-second-temple Jewish

---

66. That Jesus' inner circle included two men with Greek names—Andrew and Philip—does not indicate that they were Gentiles, but rather that his concern for Israel did not exclude those whose families had been Hellenized somewhat. In fact, apart from these two men, there is no clear evidence that Jesus was interested in appealing to Hellenized Jews either.

67. Feminists, on the other hand, have emphasized the story's attitude toward the alien woman. See, e.g., Kwok Pui-lan, *Discovering the Bible in the Non-Biblical World,* chap. 6: "Woman, Dogs, and Crumbs."

68. Jeremias, after first exploring in detail the evidence showing that Jesus restricted his mission to his people and that he spoke harshly of Gentiles, saw this too and claimed that Jesus removed "the idea of vengeance [against Gentiles] from the eschatological expectation"; he went on to argue, however, that Jesus implicitly included Gentiles in his hope for the future. To do so, however, Jeremias must find evidence in all sorts of unsuspected places (*Jesus' Promise to the Nations*).

life and hope. Part 2 ventured to identify some elements that gave his mission its distinct and characteristic profile. Thus the chapter has been given over to history—to both the study of Jesus in the history of modern scholarship and the study of Jesus in his own historical setting. This twofold concern for history puts the theme of part 3 in context, but pursuing it requires a shift into a mode of discourse that, while being informed by history, is primarily theological because historical considerations alone cannot answer the question, Why should Gentiles care about the sort of Jew Jesus was?, or, What is the import for Gentiles of Jesus' focus on Israel?

Historical ironies and theological insight. One historical irony emerges from the juxtaposition of three facts already noted. (a) Jesus has been, and remains, the central figure in Christianity, even in some of its currently attenuated forms. In its classical forms, believers offer prayers to God "in the name of Jesus"; they regard him as simultaneously the model human and the enfleshed Logos, the self-communication of God; they accept his teachings as normative. (b) Persistently Christians have affirmed that Jesus is the messiah, the one in whom God's purpose and promise to Israel are fulfilled, and they have affirmed this as persons of all sorts who remained Gentiles, not as proselytes entering Judaism. (c) At the same time Jesus both ignored the Gentiles whom he could easily have included in his mission and spoke disparagingly of them. Clearly, then, the relation of Christian Gentiles to Jesus does not depend on his attitude toward Gentiles during his lifetime but exists as a historical reality in spite of it. Ferreting out the historical processes by which this irony emerged would probably show that the Jewishness of Jesus was not given its due. That, however, need only be surmised here because the present task is to understand this irony in light of the current, though tardy, insistence that Jesus was so thoroughly and passionately Jewish that he saw his vocation as directed to Israel alone.

Undertaking this task points to a second irony implied in the first: It is precisely Jesus' concentration of his mission on Israel that grounds his permanent significance for Gentiles. This point comes into focus when we think backward toward Jesus. To begin with, for Gentiles who are, or become, Christians, Jesus is the link that connects them to Israel's scripture and to the God to whom it points. Conversely, Gentiles who are not Christians are in effect bystanders and observers of Jesus and his heritage, a situation which Ephesians 2:12 describes as "separated from Christ, being aliens from the commonwealth of Israel, and strangers to the covenants of promise, having no hope and without God in the world." Although this passage is a highly charged theological statement, it is also a simple historical fact. And it is neither Buddha nor a generic "concept of God" that links Gentiles to Israel's God but rather Jesus. And he could not do this had he been as indifferent to his heritage as he was to the Gentiles, or had he advocated a perspective that reflected discomfort with it, or had he promoted a "philosophy of life" that incorporated his heritage into something else, something less Jewish and more cosmopolitan. Had he been indifferent or uncomfortable, he would have remained in Nazareth and perhaps sought a sage who could help him with his "problem"—and no Gentile would ever have heard of him.

A third irony is now in view: The defining promise of God to Abraham pertaining to the "nations" ("in you all families of the earth shall be blessed," Gn 12:3; see also 22:18; 26:4; 28:14) becomes historical reality when through Jesus, Gentiles—precisely as Gentiles, not as proselytes—worship the God that Abraham, Moses, Isaiah, and Jesus worshiped and whose will they sought to do. Two historical reminders put the significance of this into relief. First, ever since the first century of the Common Era, Gentiles could have entered the Jewish heritage by conversion or, if they lived in the cities of the empire where diaspora synagogues were found, could have associated themselves with it without actually converting but by becoming "God-fearers" who attended the synagogues and submitted their morals—and perhaps their diets as well—to the teachings of the Torah. Some did, of course, but they scarcely constituted a "trend" that would have turned the promise into historical reality. Second, although some strands of Jewish apocalyptic eschatology envisioned the Gentiles coming to Zion as part of the scenario of the glorious future, what actually happened was somewhat different, and the difference proved to be decisive. Largely through Paul, Gentiles did become, in growing numbers, beneficiaries of the Abrahamic promise by believing the news that the glorious future has begun in Jesus, though it is not yet completed; as Paul saw it, since the Jesus event was God's eschatological act, there is no need to wait until it is completed before inviting Gentiles into the fold. Paul described the result as follows: "you turned to God from idols, to serve a living and true God [as "God-fearers" too had done] and to wait for his Son from heaven [which only those who believed the gospel were doing], whom he raised from the dead—Jesus, who rescues us from the wrath that is coming [the Great Judgment]" (1 Thes 1:9–10). In defending his mission to Gentiles, Paul insisted that Gentiles who were baptized into Christ also became participants in the one through whom God kept the promise to Abraham (Gal 3:26–29). The result was not a gentile Jesus cult alongside Israel but a newly enlarged people of God consisting of Christian

Jews and Christian Gentiles, praying, praising, and eating together. Paul insisted that "Christ became a servant of circumcision [i.e., of Israel] on behalf of the truth of God, so that the promises to the patriarchs could be confirmed, so that the Gentiles would praise God [too]" (Rom 15:8).

So the third historical irony is that Gentiles—whether first-century Greeks and Celts, medieval Teutons and Slavs, or modern Africans and Asians—have indeed learned to read the story of Israel and of Israel's God as their story too and that this occurred not because they became Jews by conversion, nor because they asked to become part of God's people in some way short of conversion, nor because Jesus had been eager to associate with Gentiles, but solely because they believed the gospel about him. And there would have been no gospel about him had those who knew him best not believed that he had been so intensely loyal to God's Israel that Israel's God ratified and transfigured him by resurrecting him from the realm of the dead.

Gentiles and "Israel." It is important to clarify in theological terms what is entailed in saying that Jesus is the Christian Gentiles' link to "Israel" and to do so in a way that takes seriously Jesus' own commitment. Because his commitment was to "Israel," recovered by God as "the people," his mission did not align itself with any group even though in some ways his convictions were closer to those of the Pharisees. For the same reason he had no interest in advocating a program for restructuring existing institutions, though he did not eschew criticizing specific aspects of them. What he called for, and sought to embody, was a kind of life that would reflect God's reign actualized, and this indeed required changes in the ways villagers related to each other (see chap. 3). Animated by the conviction that the definitive actualization of God's reign was beginning in his mission, he took his beat more from the character and will of God as attested in scripture. Jesus, therefore, does not link Gentiles to any of the Judaisms of his day, nor to the figures associated with them, such as the Teacher of Righteousness, Hillel or Shammai, John the Baptist, nor to earlier ones such as Judas Maccabaeus. Rather, for Gentiles he is the link to Hebrew scripture behind them all, to its understanding of God's people as the instrument chosen to actualize God's will and thereby disclose it to the nations, and to the one Creator who pursues righteousness and keeps promises. And because Jesus is the Gentiles' link to Israel's scripture, he is also the lens through which they read it and see into the character and will of God (see chap. 4).

This understanding of the enduring—indeed, the constitutive—significance of Jesus for Gentiles is preferable to saying that he links them to

"Judaism" because it is more precise. For one thing, *Judaism*, being the Angli-
cized form of the Greek *Ioudaismos*, is a word Jesus probably had no occasion
to use. As a comprehensive term it was probably coined to distinguish Jewish
faith and Torah-observant ethos from its alternatives, not to state Jewish self-
understanding (see, e.g., 2 Mc 2:21; 4 Mc 4:26; Gal 1:13–14; Ign. *Magn.* 8.1;
10.3). That Jesus connects Gentiles to "Judaism" in this sense is, of course, precisely what Paul's opponents, especially in Asia Minor, insisted on and what the
apostle rejected, though without disparaging "Judaism" itself.[69] Moreover, even
today "Judaism" embraces such a variety of beliefs and practices, from the vigorously orthodox Hasidim to the Reconstructionists, that it would be more con-
fusing than clarifying to say that Jesus links Gentiles to "Judaism." Further,
what bound and still binds together the various forms of Jewish faith and obedience is ethnic identity, the continuity of a people by lineal descent. This ethnic factor too makes it as inappropriate to say that Jesus links Gentiles to
"Judaism" as saying that Gentiles who "believe in Jesus" are "honorary Jews."

Concluding remarks.   It would be odd indeed if a chapter on Jesus the
Jew in a book titled *Who Is Jesus?* were to conclude without at least a few observations about his role in the ongoing conversation between Jews and Christian
Gentiles. That complex and emotionally freighted theme cannot even be outlined here; it must suffice to identify three considerations that emerge from
what has been discussed here.

First, conversations between Jews and Christians about Jesus might be more
fruitful if Christians were more sensitive to the fact that the unusual and perhaps defining factors about Jesus pose the same theological questions for Christians today as they did for his fellow Jews then. The more Jewish and Christian
scholars agree in historical matters about Jesus, the more unavoidable becomes
the question Was he right? One thinks, for instance, of his independence from
tradition, his conviction that God's kingdom is irrupting , and his confidence
about his vocation. It is understandable that scholars in the Christian tradition,
even if loosely related to it, would assume (often tacitly) that Jesus was right.
However, the effect of situating him as carefully as possible in the web of second-temple Jewish life would be more convincing, and certainly more chal-
lenging, if the point of view of those who heard him skeptically or dismissed
him for being wrong-headed were presented sympathetically. After all, they had
intelligible reasons for doing so, and some surely thought they were more faithful to God than he. It is precisely in such matters that Jewish colleagues can

69. See Martyn, *Galatians*, 154.

contribute most to the shared study of Jesus—not by arguing but by reminding their non-Jewish colleagues of the extent to which the latter's views of Jesus, like their own, are ultimately judgments of faith, whether avowed or simply inherited. That developing this aspect of the study of Jesus requires of all participants a matured self-confidence freed from apologetics and defensiveness is obvious, as is the likelihood that attaining it requires self-discipline and patience.

Second, even if Jews increasingly incorporate Jesus into their own history, their relation to him will differ significantly from that of Christian Gentiles. While this is to be expected, it should not be forgotten that this ongoing disagreement about Jesus differs fundamentally from that between Christianity and Hinduism, which can regard Jesus as one of many avatars, because theologically the Jewishness of Jesus has made this disagreement about him rather like a family quarrel. Through him both the framework within which and the categories with which Christian Gentiles think about God, the world, the nature of human existence, Israel, and therefore about Jesus have been reshaped decisively and irreversibly because they are rooted in the same Hebrew Bible, even though it is read differently. Indeed, whenever this biblical understanding and way of thinking are neglected, let alone demeaned, the Christianity of Gentiles begins to look more like another pagan religion, albeit focused on Jesus, and what is described in Ephesians 2:12 is reversed to status quo ante ("aliens from the commonwealth of Israel, and strangers to the covenants of promise, having no hope and without God in the world").

The final observation concerns the horizons against which the shared study of Jesus the Jew should move. Given the origins of the Jesus quest in the Enlightenment and its flowering according to the canons of modern historiography in the North Atlantic scholars' community—a fact to be recognized, not a sin to be confessed—it is only natural that Jesus' on-going significance for Gentiles was construed as his import for the Christian heirs of Greco-Roman culture. Today, however, they are rapidly becoming the minority in the global Christian community. Still, that Jesus links Gentiles to Israel is as true today as it was in the first century. However, the shape and the consequences were one thing when the Gentiles in view were the neighbors in the Greco-Roman cities where Jews had long been at home and quite another when they are Asians and Africans who may never have seen Jews except on television and who wonder why it is essential that Jesus link them to the scripture of another non-Christian religion and not simply, and understandably, to the New Testament alone. Even if the theological issues are the same—or better, precisely because they are—the circle of participants in this discussion, as well as its horizon, should be expanded to include the worldwide community of Christian Gentiles, because "the scandal of particularity" is more scandalous today than ever. When that expansion occurs, the question Who is Jesus? will receive new answers, some of which will be as promising (and problematic) as those given by the converts in the Roman Empire.

CHAPTER THREE

The Embodied Future
Jesus the Teacher

The Jesus discovered in the quest was above all a teacher. This is hardly surprising since the gospels report that he taught and what he taught, as well as what he did. But the real reason for the quest's massive emphasis on Jesus' teaching is found in the quest itself. From the start the Deists emphasized Jesus as the teacher of the elemental truths of natural religion, which they too emphasized, such as divine providence, immortality, and timeless moral principles. The subsequent quest rejected this understanding of Jesus yet continued to emphasize his teachings, partly because the miracles had been set aside as unhistorical, as had the bulk of Jesus' teachings in John. If critics were to find solid evidence with which to portray Jesus at all, it would be in the genuine teaching material in the Synoptics. And since the genuine was the distinctive, it is not surprising that the parables emerged as the crème de la crème.[1] So important have the teachings of Jesus been, and still remain, that to a considerable degree the history of the quest is the quest of Jesus the teacher.

In seeking the authentic teachings of Jesus some scholars recently placed unusual, if not inordinate, emphases not only on the *Gospel of Thomas* but also on a document that does not exist but must be reconstructed from those places in Matthew and Luke where the same material appears but which is absent from Mark, namely Q. Although the existence of Q has been doubted

---

1. Perrin expressed the views of many: "the parables represent by all odds the most markedly individualistic characteristic of the teaching of Jesus; both in form and in content they were highly original and strongly stamped with the personality of their author." He has in mind, of course, not the parables as they stand ("constantly modified in the tradition") but as restored to their (allegedly) original wording *Rediscovering the Teaching of Jesus*, 22.

as well as denied,[2] most students accept Q as the hypothesis that accounts best for the phenomenon. What makes Q distinctive and important is that it consisted almost entirely of Jesus' teachings and had no story of Jesus' passion and resurrection. Moreover, since Q probably was compiled in Palestine circa 50 C.E., about two decades before the oldest gospel (Mark) was written, Q puts one closer in time to Jesus than does any other source. And since historians have long assumed that the reliability of a source decreases as the length of time between the event and the report increases, the significance of Q for the study of Jesus is obvious. Indeed, in 1906 Harnack's influential study of Q reached a conclusion that anticipated much that is said today: Not only is Q more important than Mark generally, but "above all, the tendency to exaggerate the apocalyptic and eschatological element in our Lord's message [an allusion to Schweitzer] and to subordinate to this the purely religious and ethical elements, will ever find its refutation in Q."[3] In fact, it is largely on the basis of Q that some scholars today deny the apocalyptic element in Jesus' teaching altogether. Since this is a pivotal issue for understanding Jesus' teaching, it is important to note briefly the analysis of Q on which this view, and other inferences, depend.

Some of the sayings in Q do, of course, have an apocalyptic cast; others are short, aphoristic sayings; and still others show an interest in Jesus himself (the temptation story). Moreover, repeatedly the same material is worded differently in Matthew than in Luke and is found at different points in their narratives as well. Instead of explaining these two phenomena by viewing Q as one or more collections transmitted orally to the Evangelists, some contend that both result from editing a *text* and proceed to reconstruct what Matthew and Luke used.[4] Even before this work was finished, the stature of Q was enhanced by renaming it "the Sayings Gospel of Q," and four important conclusions were drawn. (a) On the basis of consistency in both form and content, some investigators found three distinct strata reflecting stages in the development of the text: Q^1 (aphoristic sayings devoid of apocalyptic thought), Q^2 (apocalyptic sayings that reflect the rejection of those who prop-

2. For a full discussion, see Tuckett, *Q and the History of Early Christianity*, chap.1.

3. Harnack, *The Sayings of Jesus*, 250–51.

4. For a decade James M. Robinson has energized an international team devoted to this task, publishing the results annually in *Journal of Biblical Literature*. The revised work is appearing in a series of volumes, *Documenta Q*. These volumes report not only the critics' assessments of each saying, excerpted from the literature since 1838 when the Q hypothesis was first proposed, but also the team's judgments about degrees of probable genuineness, though not color coded.

agated Q^1), and Q^3 (the temptation stories).[5] (b) The sayings that are most likely to be authentic are in the oldest stratum. (c) Since Q had no passion and resurrection stories, the "Q people" had no interest in Jesus' death and resurrection and did not understand them as redemptive events, as did Mark and Paul. It has also been claimed that in the canonical gospels "the historical Jesus . . . was actually lost from sight by the heavy overlay of golden patina. . . . [But] [h]ere the real Jesus, who actually lived in history, has his say."[6] Such a verdict would surely have surprised the Evangelists. (d) The original "Q people," like Jesus, were itinerants whose lifestyle and message were like those of the Cynics.[7] In short, "the people of Q were Jesus people, not Christians."[8] Many current Q enthusiasts draw important conclusions about Jesus,[9] though Vaage declines to talk about the Jesus who lies "behind" the oldest stratum of Q.[10]

The confidence with which today's "Q people" reconstruct the past on the basis of inference and assumption is remarkable. That one can use a short text—quite apart from the fact that it must first be reconstructed totally—to recover a community's beliefs and self-understanding, including what it did not believe and care about, is plausible only if one assumes that communities are completely congruent with a given text—i.e., that this single text contained everything they believed and thought. But it is at least doubtful whether such a community ever existed—doubly so in this case if the original Q group was a movement and not a tightly controlled sect. Moreover, the more Jesus is seen solely through the lens of the alleged earliest stratum of Q, the more he is isolated from the Jewish patrimony that informed and animated him and so becomes less and less "comprehensible and crucifiable" (to borrow Wright's apt phrase). Fortunately, one can work with the Q hypothesis without buying everything that has been sold recently in its name. In this chapter Jesus the teacher is not simply the Jesus of Q or of its alleged earliest stratum.

The theme of this chapter is Jesus the teacher of the kingdom of God, a theme attested in Q and which according to the earliest gospel was the warrant

---

5. Kloppenborg, *The Formation of Q*. Mack, *The Lost Gospel*, not only prints "The Original Book of Q" (73–80) but also follows it with "The Complete Book of Q" (81–102), in which the three strata are identified.

6. Robinson, "The Real Jesus of the Sayings Gospel Q," 136.

7. Other scholars, however, do not find the alleged similarities between Q and Cynics convincing. See, e.g., Tuckett, "A Cynic Q?"

8. Mack, *The Lost Gospel*, 5.

9. See, e.g., Horsley, "Q and Jesus."

10. Vaage, *Galilean Upstarts*, 7.

for his appeal: "The time is fulfilled, and the kingdom of God is at hand; repent, and believe in the gospel" (Mk 1:15). This is almost certainly the formulation of the Evangelist, but that does not mean that it distorts Jesus' own leitmotiv, even though many of his sayings neither mention the kingdom nor have its imminence in view explicitly. Nonetheless, there is broad consensus that the kingdom was the horizon, the unifying ground of his diverse teachings and of his mission. The first task, then, is to understand the teaching and its role in the teacher's mission; the second is to note what is implied in speaking of God as "king"; and since history continues, the third is to ponder the ongoing significance of what Jesus expected.

The Kingdom of God as Rectifying Power

Speaking of the kingdom.   Although it is not disputed that the overarching theme of Jesus' teaching and action was the kingdom of God, what he meant by the phrase is disputed; he never defined it. A suggestive clue, however, is found in the Matthean version of the Lord's Prayer, where the petition that the kingdom "come" is followed by "Thy will be done on earth as it is in heaven" (Mt 6:10). Although this line is a Matthean addition to the single petition (as found in Luke), it does not obscure or distort the meaning. The common insistence that the abstract Greek noun *basileia* (Aramaic: *malkutha*) refers to God's reign, not to God's realm, should not be escalated into a sharp contrast, for if God reigns when the divine will is done on earth, earth too becomes part of the monarch's realm as heaven already is. Praying for its "coming" implies, of course, that this is not yet the case, though God is king in heaven. God does not become king when the divine will is done by earthlings; rather, the transition on earth will dissolve the contradiction between what now is and what ought to be. The petition implies that when the heavenly kingship becomes God's reign on earth, the human condition will be healed and God's intent, inherent in Godhood itself, will be actualized. Because such a way of imaging God's relation to the world and to the human condition has a narrative character—beginning (the past), middle (the present), end (the future)—one can call this understanding "mythic."

What we must struggle to understand, given two millennia of usage, Jesus apparently grasped intuitively, for he used the phrase naturally and easily; there is no evidence that he hesitated to use it or found it difficult. According to the gospels he used it in various ways, some of which may strike us as odd, as it probably did those who heard him. At times the kingdom of God is a place that one "enters" (Mt 19:23) and where people share meals (Mt 8:11). At times it is an entity that "belongs" to certain people (the poor, Lk 6:20), that can be "given" (Lk 12:32) and "received" (Lk 18:17), and that can be subjected to violence (Mt 11:12). It is also the subject of verbs of movement: it "comes near" (Lk 10:9) or "comes upon" a person when demons are expelled (Mk 12:28). Moreover, Jesus suggested some aspect of it by comparing it with ordinary situations such as seeding (Mk 4:26–29) and putting leaven into bread dough (Mt 13:33), just as he used an extraordinary situation such as finding buried treasure (Mt 13:44) to suggest the proper response to it. He apparently put his own stamp on a familiar phrase.[11]

Such a range of usages has a certain parallel to the ways we use the word *administration*; it too is an abstract noun ('the administration of that program was inadequate") that we also use to refer to a specific power structure ("the Kennedy administration"). In December 1992 people spoke also of the administration that is "coming" and that many sought to "enter." Likewise, images drawn from various human situations were used to characterize those who responded to its coming ("scrambling to get on board"). So too "the administration" is used as the subject of various verbs: it acts, speaks, intervenes, avoids, conceals, hopes, etc. And of course from mid-November 1992 on, the incoming administration caused things to happen before the new president was inaugurated.

Moreover, Jesus' language about the kingdom of God accords with Norman Perrin's contention that the phrase is not a concept but a particular kind of symbol—not a steno symbol that always specifies exactly the same thing (like % or

---

11. Since the phrase "kingdom of God" is neither found in the Old Testament nor common in the literature of the second temple era, just how familiar the phrase was is not clear. What is clear is that there is no evidence that Jesus thought he needed to provide a correct explanation of it before he could use it; neither the formula "You have heard it said . . . but I say to you" (Mt 5:21) nor an equivalent appears in the canonical gospels with regard to the kingdom of God. Chilton has pointed out that where some passages in Isaiah (29:23; 31:4; 40:9; 52:7) refer to God or to God's reigning, the Targum (the oral paraphrase made in the synagogues) uses "the kingdom of the Lord of hosts" or "the kingdom of your God." He concludes cautiously that "evidence points only to the conclusion that some interpretive traditions, later incorporated in the Targum, had a formative influence on the wording of some of the sayings of Jesus." But when he avers that "the kingdom teaching of the Targum is exegetically based while that of Jesus is experientially based," he draws too sharp a contrast, for it is likely that the idiom of the synagogue affected also Jesus' experience of the kingdom (*A Galilean Rabbi and His Bible*, 58–59, 70, 63, resp.).

pi) but a "tensive symbol" that evokes and provokes thought.[12] Eugene Boring's formulation is apt:

> The "kingdom of God" is thus
> (1) that tensive . . . symbol
> (2) which evokes the myth
>   (a) of God the creator
>   (b) who has been active in history to preserve his people, and
>   (c) who will soon act definitively . . . and reassert his rule over his rebellious creation which is at present *de jure* his kingdom, but will become *de facto* his kingdom only through this eschatological act.[13]

Although the Greek *eschatos* means last in a sequence (as in Mk 12:22) or rank (as in Mk 10:31), in theological discourse the "eschatological" refers not to termination (as in "the end of the world") but to telos, the goal or consummation of God's purposes and activities. The expected *eschaton* takes on an "apocalyptic" cast when God's consummating action abruptly intervenes (irrupts, breaks in) in an increasingly rebellious scene, bringing both definitive judgment and salvation. Jewish apocalyptic eschatology provided a stock of images to which Jesus could allude.

It is also important to see that concepts or ideas function best when they are precise and that they become precise by eliminating ambiguity. Tensive symbols, on the other hand, function best when they are polyvalent, when they evoke multiple associations and images, and so embrace ambiguity and invite further thought; they appeal to the emotions as well as to the mind; they stimulate the imagination and energize the will. Moreover, because a symbol in its native habitat evokes known images and associations even when it reconfigures them,[14] it can be used effectively—without explanation—to modify common associations. So then Jesus probably did not define "the kingdom of God"

---

12. Perrin, *Jesus and the Language of the Kingdom*, 15–34, adapting Philip Wheelwright's view of a "tensive symbol." Sanders, however, insists that "kingdom of God" is a concept (*Jesus and Judaism*, 126).

13. Boring, "The Kingdom of God in Mark," 131–32.

14. Riches notes that "Jesus had to use terms which were understood by his contemporaries or they could not have understood him at all; but he had to use them differently if he was to say anything new." He claims therefore that "Jesus changed the conventional associations of the kingdom" by speaking of it in the context of his whole ministry (*Jesus and the Transformation of Judaism*, 100; see also 187).

because he trusted the phrase to function effectively even when he used it in unconventional ways, rather like an allusion functions in a community of shared discourse; in a changed community, however, explanations are required, as in footnotes explaining the allusions in John Milton's poetry. When scholars try to "explain" what Jesus was talking about when he used "the kingdom of God," they cannot avoid using concepts. The purpose of the concepts, however, is not to replace the mythic language of "kingdom of God" but to free it from inappropriate encumbrances so that it can function more nearly as it was supposed to in the first place. The polyvalence of tensive symbols implies that no single concept is mandatory. The concept used here is rectifying power, and since it has to do with what is anticipated, it is appropriate to call it the rectifying power of the impinging future. If this is what Jesus meant by "the kingdom of God," the place to begin is with its tenses.

The tenses of the kingdom. For a hundred years the Jesus quest has been coping with Schweitzer's contention that "Jesus' ministry counted *only* upon the eschatological realisation of the Kingdom."[15] In the English-using world the most influential repudiation of Schweitzer was C. H. Dodd's "realized eschatology"—the claim that for Jesus the kingdom was not near but here;[16] in Germany, Jeremias modified this to say that the kingdom was "in the process of realization."[17] After World War II Kümmel claimed that it was both near and here,[18] a view endorsed recently by Flusser, who holds that the rabbis too thought it was both present and future but from a different perspective: for Jesus it was present because of something that happened. He claims that Jesus "is the only Jew of ancient times known to us who preached not only that people were on the threshold of the end of time, but that the new age of salvation had already begun."[19] Recently, however, some American scholars have virtually eliminated the future from Jesus' message of the

15. Schweitzer, *The Mystery of the Kingdom of God*, 92, his italics. For Schweitzer, "eschatology" was simply "apocalyptic." For a useful overview of the issues, see Willis, "The Discovery of the Eschatological Kingdom."

16. Dodd presented his view in his 1935 Shaffer Lectures at Yale, *The Parables of the Kingdom*. See also Hiers, "Pivotal Reactions to Eschatological Interpretations."

17. Jeremias, *The Parables of Jesus*, 230. Jeremias notes that he learned the phrase "sich realisierende Eschatologie" from Ernst Haenchen and that Dodd agreed with it. Later Jeremias wrote that "the consummation of the world is near. Indeed it is very near," and that "the time of expectation is at an end; the time of fulfilment [*sic*] has dawned" (*New Testament and Theology*, 102, 108).

18. Kümmel, *Promise and Fulfillment*.

19. Flusser, *Jesus*, 110.

kingdom. Crossan,[20] for example, claims that Jesus rejected apocalyptic eschatology (259) and that one should understand him in terms of a "kingdom performed rather than just proclaimed" (249)—a false alternative if he "had both
an ideal vision and a social program" (349) that he put into effect by his shared
meals. Borg's claim that "the majority of scholars no longer think that Jesus
expected the end of the world in his generation"[21] is doubly misleading because
the world's cessation was never the point, and the majority to which he refers
turns out to be the Jesus Seminar! On the other hand, when Sanders lists "the
most secure conclusions" he puts first, "Jesus expected the kingdom in the near
future"; he also considers it "possible—no more" that Jesus saw the kingdom
arriving in his words and deeds.[22] Others, this writer among them, argue that it
is more than possible.

Before proceeding, it is useful to reflect on the question Did Jesus think the
reign of God is now imminent or that it was now immanent, near or here? The
answer requires attending to both the content of his words and the character of
his mission, for it was more than a vehicle for transmitting verbally his view of
the kingdom; it was also itself an expression of that understanding. The more
one insists that he understood the kingdom's arrival as transforming socioeconomic conditions and ending Roman hegemony, none of which was actually
happening, the more likely it becomes that he announced not the kingdom's
presence but its nearness and called for an appropriate anticipatory response.
Had God's reign, so understood, been *here*, there would be no need to announce it, for its presentness would have been manifest. Conversely, a reign
that must be announced and interpreted, because otherwise no one would
know about it, is either not yet fully manifest or is inherently, constitutively, not
manifestable because it is God's rule in the human heart—in which case Jesus'
mission would have concentrated on inward personal piety. But the shape of
his mission and his words about the kingdom cannot be separated; therefore his
sense of the future and the present constitute a unity as well.

20. Crossan, *The Historical Jesus*; the numbers in parentheses refer to this book.

21. Borg, *Jesus: A New Vision*, 14.

22. E. P. Sanders, *Jesus and Judaism*, 156; also 153, 232. Because Sanders refuses to rest
his case on Jesus' sayings (ibid., 132), he relies on broader historical considerations. Moreover, like Crawford, he thinks that even the three sayings commonly regarded as showing
that Jesus expected an imminent event (Mk 9:1; 13:30; Mt 10:23) might not be genuine
and that Lk 17:21—the text widely regarded as evidence that Jesus thought the kingdom
was here—shows that it is only "possible" that he thought it was actually present. See Crawford, "Near Expectation in the Sayings of Jesus" (a critique of Kümmel).

Jesus did not, however, make these unities the subject matter of his teaching. Rather, these unities of word and deed, future and present, are so built into his mission that they shaped it intuitively. According to the gospels, he spoke of such matters when specific circumstances required him to, as will be noted below. There is no evidence that Jesus did what his interpreters deem essential today: explain discursively how the tenses of the kingdom are related. It is useful to bear such considerations in mind as we turn to the sayings that have been used to argue that Jesus spoke of the kingdom only in present tense.

According to the Q material used in Luke 11:29–32 and Matthew 12:38–42, Jesus expected the eschatological judgment when both the queen of the South (who had come to hear Solomon's wisdom) and the Ninevites (who had repented in response to Jonah's preaching) will condemn Jesus' generation for not responding to him, despite the fact that "something greater" than Solomon and Jonah "is here." Jesus, however, neither explained what that "something" was, even though it is utterly decisive for one's future, nor actually said that the kingdom of God is here. This saying, combining warning with assertion, was surely provoked by some circumstance, though it remains unknown; the same is probably true of the alternative form of the tradition in Mark 8:11–12.[23]

The likelihood that Jesus said various things about his mission and its relation to the kingdom is strengthened by the cluster of sayings about John the Baptist in Matthew 11:2–19 and Luke 7:18–35 and 16:16, which both Evangelists adapted from Q. Three parts of this cluster merit attention here.

---

23. It is exceedingly difficult to sort out and sketch the history of the transmission of these sayings. According to Luke, "when the crowds were increasing," Jesus rebuked "this generation" for seeking a "sign" (presumably a legitimating act), having noted this earlier in verse 16, and declared that the only sign will be that of Jonah. According to Mk 8:11–12, Jesus was exasperated by the Pharisees' request for a sign: "he sighed deeply in his spirit and said, 'Why does this generation ask for a sign? Truly I tell you, no sign will be given to this generation.'" Luke inserts an explanation between Jesus' declaration and the saying about the queen of the South: "For just as Jonah became a sign to the people of Nineveh, so the Son of Man [presumably Jesus] will be to this generation." According to Matthew, Jesus' rebuke is directed to the scribes and Pharisees who ask for a sign—an inference from the saying itself: "An evil and adulterous generation asks for a sign, but no sign will be given it except the sign of Jonah." As in Luke, Matthew also inserts an explanation: Jonah's three days and nights "in the belly of the sea monster" is a sign of the Son of Man's stay "in the heart of the earth" before the resurrection. Later Matthew repeats the point: no sign but Jonah (Mt 16:1–4). There is no convincing reason why Jesus could not have denied any sign on one occasion and made Jonah an exception on another, each time reflecting what he thought was appropriate. For a discussion of the critical issues, see Fitzmyer, *Luke*, II, 930–38.

The first concerns Jesus' response to the question that John's disciples put to him at the Baptizer's behest: "Are you the one who is to come or are we to wait for another?" (Mt 11:2–3; Lk 7:18–20). According to both Matthew and Luke, Jesus replied, "Go and tell John what you hear and see: the blind receive their sight, the lame walk, the lepers are cleansed, the deaf hear, the dead are raised, and the poor have good news brought to them. And blessed is anyone who takes no offense at me."[24] The list of wonders is not accidental but alludes to what was promised in Isaiah 26:19 regarding the resuscitation of the dead; in 29:18–19 regarding the deaf and blind; in 35:5–6 regarding the blind, deaf and lame; and in 61:1 concerning good news to the oppressed. Even though Isaiah says nothing about lepers[25] or exorcisms, the point is clear enough: Jesus saw his healings and preaching of good news as the fulfillment of the Isaianic prophecies—i.e., as the eschatological event, though not a word is said about the kingdom of God. Moreover, Meier rightly notes that "Jesus' response focuses upon the precise points at which his own ministry strikingly diverges from and goes beyond John's."[26]

Second, the sayings that follow do speak of the kingdom (Mt 11:7–11; Lk 7:24–28).[27] After identifying John as the "messenger" that scripture (cf. Ex 23:20; Mal 3:1) promised would "prepare the way" for God's coming, Jesus declares, "Truly I tell you, among those born of women, no one has arisen greater than John the Baptist; yet the least in the kingdom of God is greater than he." In other words, great as John is as the fulfillment of prophecy, he is still "less" than the "least" in the kingdom because being "in" the kingdom surpasses being even the greatest on the outside.[28] Although this saying is often regarded as evidence that Jesus thought the kingdom to be here, it actually says

24. Although both gospels have included such deeds in their story to this point (though only Matthew reports the healing of blindness and neither reports a healing of deafness), neither has the stories in the sequence of Jesus' words. Jesus' reply, therefore, cannot be attributed to the Evangelists. Only Luke reports that before Jesus answered the emissaries, "There and then he healed many sufferers from diseases, plagues, and evil spirits; and on many blind people he bestowed sight" (Lk 7:21, REB). NRSV, however, reads, "Jesus had just then cured," thereby subverting Luke's point: Jesus made sure that the emissaries saw the healings.

25. These actions may allude to Elijah who raised the dead (1 Kgs 17) and Elisha who healed leprosy (2 Kgs 5); if so, mentioning these wonders would suggest that Jesus is their kind of prophetic figure. See Tuckett, *Q and the History of Early Christianity*, 222–23.

26. Meier, *A Marginal Jew*, II, 133.

27. For the structure of this material, see Meier, *A Marginal Jew*, II, 137–38.

28. The *Gospel of Thomas* has: "Jesus said, 'From Adam to John the Baptist, no one born of woman is greater than John the Baptist. . . . But I have said that anyone among you who becomes as a child will know the kingdom and will become greater than John.'"

nothing about its presence. The saying would be just as true in the future, and Jesus does not say whether anyone is presently "in" the kingdom. The "near or here" issue is simply not addressed.

Third, the creator of Matthew may have sensed this, for at this point he inserted a Q saying found elsewhere in Luke: "From the days of John the Baptist until now the kingdom of heaven has suffered violence, and the violent take it by force. For all the prophets and the law[29] prophesied until John came; and if you are willing to accept it, he is Elijah who is to come" (Mt 11:12–15). The Lukan version differs significantly: "The law and the prophets were in effect until John came;[30] since then the good news of the kingdom of God is proclaimed, and everyone tries to enter [literally, enters] it by force" (Lk 16:16). This notoriously difficult passage does imply that the kingdom is somehow present, for only so could one "take it by force" (Mt) or "enter it by force" (Lk). Beyond that nothing is clear.[31] The Lukan version elicits questions such as: Why would one forcefully enter what is proclaimed as good news? Moreover, in what sense does "everyone" enter it this way? The Matthean version offers even more problems; e.g., does "suffered violence" rightly translate *biazetai*?[32] What does it mean to take the kingdom "by force"? Who are "the violent" who

29. This unique sequence (prophets before law) probably is the Evangelist's deliberate change, reflecting his view that the law too is prophecy. See Davies and Allison, *A Critical and Exegetical Commentary on the Gospel According to Saint Matthew* (herein cited as *Matthew*), II, 256–57.

30. The text has no verb; in supplying it, the translators disclose their interpretation. REB: "were"; NIV: "were proclaimed"; NJB evidently "corrects" Luke: "Up to the time of John it was the Law and the Prophets"; so too CEV: "people had to obey the Law of Moses and the Books of the Prophets."

31. For a discussion of the exegetical and historical problems, see Meier, *A Marginal Jew*, II, 157–63; a more exhaustive discussion is offered by Chilton, *God in Strength*, 203–31.

32. *Biazetai* can be either passive or middle voice. In Lk 16:16 it is middle and so is rendered "everyone enters it by force" (or "forces a way in," REB); "is trying hard to get in" (CEV); "enters it violently" (RSV). If it were passive, it would say "everyone is forced into it" (preferred by Fitzmyer, *Luke*, II, 1114, who softens it to "pressed into it"). Exactly the same form of the verb is used in Mt 11:12. If here too it is a middle verb, then the clause is to be translated as "the kingdom of heaven comes forcibly [or violently]"; if it is a passive, it says that the kingdom "has suffered violence." Since the next clause uses the noun *biastai* (the violent ones) as the subject of the verb *harpazousin* (seize forcibly, as in robbery or plunder), the NRSV is probably correct: "the kingdom of heaven has suffered violence, and the violent take it by force."

do so?[33] Is this a positive or negative reading of the situation—i.e., is Jesus celebrating the arrival of the kingdom and the vigorous response to it or lamenting what is happening? In short, although this passage mostly tantalizes, it does imply that since John the Baptist the kingdom of God is no longer only something expected in the future; beginning with John its tense has changed.[34]

There is, in fact, only *one* saying in which Jesus asserts the presence of the kingdom, and it is reported only in Luke 17:20–21: "Once Jesus was asked by the Pharisees when the kingdom of God was coming, and he answered, 'The kingdom of God is not coming with things that can be observed; nor will they say, "Look, here it is!" or "There it is!" For, in fact, the kingdom is among (*entos*) you.'" A variant version is found in Thomas.[35] Not surprisingly, this is *the* proof-text for the noneschatological Jesus.[36] But such a conclusion is easier to reach if one ignores the hand of the Lukan Evangelist in both the composition of the larger context (17:20–18:8) and in the wording of the short story itself. (a) In 17:20–21 the use of "coming" in both the question and the answer indi-

33. For major alternatives, see Davies and Allison, *Matthew*, II, 254–55; they reject the view that the violent are political revolutionaries, proposing instead that the saying's horizon is the eschatological conflict between good and evil, and that the violent are "those who, through opposition to the heralds of the kingdom, close that kingdom to others." This is too vague to be convincing. Breech thinks they are those who so resisted the kingdom, as "the mode of being human that he [Jesus] shares with John," that they felt "that there was something to be destroyed if they were to escape the subjection they felt in the face of freedom" (*The Silence of Jesus*, 30); this is more imaginary than imaginative.

34. So also Tuckett, *Q and the History of Early Christianity*, 137.

35. In the *Gospel of Thomas* elements of this saying appear in two sayings. According to Logion 3, "Jesus said, 'If those who lead you say to you, "Look! The kingdom is in heaven," then the birds of heaven will precede you. If they say to you, "It is in the sea," then the fish will precede you. But the kingdom is within you and it is outside of you. If you will know yourselves, then you will be known, and you will realize that you are children of the living Father. But if you do not know yourselves, then you will dwell in poverty and you are poverty.'" According to Logion 113, "Jesus' disciples said to him, 'When will the kingdom come?' Jesus answered, 'It will not come by waiting for it. People will not say, "Look! Here it is!" or "There it is!" But the kingdom of the Father is spread out upon the earth and people do not seek it.'"

36. Breech, for example, argues that here "Jesus maintains a deafening silence" with respect to Johannine eschatological prophecy, repudiates apocalyptic conceptions, and ignores the Jewish expectations that God will intervene on behalf of his people and instead "locates the kingdom" in the experience shared by those who live as free persons by "a trans-personal power" (*The Silence of Jesus*, 37–39).

cates that the Evangelist inferred the question from the answer and attributed the former to the Pharisees, who ask a straightforward question without any evident motivation. (b) Likewise, the rejected "Look, here it is!" and "There it is!" (v. 21) is repeated in the sayings that follow, addressed, however, to the disciples concerning the future coming of the Son of Man (17:23–18:8). To create this discourse about the coming of the Son of Man, framed by 17:22 and 18:8, the Third Evangelist added peculiarly Lukan sayings[37] to Q.[38] (c) The Pharisees' straightforward When? is not actually answered. Instead Jesus' reply first deals with the How? ("not with things that can be observed," taken up in the sayings about the Son of Man) and with the Where? ("The kingdom . . . is among you"); the same question reappears suddenly at verse 37 where the *disciples* ask, "Where, Lord?," to which Jesus replies enigmatically with a proverb, "Where the corpse is, there the vultures will gather"—as if to suggest (to Luke's reader) that the "Where?" in verse 21 and the proverb are to be seen together. But the point is anything but obvious. To conclude, the Evangelist has made Jesus' reply to the Pharisees' question about the time of the kingdom's coming into the springboard for his teaching the disciples about the sudden, incalculable coming of the Son of Man. It is not clear whether this juxtaposition of the kingdom and the Son of Man is to be understood disjunctively or conjunctively—whether the Evangelist understood Jesus to be changing the subject (and audience) or whether he thought Jesus was explaining privately that the kingdom's coming would coincide with the arrival of the Son of Man.

Even if the occasion of verse 20 was inferred by the Evangelist, he might have used an isolated saying of Jesus transmitted without any narrative setting or with one that the Evangelist replaced with his own. Either way it remains impossible to know what or who had elicited from Jesus this unparalleled assertion that God's kingdom "is among you" (most scholars agree that *entos* means "among" not "within"). In its present (Lukan) setting it challenges the Pharisees to discern the kingdom's presence in their midst, implying that it is there because Jesus is there. Indeed, this would have been its effect on whoever might have elicited this unique declaration. In any case, it would be unwise to make this saying the keystone in the arch of a noneschatological Jesus.

37. In addition to the framing references to the coming of the Son of Man in 17:22 and 18:8, peculiar to Luke are the predicted passion of the Son of Man (17:25), comparison with the days of Lot (17:28–32), and the parable of the persistent widow, used to encourage persistent prayer and steadfast hope (18:1–8a).

38. Except for the parallel to Lk 17:33 in 10:39, the Q materials are found in a quite different context in Matthew—in chapter 24, the expansion of the "little apocalypse" in Mark 13.

Unless one is prepared to deny that the earliest form of the Lord's Prayer can be traced to Jesus—as does Crossan, who asserts also that "there is nothing apocalyptic about it"[39]— its petition "Thy kingdom come" indicates clearly enough that Jesus did not think it was already here and that whatever its present expressions, its arrival remains something to be prayed for. Earlier in this chapter, moreover, it was noted that many of Jesus' teachings do not mention the kingdom or its coming; it was also claimed that the kingdom was the "unifying ground" of his work. So the question emerges: What unifies the eschatological and the noneschatological teachings?

One can adopt Harnack's imagery and regard the eschatological sayings as the husk and the noneschatological wisdomlike sayings as the truth-bearing kernel; or one can follow Rudolf Otto, who claimed that there is an essential irrationality of all apocalyptic eschatology: one expects both an imminent end and yet assumes that life will continue as before.[40] Or, like Crossan, one can note that there are diverse ways of talking about the kingdom, an apocalyptic one that looks to the future and a sapiential (wisdom) one that emphasizes the present (though the cited evidence for the latter is sparse), and then proceed to ignore the former because the one is as world-denying as the other.[41] None of these is satisfactory, however, because none gives due weight to the positive theological understanding of God's reign that underlies them both and so cannot show why or how they belong together.[42]

More promising is Amos Wilder's argument that the eschatological strand serves as the "formal sanction" for Jesus' ethics,[43] while the "substantive sanc-

39. Crossan, *The Historical Jesus*, 293–94.

40. Otto, *The Kingdom of God and the Son of Man*, 59–63.

41. Crossan, *The Historical Jesus*, 292.

42. Six decades ago Windisch noted that it was Jesus' idea of God that determined both his wisdom and his prophetic message, "and in both [he] intensifies the demand for radical detachment from all that is outside the sphere of the divine. . . . Both the wisdom and the eschatology of Jesus' teaching are heightened to radical demand, and this fact is one of the most important in accounting for the combination of these two forms of proclamation" (*The Meaning of the Sermon on the Mount*, 40).

43. Wilder regarded the eschatological material as "myth" or "fictions" naively held, a "picture of the asserted sovereignty of God" that sturdy faith demanded in the face of reality, "the appeal of the ethical consciousness against things as they are, and the incontrovertible assurance of faith that God will act"; the eschatological sanction is "always in the form of a fictional or formal sanction" (*Eschatology and Ethics*, 26, 36, 134 resp.).

tion" (more accurately called a "warrant"[44]) is the nature of God. At the same time, however, Wilder pointed (perhaps unwittingly) to a factor that makes it untenable to regard the eschatological element as a purely "formal sanction." He noted that for Jesus "a new situation has arisen with the presence of the Baptist and Jesus" (147, italicized) because of "the new relation to God in the time of salvation" (161)—namely, "the presence of the promised time of the new covenant and the corresponding new relation to God" (183). Therefore, the person who accepts Jesus' message "is a self profoundly altered by the situation into which it has been plunged by the power of the *aeon* to come" (211). In short, "obedience [to Jesus' teaching] is itself part of the positive gift of the kingdom" (113). This is on target, for if a person in the new situation lives by the power of the coming *aeon*, what Machovec calls "living off the future,"[45] then in Jesus' teaching the "picture of the asserted sovereignty of God" *is* coming into view. Because living "by the power of the *aeon* to come" is what Jesus' mission was about, he could indeed claim that something greater than Solomon was present because it produced "a self profoundly altered."[46]

In Jesus' teachings the "picture of the asserted sovereignty of God" becomes concrete in various ways, though they can be classified as eschatological or sapiential. Among the former are sayings such as "All who exalt themselves will be humbled, and all who humble themselves will be exalted" (Mt 23:12) and "Those who try to make their life secure will lose it, but those who lose their life will keep it (Lk 17:33; see also the varying formulations in Lk 9:24; Mt 10:39, 16:25; Mk 8:35). Likewise, Jesus promises that the currently hungry will

---

44. That which provides the real, intrinsic basis for an exhortation is its warrant, whereas a sanction is an external consideration adduced to reinforce the exhortation, such as a reference to honor or shame. For instance, "Whoever says, 'You fool!' shall be liable to the hell of fire" (Mt 5:22) is an eschatological sanction in the form of a threat, whereas "Your Father who sees [your almsgiving] in secret will reward you" (Mt 6:4) is a sanction as promise; both reinforce the seriousness of choosing right behavior but do not provide its real ground. But when Jesus urges love of enemies in imitation of the Father who sends sun and rain on the evil and good alike, he provides a warrant: act like God acts. For additional comments on warrants and sanctions, see Keck, "Rethinking 'New Testament Ethics,'" 11–14.

45. Machovec, *A Marxist Looks at Jesus*, 91.

46. Vermes claims that "in a real eschatological atmosphere the change is total. The future to all intents and purposes is abolished and replaced by imminence, immediacy and urgency. . . . There is no second chance for one convinced that the kingdom of God is at hand. . . . The religion of Jesus the Jew is a rare, possibly unique, manifestation of undiluted eschatological enthusiasm" (*The Religion of Jesus the Jew*, 189–90).

be sated by God[47] and that those who are "full now" will hunger then (Lk 6:21, 25). Precisely this change, which some scholars call the "eschatological reversal," shows just how far off-base is the portrayal of Jesus as a Cynic, because for a Cynic "hunger might be alleviated in the present; but a life of poverty . . . was what was explicitly embraced and welcomed," as Tuckett rightly notes.[48] At the same time the kingdom will bring also vindication of what is presently good and right. Those who do not judge others now will not be judged; those who do not condemn will not be condemned; the forgiving will be forgiven, and to those who give it will be given amply (Lk 6:37–38). Not even a cup of water given to "one of these little ones" will be unrewarded (Mt 10:42). The presently "pure in heart" will see God then (Mt 5:8).

Both the inversion of the currently wrong and the reward for the currently right express the two sides of the kingly rule of God actualized; the inversion ends the marks of the present resistance to God's rule, and the reward confirms that God is, and always has been, king. There is no contradiction, nor even serious tension, between a sapiential assurance that "every sound tree bears good fruit" and the apocalyptic warning that "every tree that does not bear good fruit is cut down and thrown into the fire" (Mt 7:18–19). The wisdomlike sayings that express insight into the way things really are and the apocalyptic sayings that express what will be cannot be separated because what will be is the future brought about by the God who is already king and in no way is waiting to become king. In short, the nonapocalyptic, nonfuturist teachings of Jesus, whether expressed sapientially or mandatorily, assume that God's kingly rule always "is," so much so that the divine sovereignty provides for the birds, decks the lilies in splendor (Mt 6:25–34; Lk 12:22–31), and rules the creation so sturdily that Jesus can ask his hearers to grasp what the imminent rule is like by observing "natural" phenomena: seed time and harvest (Mk 4:26–29), the change of weather (Mt 16:2–3; Lk 12:54–56), and the permeating power of leaven (Mt 13:33; Lk 13:20–21). It is not accidental that Jesus grounds his view of marriage and divorce in creation, implying that the ethos that responds to the kingdom is nothing other than what has been God's will all along (Mt 19:3–6).

The significance of this complementarity of the imminence and the immanence of God's kingly reign is often overlooked; where this occurs it is all the

47. The translation of *chortasthēsesthe* as "you shall be satisfied" is misleading, for it implies that one will be content or pleased with a desired result. But the Greek verb is in the passive, implying that it is God who brings about the result. Since the text refers to food, NRSV renders the verb "for you will be filled"—by God.

48. Tuckett, *Q and the History of Early Christianity*, 141, n. 9.

easier to portray Jesus' understanding of the kingdom's coming in terms that so heavily accent its transformative, revolutionary (not necessarily insurrectionist) impact that scarcely any trace of continuity remains between life before its arrival and afterward, nor is there much room for the kingdom as the actualizing of God's promise to Israel. Crossan, for example, declares that the food laws, which were of concern not only to the scrupulous Pharisees but were a part of the Torah revered by all, were subverted by Jesus, who ignored them; when he also asserts that for Jesus the kingdom "rendered sexual and social, political and religious distinctions completely irrelevant and anachronistic,"[49] he clearly implies that the kingdom is so thoroughly "world-negating" that it completely abolishes all threads of continuity with the values and structures that, despite undeniable abuses and distortions, have sustained human communities and have kept life minimally humane and nurtured love and justice in the face of cruelty and oppression. The coming of such a kingdom of God would not begin the reign of the Creator who has always been the ground and warrant of the good, but of another Being who through Jesus rescues persons from a wholly evil present world. Were that the case, then Marcion, who made just this claim in the second century, would smile and say, "I told you so!"

But for Jesus, the coming of God's kingdom was world-negating only as the necessary dimension of its essentially world-affirming character, for the actualizing of God's reign means that all things are finally made right, thereby negating what is currently skewed. This rectifying impingement is what made the news of God's imminent kingdom essentially good.

God's kingdom as rectifying impingement.   Because "kingdom of God" symbolizes God's relation to the created order as a theocracy in which God's will is no longer only a command but a condition in which all resistance is overcome, its actualization is an exercise of divine power that can be imaged spatially as "coming near" and temporally as "coming soon." Further, because power is exercised only in relationship, God's kingship is a field of force that orders and shapes, and if necessary realigns, relationships between the sovereign and whatever is in range of the sovereign power; this is similar to the way iron filings on a sheet of paper begin to fall into a pattern in response to the magnetic field when a magnet under the paper comes near. So too God's kingdom changes things before it actually arrives. When it impinges on the present, rectification begins. And since for Jesus it is the creator's kingdom that rectifies, its impingement affects both the material self and the moral self—i.e., Jesus the teacher both brought healing and redefined repentance. Apparently Mark recognizes this connection, for it reports

49. Crossan, *The Historical Jesus*, 263, 298.

that the congregation expressed its amazement at Jesus' exorcism in the synagogue by saying, "What is this? A new teaching! With authority he commands even the unclean spirits, and they obey him" (Mk 1:27).

Today there is more agreement that Jesus healed people from time to time than there is about the nature of his healings and their significance in his mission. The late Morton Smith rightly asserted that "the gospels represent Jesus as attracting attention primarily as a miracle worker, and winning his followers by miracles. The gospels do so because he did so."[50] Smith's assertion, though stated carefully, can be misunderstood all too easily. That Jesus' wonder-working power attracted attention is clear; that he did wonders in order to acquire followers or gather a crowd is precisely what the Synoptics do not show (nor did Smith say). Of concern here are not the "nature miracles" (e.g., walking on water) but the exorcisms and healings, which the Synoptics restrict to Jesus' mission in Galilee. The reports vary greatly in length, detail, circumstance, and function. All of the stories, like Jesus' teachings, were told and transmitted from the standpoint of Christian faith, so it is not surprising that the critics' assessments of their historical reliability vary greatly.[51] What matters here, however is

50. M. Smith, *Jesus the Magician*, 10. For an appreciative critique of Smith's contention that Jesus was a magician, see E. P. Sanders, *Jesus and Judaism*, 165–69. Jesus' fame as an exorcist is emphasized repeatedly in the gospels; see, e.g., Mk 1:21–37; 3:7–10. According to Lk 5:1–11, but not according to Mk 1:16–20, Jesus' role in the marvelous catch of fish prompted Peter, James, and John to become his disciples. S. Davies goes farther: "most of Jesus' associates, male and female, became 'followers' after he had cured them of demons and/or illness. . . . It does not stand to reason that Jesus could simply 'call' and, by virtue of that fact alone, men would follow, leave their homes, jobs, families to live indigently and itinerantly in his company" (*Jesus the Healer*, 107).

51. Meier, for example, after discussing each of the healing stories in great detail, concludes that some "have a good chance of going back to some event in the life of the historical Jesus—however much they may have been reworked and expanded by Christian theology." These are the following: two healings of paralysis (Mk 2:1–12, par.; Mk 5:1–9), three of blindness (Mk 10:46–50, par.; 8:22–26; Jn 9:1–7), one each of a deaf mute (Mk 7:31–33) and an unspecified illness (Mt. 8:5–13, par.; Jn 4:46–54). Of the seven exorcism stories, he thinks that only two probably rest on actual events (Mk 9:14–29; Lk 8:2) and that perhaps three others do (Mk 1:23–28//Lk 4:33–37; Mk 5:1–20; Mt 12:24//Lk 11:14–15) (*A Marginal Jew*, II, 726, 661). On the other hand, S. Davies, appealing to cross-cultural studies of possession and trance, as well as of altered states of consciousness (and changed ego identity resulting from spirit-possession), argues that "the events given and implied in Mark's account, including various 'supernatural' events, happened much as Mark says they happened" (*Jesus the Healer*, 55–56).

not so much the accuracy of the individual stories[52] as the fact that Jesus was a kingdom-shaped teacher who also healed and exorcised the demonic. He did not, of course, explain either his motivation (e.g., a powerful desire to help people[53]) or the theological rationale which held together his understanding of the kingdom and his wonder-working. That rationale can only be deduced from his actions and from what he occasionally said about them. Here too, of course, one cannot claim to have discerned Jesus' own thinking; in fact, he might not have reasoned analytically about the rationale at all.

The Synoptics (apart from their generalizing summaries) imply that Jesus' teaching activity was proactive but his healing and exorcistic activities were reactive; that is, he took the initiative in teaching but did not seek out the diseased and possessed. He did not need to, for they sought him and confronted him with their pleas for help. Mark 1:35–38 reports that when told that people were looking for him because on the previous evening "he [had] healed many who were sick with various diseases, and cast out many demons," he resolutely said, "Let us go on to the neighboring towns, so that I may proclaim the message there also; for that is what I came out to do." Even if this is the Evangelist's own formulation, it accords with what is implied in the healing and exorcism stories themselves: For Jesus, these activities flowed from the message, not the reverse; he was not a healer who found he had something to say but a teacher who found it necessary to heal. In other words, while Jesus discovered that healing and exorcism were expressions of the kingdom's impingement, he also knew that they did not necessarily imply the kingdom's coming. After all, there were other healers and exorcists in Galilee.

Jesus pointed this out when he defended his exorcism against the charge that he was in league with the devil: "He casts out demons by Beelzebul."[54]

52. For a discussion of each exorcism story, see Twelftree, *Jesus the Exorcist*, 53–127.

53. Only one story reports that Jesus was moved by pity for a diseased person—the "leper" (Mk 1:41)—*if* one decides that the best text reads *splangthnistheis* ("moved with pity," NRSV) and not *orgistheis* ("moved with anger," REB); the latter should be preferred because it is the more difficult reading and so would have been changed to "pity" whereas the reverse is highly improbable. Nonetheless, Jesus surely was a compassionate person. Interestingly, however, when Mark says he had compassion on the crowds, the reason was "because they were like sheep without a shepherd," not because there were many with illness; so he "began to teach them many things" (Mk 6:34). Later it was hunger, not illness, that prompted him to say, "I have compassion on the crowd" (Mk 8:1–2, the lead-in to the story of the miraculous feeding).

54. The accusation, though not attributed to the same people, is found in Mark (3:22, scribes), Luke (11:15, some of the crowd that had just seen one of his exorcisms), and

According to Q (Mt 11:27–28; Lk 11:19–20), Jesus first responded by pointing out the self-contradiction of the charge and then said, "Now if I cast out demons by Beelzebul, by whom do your exorcists [literally, your sons] cast them out? Therefore they will be your judges. But if it is by the finger of God [Mt: Spirit of God] that I cast out demons, then the kingdom of God has come to you." In this two-pronged reply Jesus first demolishes the accusation as a nonstarter: If you accuse me of using Satanic power to expel demons, you must accuse other exorcists as well, and they will condemn such calumny. Then he claims that through *his* exorcisms God's kingdom is brought *to the accusers* (and presumably to the possessed as well, though not in the same way). Thereby he reverses the flow: now the accusers must decide whether he is in league with God or Beelzebul. The same self-contradiction (Mt 12:25–26; Lk 11:17–18), like the accusation, is reported also in Mark 3:22–26, where its figurative character—neither a kingdom nor a house [dynasty or family?] divided against itself can stand—prompted the Evangelist to say that Jesus spoke "in parables" even though the point is stated clearly at the outset: "How can Satan cast out Satan?"

All three gospels report yet another reply which, though stated differently in each case, offers the same positive interpretation of Jesus' exorcisms: Before plundering a strong man's house, one must first tie him up (Mt 12:29; Mk 3:27; Lk 11:21–22). In other words, Jesus' exorcisms, far from being done with Satanic power, are events in which he overcomes Satan's power and liberates those in his possession, restoring them to community and rehabilitating them as responsible persons under the sovereignty of God. This is the point made also in a healing story found only in Luke 13:10–17, whose key saying may well represent Jesus' view despite the Lukan rhetorical setting in which it is found.[55] To the objection that he healed a severely disabled woman on the Sabbath by laying hands on her (making his deed a forbidden "work"), Jesus responded with an analogy based on reasoning from the lesser to the greater: If each of you unties animals on the Sabbath in order to lead them to water, "ought not this woman, a daughter of Abraham whom Satan bound for eighteen long years, be set free from bondage on the Sabbath day?"

Several things can be inferred from these sayings: (a) Jesus assumed that all exorcisms relied on God's power, not Beelzebul's. (b) What distinguished *his*

Matthew (12:24, Pharisees who heard of Jesus' exorcisms). All three Evangelists append various sayings to Jesus' reply. The tradition-history of this material is complex, for at some points what is in Mark was also in Q.

55. Fitzmyer too declines to dismiss the story as a sheer church creation (*Luke*, II, 1010–12).

exorcisms was their relation to the coming of God's kingdom, their eschatological significance; apart from this connection, Jesus would have been just another
thaumaturge, and he knew it—better than anyone else, in fact. (c) That significance could not simply be "read off" the exorcisms but must be believed when
it is announced as a mark of the kingdom's coming; the exorcisms do not authen-
ticate Jesus' message and mission but express it. (d) Since it is he who announces
the kingdom, the significance of the exorcism cannot be believed without believing him. (e) As God's agent ("finger"), he is engaged in a struggle against Satan
to restore God's sovereignty over those who now are in bondage to demonic
power; by this restoration God's kingly reign already impinges on a particular person's present, making it right. (f) If in exorcism Jesus regarded himself as God's
"finger," translating the news of the kingdom into action, he also implied that it
was his vocation to embody the future by making it present as a sign of what is
yet to come. (g) Because he did not explain this rationale but simply acted on it
(unless challenged), Mark's report (omitted by Matthew and Luke) is probably
reliable; understandably, Jesus' family "went out to restrain him, for people [lit-
erally, they] were saying, 'He has gone out of his mind'" (Mk 3:21).

Although the exorcisms and healings were for Jesus expressions of the kingdom's coming, the kingdom's primary import was moral—i.e., a changed life.
What has often been called, wrongly, Jesus' "ethics" (see chap. 5) is really his profile of repentance. To be sure, it was the Evangelist who formulated the theme of
his message in which the call to repentance flows from the coming of the kingdom (Mk 1:15), as noted earlier. But he got it right, even though the narrative
that follows never has Jesus use either the verb *repent* or the noun *repentance*.[56]
Jesus does use this terminology occasionally in Matthew, in Luke more frequently, since it is found in sayings peculiar to this gospel (Lk 13:1–5, 15:7,10,
16:30), and in Lukan modifications of Q (5:32; 17:3–4). This means that solid
evidence for Jesus' use of repentance language is provided only by Luke 13:1–5
and the Q saying in Luke 10:13–14, which appears in a different setting in
Matthew 11:20–24.

Luke 13:1–5 follows the Q saying in 12:57–59 (Mt 5:25–26) that urges the
accused to settle out of court lest the judge put the accused in (debtor's) prison
until the last penny is paid—implying that drastic action is required now before
the imminent Judgment Day. At that moment Jesus is told "about the Galileans
whose blood Pilate had mingled with their sacrifices"—i.e., they were cut down
in the temple area. Though this is "the kind of provocation one would report

56. Interestingly, Mark says that the disciples whom Jesus sent on a mission "proclaimed
the need for repentance," though his instructions had not mentioned it (Mk 6:7–13).

to a political figure on the brink of a holy revolution,"[57] Jesus neither denounces Pilate nor bemoans the Galileans' tragedy; he instead addresses those who told him of it: "Do you think that because these Galileans suffered in this way they were worse sinners than all other Galileans? No, I tell you, unless you repent, you will all perish as they did." Then he makes the same point by alluding to another tragedy: "Or those eighteen who were killed when the tower of Siloam fell on them—do you think that they were worse offenders than all others living in Jerusalem? No, I tell you; but unless you repent, you will all perish just as they did." Jesus not only refuses to interpret either death by assassination or by accident as God's punishment of the unusually sinful but threatens his hearers with comparable death unless they repent. Fascinating as this response may be, its logic is too obscure to disclose what he meant by *repenting*. The response's very obscurity, however, argues for its genuineness.[58] What is clear, however, is that Jesus assumes that all must repent.

More promising is the Q saying in Luke 10:13–15: "Woe to you, Chorazin! Woe to you, Bethsaida! For if the deeds of power [*dynameis*] done in you had been done in Tyre and Sidon, they would have repented long ago. . . . But at the judgment it will be more tolerable for Tyre and Sidon than for you. And you, Capernaum, will you be exalted to heaven? No, you will be brought down to Hades."[59] The hypothetical repentance of Tyre and Sidon, like the actual positive response of the queen of Sheba and the Ninevites (Lk 11:31–32), is used as a foil to condemn the Galilean towns for failing to respond with repentance to Jesus, despite his (unspecified) mighty deeds; since Tyre and Sidon are regarded in scripture as especially wicked, the condemnation is markedly searing. This saying suggests that Jesus expected his

57. Yoder, *The Politics of Jesus*, 43.

58. The logic of the suggestion that the story is a Lukan invention based on Josephus's reports of Pilate's (later) military action against Samaritans (*Antiq.* xviii 4.1 # 86–87) is more obscure than the saying. See Fitzmyer, *Luke*, II, 1004–8.

59. Mt 11:21–23a is virtually identical, but vv. 23b-24 add, "For if the deeds of power done in you had been done in Sodom, it would have remained to this day [assuming that the Sodomites repented?]. But I tell you that on the day of judgment it will be more tolerable for the land of Sodom than for you." In Matthew these sayings follow Jesus' words about John. Luke, however, has the second sentence ("I tell you . . .) just before the woe to Chorazin (Lk 10:12), making it a link between the mission charge, whose ending counsels the disciples what to do if they are not received, and the woes in vv. 13–15. Actually, v. 16 would follow v. 12 more naturally.

message to elicit a positive response since it was dramatized by his mighty acts.[60]

Since the evidence for Jesus' actually preaching repentance is both sparse and ambiguous, one might easily infer that he did not call for repentance in response to the kingdom's nearness, despite Mark 1:15. Indeed, Sanders has drawn just this conclusion: "There is not a single piece of information about Jesus that indicates that he . . . called for *general* repentance *in view of* the coming kingdom." Indeed, "there is not a significant body of reliable sayings material which *explicitly* attributes to Jesus a call for *national* repentance." Sanders does not, of course, deny that Jesus affirmed the importance of individual forgiveness, as in the Lord's Prayer, but he does insist that "while looking for the restoration of Israel, he did not follow the majority and urge the traditional means toward that end: repentance and a return to the observance of the law."[61] Moreover, Sanders points out that for individuals, forgiveness by God ("always available to those who return to the way of the Lord") normally required restitution as well as repentance, to be demonstrated by a sacrifice in the temple. What was remarkable about Jesus, then, was that he offered sinners "inclusion in the kingdom not only *while they were still sinners* but also *without* requiring repentance as normally understood. . . . It was Luke who emphasized the reform of the wicked who accepted him." This, in fact, was "the novelty and offense of Jesus' message," for no one would have been offended by a summons to repent.[62]

Sanders is right in what he denies—that Jesus called for national repentance, as normally understood, in response to the kingdom's coming—but wrong in what he goes on to say about individuals—that Jesus "simply did not deal in detail" with the changed behavior of those who accepted his message "because he understood that John had taken care of that part of the overall task" (323, 322, resp.). Since Sanders thinks that Jesus did expect the kingdom to come imminently by God's dramatic action (320), it is appropriate that this response to Sanders take as its starting point his own correct observation, "New ages by definition must alter the present" (319).

60. Some, however, think this saying belongs to the second stage of Q, that which reflects the rejection of the Q people, not Jesus himself. So, e.g., Chilton, *Pure Kingdom*, 129 and Vaage, *Galilean Upstarts*, 108.

61. E. P. Sanders, *Jesus and Judaism*, 110, 111, 119, his italics.

62. Ibid., 206–7, his italics. Sanders's premonition that his view "will not be a popular one" (208) has been substantiated. See, e.g., Chilton, "Jesus and the Repentance of E. P. Sanders."

To begin with, by holding it certain that Jesus expected the kingdom but no more than possible that he saw it arriving in his mission (see above, p. 72), Sanders virtually precludes seeing the new age's impingement on the present. But if Jesus were convinced that since John the situation with respect to the kingdom has changed (see above, p. 76)—so much so that in fact he saw himself as God's "finger" expressing its character in advance—then what he expected of those who believed him would naturally differ from what John expected. John had announced the coming judgment and required repentance and baptism to be ready for it, and Jesus, in accepting his baptism, had accepted his message as well. But the omission of baptism from his own mission implies a change in both what he announced and what he expected of those who accepted it. In other words, because the focal point of Jesus' message was not the imminent judgment but the kingdom—so imminent that it already changed the present of those who allowed themselves to be grasped by the news of its nearness—baptism was unnecessary and repentance was transformed from readiness for disaster into response to God's coming. For those who ignore or reject Jesus' message, his good news of the kingdom would turn into bad news of judgment, for one cannot spurn the impending actualization of God's reign with impugnity. The lives of those who believed John were rectified by repentance in order to face the future prepared; the lives of those who believed Jesus are presently rectified by responding to the future's present impingement. It may be that Jesus avoided the traditional terminology of repentance, and the practices associated with it, because it was no longer the appropriate word for the response he sought to the message he brought.

The logic of repentance, as commonly understood then, diverged from the logic of Jesus' message. In the Hebrew Bible, and subsequently as well, the word for *repent* is *shub* (*repentance: teshubah*), "turn," "turn back" (and hence away from). The prophets, convinced that the nation had abandoned the God of Moses for alien deities and their ways, used this language to call God's wayward people back to its formative faith and practice. This core meaning endured. In other words, the logic of repentance inherently assumes that the norm to which one turns lies in the past, in the character, commitment, and will of God disclosed in Israel's decisive history and authoritative scriptures. As Jesus saw things, however, responding to the kingdom's coming turns one to the future, even though God's coming reign neither displaced nor replaced the God of Abraham, Moses, the prophets, and sages. The "turning" Jesus called for was not a return, marked by remorse and determination to do better, to what had been abandoned, as appears to have been the case for John; it was rather a "turning," marked by daring and joy, to the future when what was articulated in the past would be actualized decisively and definitively. Living now by that future is what makes it truly eschatological. Clearly, Jesus did not offer such explanations, nor is it likely that he even thought about them; that, however, does not matter. What does matter is whether differentiating the logic of traditional repentance from the logic of Jesus' word about the kingdom suggests a plausible explanation of what Jesus instinctively did and did not do. There is no evidence that he gave much thought to finding just the right word or phrase that would sum it all up — though "kingdom of God" signaled quite well what was afoot.

If one bears in mind that *shub, teshubah* is "turning Godward" — i.e., "turning one's life toward the impinging reign of God" — there is no reason why one should not say that "repentance" was precisely the response Jesus sought and instanced in his moral teaching. Seen in this light, the "ethics" of the Sermon on the Mount, for example, are neither timeless principles or ideals nor requirements for admission to the kingdom, but rather specific indications of what a Godward turned life calls for. The Godward life is indeed eschatological but precisely not an "interim ethic" as Schweitzer claimed. What Jesus portrayed was a daring prolepsis of the future in the present, not as a way of hastening the future or as a program for restructuring society (though social relations would indeed be restructured for those who were grasped by what Jesus envisioned) but as a way of claiming the future boldly. This was not Harnack's "eternity in the midst of time" but the future's rectification in the present. Chilton put it this way: "Subversion of conventional morality is inevitable if what is final and transcendent has become available in the present."[63]

Schweitzer ruptured the idealist understanding of the kingdom of God in Jesus' teaching and exposed its future character instead, but the subsequent debates about the time of its coming have overshadowed the more significant question: *Whose* kingship is so imminent that those who believed this news were empowered to live now in its name? The question manifests the assumption, especially in antiquity, that the reign reflects the character of the sovereign. Accordingly, to know what the kingdom of God is like, and what it effects, is to know what God is like, and vice versa.

The King as Father

Jesus the teacher did not lecture. Matthew, to be sure, does present him delivering five discourses, each devoted to its own theme (chaps. 5–7, 10, 18,

---

63. Chilton, *Pure Kingdom*, 80.

23–25), but scholars agree that they assemble sayings spoken on diverse occasions that are no longer recoverable. As a Jewish sage Jesus used proverbs, epigrams, parables, terse retorts, and counterquestions to convey his message.[64] These oral forms of instruction suggest that his teaching was largely ad hoc, elicited by specific situations, some of which the tradition mentioned as the setting for the saying, others of which were inferred from the saying by the Evangelist, but most of which remain unknown. The point is that Jesus' teaching was delivered in bits and pieces, not as explanatory discourses or disquisitions on a theme as we find in writings by theologians such as Philo or Paul. Even if Jesus' understanding of God's kingdom undergirds everything he says and does, assembling his references to "God" would yield but a severely truncated corpus of his "theology." The task here, though, is to ascertain how the image of God as king and father, as one who controls and as one who cares, are related even though both do not appear in the same saying. The subject matter is, in fact, the theological counterpart to the relation between God's kingship being atemporal because God *is* king and God's kingship as an event in time because it is "coming."[65]

Both images have recently become as much of an offense in some quarters as the cross. Indeed, hierarchy and patriarchy have been linked and identified as the root to which the ax of liberation is at last being laid (*pace* John the Baptist, Mt 3:10). The subject matter is taken up here, however, neither in order to swing the ax once more nor to forbid swinging it but to understand what is implied in Jesus' use of these images. Although both *king* and *father* are terms characteristic of his teaching, he did not inaugurate the use of either of them but gave them his own emphasis.

God the king.   Jesus had neither to explain nor justify speaking of God as king, for this image was deeply embedded in the religious tradition that formed him.[66] Today, when kings are symbols of sovereignty more than exercisers of it, it is useful to remember that in antiquity the king had supreme power, and though he usually ruled in concert with the nobles, a constitutional monarchy was unheard of; and people were subjects, not citizens. Given that the mon-

---

64. For a discussion of the various aspects of Jesus the sage, see Witherington, *Jesus the Sage*, chap. 4 and Scott's suggestive "Jesus as Sage."

65. Fitzmyer notes that "the 'coming' of God's kingdom is not an Old Testament notion" (*Luke*, II, 904).

66. For a useful overview, see Whitelam, "King and Kingship," especially "Yahweh as King" (43–44); Duling, "Kingdom of God, Kingdom of Heaven"; and de Jonge, *God's Final Envoy*, chap. 4.

arch was at the apex of the power pyramid, it is understandable that the way power was exercised—or not exercised—shaped the whole society. The "consent of the governed" was not the ground of the king's authority but the reflex of the way he exercised it. These rudimentary reminders suffice to suggest that in the biblical and Jewish tradition calling God "king," and using related language, did not express misgiving, objection, or contempt but rather acknowledgment, assurance, and hope, on the one hand, and God's rightful claim to human obedience, service, and honor, on the other hand. To refuse these or to give them sullenly was therefore to contest God's right to rule unchallenged. Accordingly, the image of God on the throne pictures a quite different relation to the world than does an image of a person "in the chair."

Although God's kingship was basic to the religion Jesus inherited, apart from "the kingdom of God" references to God as king are noticeably marginal in his sayings. They are totally absent from Mark. In the double parables of Luke 14:25–35 the king does not represent God but, like the man who set out to build without first counting the cost, is a negative example for the disciples, for he undertook a war he could not win. It is only in Matthew's version of the parable of the Great Supper (Mt 22:1–14; Lk 14:15–24 [Q]) that the host is a king who represents God's actions in the history of salvation (in Luke the host is simply "a man" who gave a great banquet). In fact, there is only one parable in which the king represents God, the story of the forgiven servant who refuses to forgive and so forfeits his own forgiveness when the merciful, forgiving king turns into a merciless judge. Found only in Matthew (18:23–35), the parable climaxes the teachings about the need for the forgiven Christians to forgive each other, as in the Lord's Prayer. The concluding line uses distinctly Matthean language: "So also my heavenly Father will do to every one of you, if you do not forgive your brother from the heart."[67] This sparse evidence suggests that while Jesus had no hesitation in speaking of God's kingly rule, imaging God as king was not the point of his teaching; he did not have to instruct people on *that* point. What is implied in his image of God as king must therefore be smelted out of other ores.

The king whose kingdom is evoking the Godward turn is the holy God of Israel. Nowhere is this disclosed more succinctly than in the petition of the Lord's Prayer, "Hallowed be your name." In Luke's version (Lk 11:2–4; cf. Mt

---

67. That the Father is "in heaven" is stated repeatedly in Matthew (e.g., 5:16, 45; 6:1, 9, 32; 10:33; 12:50; 16:17; 18:10, 14; 23:9) but only once in Mark (11:25) and not at all in Luke; likewise, "heavenly Father" occurs but once in Luke (11:13) but often in Matthew (5:48; 6:14; 15:13; 18:35).

6:9–13; *Did.* 8.2), generally regarded as the earlier, this is the first half of a cou-
plet in which both lines have the same structure, indicating that they are not
simply items in a series: "Let your Name be sanctified / Let your kingdom
come."[68] The petitions for the coming of the kingdom and for the sanctification
of the name illumine each other: when God's kingship is actualized on earth,
God's identity as the Holy One is affirmed. The sanctification of the Name is
a theme deeply rooted in scripture and emphasized in postbiblical Jewish
thought and liturgy.[69] Characteristic is the coinherence of obedience to God
and the sanctification of the Name, expressed already in Leviticus 22:32–33:
"So you shall keep my commandments and do them: I am the LORD. You shall
not profane my holy name, that I may be sanctified among the people of Israel;
I am the LORD; I sanctify you." Even more explicit is Ezekiel 36:23: "I will sanctify my great name, which has been profaned among the nations, and which
you have profaned among them; and the nations shall know that I am the LORD
. . . when through you I display my holiness before their eyes." This passage
goes on to promise that God will cleanse Israel, give it a new heart and a new
spirit, and "make you follow my statutes" (v. 27)—i.e., see to it that the divine
will is "done on earth as it is in heaven." Moore's concise statement makes the
point well: "God 'hallows his name' (makes it holy) . . . by doing things that
lead or constrain men to acknowledge him as God. And as it is God's supreme
end that all mankind shall ultimately own and serve him as the true God, so it
is the chief end of Israel . . . to hallow his name by living so that men shall see
and say that the God of Israel is the true God."[70] This entire insistence that

68. The Matthean version adds a third line ("let your will be done on earth as in heaven"),
which explains the second, and implicitly the first as well (Mt 6:9–10; Lk 11:2). The verb in
each line has the same form: 3d sg imperative, indicating that these petitions are not simply
devout desires but urgent entreaties. The translation of the first line given above reflects four
important considerations: (a) the imperative, being in the passive voice, implies that God is
the entreated doer; (b) "let" is used in the imperatival sense of "cause to be," not in the more
common use of "permit"; (c) *hagiasthēto* is better translated as "sanctified" than as "hallowed,"
which is often used as an adjective ("her hallowed memory" = her memory is highly honored);
(d) *Name* is capitalized because in the Jewish tradition the Name alludes to the sacred identity of God (see Ex 3:13–14). The initial lines of the model prayer are often compared with the
ancient Kaddish, whose earliest formulation might go back to the first century: "Exalted and
hallowed be his great name / in the world which he has created according to his will. / May
he let his kingdom rule / in your lifetime . . . speedily and soon."

69. In addition to the preceding Note, see Davies and Allison, *Matthew,* I, 595–97 for
ancient parallels.

70. Moore, *Judaism,* II, 103.

Israel's life is to reflect the character of God is grounded in Leviticus 19:2: "You shall be holy; for I the Lord your God am holy," which Jesus paraphrased as "Be merciful, just as your Father is merciful" (Lk 6:36; Mt 5:48 has "be perfect").

In short, to pray for God's kingly rule to actualize itself is to place oneself (and the group that prays together) at the disposal of God's sanctifying action by which the Holy One facilitates the reshaping of one's life so that it reflects properly the character of God the king. Within this thoroughly Jewish understanding, Jesus emphasizes and epitomizes the divine character with one word: Father.

God the Father (Abba). That Jesus prayed to God as "Father" is beyond serious doubt, though he probably did not refer to God as Father as often as Matthew reports that he did. Despite the often-repeated claim that *Abba* is the small child's *Daddy*, the word was used also by adults to express respect.[71] Like the image of God as king, God as Father too is deeply rooted in scripture and early Jewish literature.[72] The idea appears in all three parts of the Hebrew Bible and in LXX as well.[73] It is not surprising to find the image used by Jesus also; what may be surprising is that, apart from the Matthean version of the Lord's Prayer, Jesus never refers to "our Father."[74] The Synoptics report that he spoke of "your Father" or "my Father." Of the latter all but Luke 2:49 (the boy Jesus in the temple) and Luke 22:29 are in sayings either peculiar to Matthew,[75] derived from Q (Mt 11:27), or added to it.[76] Although references

---

71. See Vermes, *The Religion of Jesus the Jew* 181–83, and especially Barr, "'Abba' Isn't Daddy.'"

72. See Vermes, *The Religion of Jesus the Jew*, 173–80.

73. Hamerton-Kelly distinguishes earlier "indirect symbolization" in which God as Father is implied (as when Yahweh calls Israel his "first-born son," Ex. 4:22) from later "direct symbolization" in which God is explicitly characterized metaphorically as "father" (e.g., Dt 8:5), sometimes combining mother traits with those of father (e.g., Dt 32:18). Of these, he asserts that "every declaration of God as Father of the people occurs either in an indictment of Israel's ingratitude or as the basis of a plea of forgiveness in the face of an indictment" (*God the Father*, 102).

74. In the Synoptics Jesus refers only once to "the Father" (Mk 13:32), to "their Father" (viz. the righteous), to "my Father's kingdom" (Mt 26:29), or to "his Father" (viz., the Son of Man, Mk 8:38; Mt 16:27).

75. Mt 7:21; 10:32,33; 16:17; 18:11,14,19,35; 26:53.

76. "My Father" is used in (a) Christological statements (Mt 11:27 [Q]; 16:17 [M]; 26:53 [M]; Lk 2:49 [L]) and in (b) future-oriented assurances and warnings (Mt 7:21 [M]; 18:11, 14, 19, 35; 20:23; 25:34; 26:29 [M]), but *not* in connection with exhortations to present activity. Instead, "your Father" is used in connection with exhortations (Mt 5:45 [M], 48 [Q]; 6:4, 15, 18 [M]; 6:32 [Q]; 18:14 [M; many mss. read "your" and D has "our"]; Mk 11:25 [cf. Mt 6:14]), and in words of assurance (Mt 7:11 [Q]; 10:20 [M]; 10:29 ["your Father's will" added to Q]).

to God as Father are found in all strands of the Synoptic tradition (Mk, Q, M, L), those most likely to be genuinely from Jesus are probably found in Mark 11:25 and the Q traditions (Mt 5:48; 6:9,32; 7:11; the genuineness of Mt 11:25 is debated—see below).

If one looks closely at those sayings that are widely regarded as genuine, four features emerge. First, the opening petitions of the model prayer (Mt 6:9; Lk 11:2) show that the Father has a Name to be sanctified and a kingdom to be actualized, neither of which one would expect of a "daddy" deity. Although Jesus does not speak explicitly of the fatherly King or of a kingly Father, his use of both *Father* and *kingdom* shows that he saw no conflict between them. It is no distortion of his thought, therefore, when Matthew 26:29 replaces Mark's "kingdom of God" (14:25) with "my Father's kingdom."[77] Nonetheless, it is noteworthy that the prayer is addressed not to the King but to the Father, implying that for Jesus the exercise of divine sovereignty is imaged appropriately in familial language.

This is totally consistent with the second feature of Jesus' use of *Father* for God, manifest in Matthew 7:11 and Luke 11:13: If you evil fathers manage to give good gifts to your children, "how much more will your Father who is in heaven give good things [Lk: the Holy Spirit] to those who ask him?"[78] Likewise, Jesus' admonition against anxiety about elemental needs assures hearers that the Father "knows that you need them" and that therefore one should "seek his kingdom, and these things shall be yours as well" (Lk 12:22–31). Precisely in the social context in which it was assumed that the father is the authority figure,[79] Jesus used *Father* to point out God's beneficence as an expression of God's character.[80]

77. According to Mk 14:25, at the Supper Jesus promised that he would "never again drink of the fruit of the vine until that day when I drink it new in the kingdom of God"; Mt 26:29 modifies this: "when I drink it new with you in my Father's kingdom."

78. Matthew adds both a reference to God's (or his kingdom's) righteousness and another saying, "Therefore do not be anxious about tomorrow, for tomorrow will be anxious for itself. Let the day's own trouble be sufficient for the day"—an admonition that follows logically from the petition for today's bread (Mt 6:33–34; cf. 6:11).

79. To claim, however, that Jesus' attitude toward women and children shows that he "neutralizes the absolute power of the earthly father by means of the claims of the heavenly Father," as does Hamerton-Kelly, who also infers that "father" was Jesus' weapon against sexism (*God the Father*, 102), is to engage in just the sort of modernizing to which Cadbury objected; see pp. 8–9.

80. One thing for which Harnack is remembered is his declaration that "the Gospel, as Jesus proclaimed it, has to do with the Father only and not with the Son" (italicized). What is less fre-

Third, God's Name is sanctified when the reliable goodness of the Father is imitated in the goodness of the disciple, even to the point of loving one's enemies. In Matthew 5:45 loving enemies and praying for persecutors makes disciples "sons of your Father who is in heaven," the One who gives sun and rain to the bad and the good; in Luke 6:34–35 loving enemies, doing good, and lending to those from whom one does not expect repayment will make one a son of "the Most High, for he is kind to the ungrateful and the selfish." The Father's mercy which is to be imitated is made concrete in his forgiveness, which is also obligatory for those who ask for it, emphasized not only in the model prayer but in Mark 11:25 as well: "And whenever you stand praying, forgive, if you have anything against any one; so that your Father who is in heaven may forgive your trespasses" (see also what follows the Lord's Prayer in Mt 6:15)—a clear warning that the Father will imitate those who refuse to imitate him. The contradiction between this saying and that concerning the Father's kindness to the selfish is more apparent than real, for the two assertions make exactly the same point: God's treatment of us must be repeated in our treatment of one another; one cannot have God as Father without having the neighbor as brother or sister.

Fourth, the obligation to imitate God the Father has no parallel in a call to imitate God the king. Indeed, precisely the opposite is required: "You know that among Gentiles those whom they recognize as rulers lord it over them, and their great ones are tyrants over them. But it is not so among you" (Mk 10:42–43a; Mt 20:25–26; Lk 22:25 has "the kings of the Gentiles . . . and those in authority over them are called benefactors. But not so with you"). If the disciples are to be "great" they "must be your servant" (Lk: "the leader like one who serves").

Two generations later the creator of Matthew used Jesus traditions to provide guidance for disciplinary procedures in a church divided, probably because its rigorists (perhaps those eager to pull the weeds out of the wheat, Mt 13:24–30

---

quently remembered is that Harnack went on to insist that Jesus "knows that through him a new epoch is beginning, in which, by their knowledge of God, the 'least' shall be greater than the greatest of the ages before; he knows that in him thousands—the very individuals who are weary and heavy laden—will find the Father and gain life. . . . these things involve no dogmatic doctrines. . . . They are the experience of an actual fact which he perceives to be already happening, and which, with prophetic assurance, he beholds in advance. . . . *He is the way to the Father, and as he is appointed of the Father, so he is the judge as well.* . . . It is not as a mere factor that he is connected with the Gospel; he was its personal realization and its strength, and this he is felt to be still" (*What Is Christianity?*, 144–45, his italics).

[M]) were insisting that strict discipline must be enforced if the community is to survive its current duress, when "many will fall away and betray one another, and hate one another. . . . And because wickedness is multiplied, most people's love will grow cold" (24:10,12 [M]). Such a situation may account for the fact that the discourse in chapter 18 emphasizes a vigorous call to *self*-discipline (Mt 18:6–9); the discourse also adds to the parable of the man who left his ninety-nine sheep to find the one gone astray, "So it is not the will of your Father who is in heaven that one of these little ones should perish" (Mt 18:12–14; Lk 15:3–7 differs). Understandably, since restoration of the strayed brother or sister entails forgiveness, Matthew prefaces the long parable of the unforgiving servant with Jesus' response to Peter's question about the limits of forgiveness: not the maximum seven times suggested by Peter but seventy times seven (or seventy-seven times; Mt 18:21–22). In using these sayings to address the late-first-century church Matthew showed the perfect tense of Jesus' sayings about God the Father.

No discussion of Jesus' teaching about God can ignore the relation between Jesus the teacher and God the taught. In fact, it is often claimed that Jesus' self-awareness of being God's son is inseparable from his calling God Abba.

Father and Son.   In the Fourth Gospel the relation of the Son to the Father is a theme essential to the significance of Jesus as the giver of life. But in the Synoptics, Jesus makes no such claims in his public ministry, despite the fact that these gospels present him as God's Son, whether because of his exceptional conception in Mary's womb (Matthew and Luke) or because God's voice said so at his baptism and transfiguration (all three Synoptics). Still, none of them includes a single saying in which Jesus claims this publically for himself. They would hardly have omitted such a saying if they had known of it. Oddly, Matthew reports that the mockery of the crucified Jesus included the taunt "Let God deliver him now, if he desires him, for he said 'I am the Son of God'" (Mt 27:41–43 [M]), though the preceding narrative contains no such saying. To the contrary, this gospel (like Luke) actually rejects the Markan report that Jesus admitted that he was God's Son when the high priest asked him and instead gives Jesus' reply as an evasive "You said it" (Mk 14:62; Mt 26:64; Lk 22:70).[81] On the other hand, Matthew reports that the disciples had

81. In Matthew, as in Mark, Jesus goes on to promise that the high priest will see the Son of Man enthroned at God's right hand and coming from [or to?] heaven, alluding to Dan. 7:13. Luke rewrites the scene: now the reference to the Son of Man's enthronement is part of Jesus' reply to the first of two questions concerning his messiahship; this prompts the second question, Are you the Son of God?, to which he replies, "You say that I am." All three gospels assume that Jsus admitted his true identity and nature.

twice called Jesus "Son of God," first as the climax of the story of Jesus and Peter walking on the sea (Mt 14:22–32) and then in Peter's confession "You are the Christ, the Son of the living God" (Mt 16:17). No response of Jesus is given to the first occasion, but according to the second (peculiar to Matthew) he evidently accepted the designation, for he said that his Father had revealed it to Peter. Still, even in Matthew identifying Jesus rightly as Son of God does not result from what he had taught about himself but from divine action, either a revelation or a miracle.[82]

There is, however, the remarkable passage in which the Matthean and Lukan Jesus speaks like the Johannine Jesus, namely Mt 11:27; Lk 10:22 (Q): "All things have been delivered to me by my Father, and no one knows the Son except the Father, and no one knows the Father except the Son and anyone to whom the Son chooses to reveal him."[83] This saying stands between Jesus' words of gratitude for the Father's revelatory work (Mt 11:25–26) and the invitation to the laboring and burdened to come to Jesus and to take up his easy yoke (vv. 28–30). Evidently Q juxtaposed three originally independent sayings, the first addressed to God (which Luke says was inspired by the Holy Spirit), the second addressed to no one that can be identified, and the third to those needing Jesus' "rest," though no hearers are specified and no response reported. In the central saying Jesus claims to be the exclusive revealer of the Father because he has given him "all things." This claim is so out of character with the rest of Jesus' words about himself (apart from the risen Jesus' words found only in Mt 28:16–20) that its genuineness has been questioned or denied outright for a long time. No historically reliable answer to the question Did Jesus make his own Sonship an explicit part of his teaching about God the Father? can rest on this foundation. Not only is it unusually specific, but it also assumes that being "Son" means mediating exclusive divine revelation. Fortunately, however, that is not the end of the matter.

The relation between teacher and taught, messenger and message, Jesus and the One he addressed as Father can be approached from another angle—the use of the idiom "son of" in Jesus' milieu. The basic, literal meaning obvi-

82. In addition to what is reported in chap. 14, in Matthew the soldiers at the cross call Jesus God's Son when they see the rocks split and graves opened by an earthquake (Mt 27:51–54 [M]).

83. The passage is often regarded as an expression of Jewish Wisdom theology such as is found in Wisdom of Solomon and Sirach. See, e.g., Deutsch, *Hidden Wisdom and the Easy Yoke.* Davies and Allison, however, find the background in Moses traditions; see their *Matthew,* II, 502.

ously refers to physical descent ("James the son of Zebedee," Mk 1:19), which can also refer to literal descent from a special ancestor ("Joseph, son of David," Mt 1:20, not to be confused with the royal title "Son of David"). This literal paternity is expressed in the angel's words to Mary "the Holy Spirit will come upon you, and the power of the Most High will overshadow you; therefore the child to be born will be called holy, the Son of God" (Lk 1:35). More common is the metaphorical meaning that rests logically on the assumption that like begets like, that fathering means reproducing oneself; therefore being a "son of" suggests replication, derivation, and hence being wholly determined by, though the distinctions are not always clear. In the Synoptics each of these metaphorical meanings is found on the lips of Jesus.

Sonship as *replication* is implied when Jesus commands love of enemies, as already noted. In addition, when Jesus accuses the Pharisees of being "sons of those who murdered the prophets" (Mt 23:31), "sons of" means *replicators*. Sonship as *derivation*, in the sense that the character and commitment of one's life are determined by that on which one is dependent for value and meaning, appears in various sayings. Reminiscent of the "sons of light" and "sons of darkness" in the Dead Sea Scrolls, Luke 16:8 has Jesus say that "the sons of this world [literally, *aeon*] are wiser . . . than the sons of light." In Luke 20:36 Jesus says that the resurrected ones "cannot die any more, because they are equal to angels, and are sons of God, being sons of the resurrection." People can also be determined by qualities, as when Jesus refers to "a son of peace" (Lk 10:6; see also Eph 2:2; 5:6—"son of disobedience"). And just as one can be a "son of the devil" by allowing oneself to be controlled by evil (Acts 13:10; see also Jn 8:44), so one can be a son of God by being a peacemaker (Mt 5:8). At no point, however, is the disciple called "the son of Jesus" or of Christ. Given this usage, the gospel traditions can portray Jesus acting as God's son, one whose life and work are so determined by God that he replicates on earth his Father in heaven. The Evangelists account for such a figure by reporting that he was God's wondrously conceived Son.[84] That "son of God" meant unqualified obedience to

84. Dunn rightly observes that in Jesus' day there was "nothing particularly unique about calling someone 'son of God,'" noting that Wis 2:13–18 uses the phrase for the righteous person. Later, in Christian usage the phrase came to imply Jesus' exclusive identity, expressible in English by capitalizing "Son" (the distinction will not work in German, which capitalizes all nouns). Dunn also notes that it was not the application of the *"title* 'Son of God' to Jesus which transformed Jesus from someone rather ordinary to someone unique. . . . It was the distinctiveness of *Jesus* which caused a rather commonplace title to gain its note of exclusiveness" (*The Evidence for Jesus*, 49–50, his italics).

God is precisely the point of the temptation stories (Mt 4:1–11; Lk 4:1–13 [Q]). They show that divine Sonship must be actualized as human sonship by obedience. These Christian stories suggest that this moral sonship was not achieved without a struggle, just as the Gethsemane story expresses the Christian conviction that Jesus was willing to pay the price of being Abba's son.

Certain aspects of the Synoptic portrait of Jesus imply that Jesus probably saw himself as God's obedient son, replicating the Father's way. In forming the Twelve he was doing symbolically what he expected God to do actually when the kingdom arrives. Likewise, the itinerant character of his mission rhymes with the conviction that the kingdom is on the move. Jesus went not only from place to place but also from one type of situation to another (even if the reported situations were inferred by the Evangelists). He taught in synagogues and in boats, in the open air; he accepted the hospitality of Levi the tax collector (Mk 2:15) and of three Simons: the former fisherman, the Pharisee, and the leper (Mk 2:15; Lk 7:36–50; Mk 14:3, resp.). When Crossan speaks of this constant movement as an expression of Jesus' commitment to a "brokerless" (unmediated) ministry,[85] he has it backward: in going from place to place it was Jesus who brought the news and the power of the coming kingdom and, in addition, dispatched his disciples to do the same (Mt 10:11–13; Lk 10:5–9). Thereby the message and its manifestations were indeed mediated by the messenger(s).

In short, both his style and his specific deeds suggest that he understood his vocation to be not only that of saying what the kingdom's coming entails but also representing it by what he did. This is just the point Morna D. Hooker made in her 1995 Shaffer Lectures at Yale, in which she analyzed a whole range of Jesus' deeds as "prophetic signs." Taking her cue from the symbolic acts of the biblical prophets, she defined a "prophetic sign" as follows: not "a visual aid intended to *assist* in teaching—rather, the dramatic *equivalent* of the spoken oracle, *not* as an efficacious act, which *causes* something to happen— rather, the dramatic *embodiment* of the divine purpose, which otherwise may well be at present hidden."[86] This suggests that Jesus subjected himself to the coming kingly rule of God so fully that his mission was more than a vehicle for a message; it became its harbinger. In a word, since one is a "son of" whatever determines one's existence, by allowing himself to be so shaped and driven by the impending reign of God that he could embody it, Jesus probably understood himself as the "son of God."

85. Crossan, *The Historical Jesus*, 346–47.
86. Hooker, *The Signs of a Prophet*, 38–39.

No one knows how he came to his sense of vocation or how he came to conclude that he must not only announce what God was doing definitively but also allow himself to become its effective analog. One can, however, note that his silence about himself is entirely appropriate for one who sees himself as the emissary who so embodies the impingement of the "not yet apparent" that his embodiment becomes translucent enough that in responding to him people actually respond to the Father as well. Not discursive explanations but parables were the proper way to point to the kingdom when he became its parable.

Jesus may also have made himself the pivotal character in a parable, the story of the wicked tenants who killed the landowner's son (Mt 21:33–46; Mk 12:1–12; Lk 20:9–19; *Thomas* 65). In the Synoptics, especially in Matthew, the story is an allegory of God's repeatedly frustrated efforts with Israel: the landowner is God, the vineyard is Israel (as in Is 5:2), the tenants are the religious leaders, the rejected slaves sent by the owner are the prophets, Jesus is the son, his murder is the crucifixion,[87] the annihilation of the tenants is the destruction of the temple, and the "others" who receive the vineyard are the gentile Christians. Since the Evangelists see in the slain son Jesus' self-reference, they append a saying about the rejected stone, taken from Psalm 118:22–23. The absence of these allegorical details from Thomas implies that it may well be closer to what Jesus said than what the Synoptics report:[88] "A [...] person owned a vineyard and rented it to some farmers, so they could work it and he could collect its crop from them. He sent his slave so the farmers would give him the vineyard's crop. They grabbed him, beat him, and almost killed him, and the slave returned and told his master. His master said, 'Perhaps he didn't know them.' He sent another slave, and the farmers beat that one as well. Then the master sent his son and said, 'Perhaps they'll show my son some respect.' Because the farmers knew that he was the heir to the vineyard, they grabbed him and killed him. Anyone here with two ears had better listen."[89] Although it has been claimed that "son" refers to John the Baptist,[90] it probably refers to Jesus; if the parable is genuine, then it is also a veiled passion prediction.

87. Matthew and Luke reverse Mark's "killed . . . threw him out" in keeping with what happened: Jesus was executed outside the city.

88. For a discussion of the many problems generated by this story, see Davies and Allison, *Matthew*, III, 174–92 and Fitzmyer, *Luke*, II, 1276–88; both have extended bibliographies. A recent, extended, defense of the story's genuineness is offered by Charlesworth, *Jesus within Judaism*, 143–53; a more compressed argument for genuineness is found in Witherington, *The Christology of Jesus*, 213–14.

89. Quoted from *The Complete Gospels.*

90. Lowe, "From the Parable of the Vineyard to a Pre-Synoptic Source."

Given the amply documented Jewish use of *son* to refer to one who is an obedient agent of God,[91] and given Jesus' understanding of his mission as well, it is not surprising that he thought of himself as God's son. What cannot be overemphasized, however, is that he neither made this tacit self-understanding the burden of his message (as in John) nor asserted it as a legitimating warrant for what he said and did. Instead he acted as the "finger of God" and spoke as the mouth of God.

Jesus' audacity did not go unnoticed. The Synoptics report that in the temple precincts he was asked directly, "By what authority are you doing these things, or who gave you this authority to do them?" Instead of answering a straightforward question straightforwardly, he came back with a counterquestion: "Did the baptism of John come from heaven, or was it of human origin? Answer me." When the questioners too avoided a clear answer and simply replied, "We do not know," he responded, "Neither will I tell you by what authority I do these things" (Mt 11:27–33, par.) Though each Evangelist stylized the story, its core meaning is surely historical: Even when questioned, Jesus refused to account for his authority.

As noted in chapter 2, Jesus taught without referring to his teacher or appealing to a teaching tradition in support of his message. When dealing with divorce, he bypassed even Moses in order to appeal to God's will in creation (Mk 10:1–2; Mt 19:1–12). In the first Beatitude he announced as boldly as possible who it is that the kingdom belongs to—the poor (Lk 6:20). Even if one allows for the likely role of the Christian tradition in formulating his pronouncements as concisely as possible, it is impossible to deny that the Matthean observation at the end of the Sermon on the Mount is on target: "He taught them as one who had authority, and not as their scribes" (Mt 7:28–29). Whoever teaches authoritatively is confident that what is taught is utterly true.

In the Jesus tradition, this confidence is expressed explicitly in those sayings that begin with the word that customarily ended prayer: *Amen*, commonly translated "truly." This appears in each of the Synoptics, though mostly in Matthew; in John it is actually doubled: "Amen, Amen, I say." No one else in the New Testament, or in early Jewish literature known to us, speaks this way.[92] The appearance of an introductory Amen does not, however, establish the genuineness of the saying that follows, for comparing Matthew 5:28 with Luke 12:59 shows that the word was added in Matthew; the same is doubtless true

91. The references are assembled and classified in Charlesworth, *Jesus within Judaism,* 149–52 and in Dunn, *Christology in the Making,* 15–16.

92. For issues in interpretation see Davies and Allison, *Matthew,* I, 489–90.

elsewhere. The point is that the prefatory Amen expresses the speaker's certitude; the Contemporary English Version catches this with its "I promise you" in Matthew 5:18,26.

Jesus' confidence is not limited to the sayings that begin with Amen but pervades his teachings and actions. Nowhere does he relativize his teaching by prefacing it with, for example, "In my opinion" or by suggesting, "You might consider looking at it this way." Nor, conversely, does he claim to be inspired or that he is saying what he heard from an angel or had seen in a visionary experience. Nor, for that matter, do the Evangelists report of Jesus what Luke says about John the Baptist: "the word of God came to him" (cf. Is 38:4; Jer 1:1; Ezek 1:3; Hos 1:1). Even if Jesus were perceived to be a prophet (Mk 8:28; Lk 7:16), and probably understood himself to have that role (Mk 6:4; Lk 13:33), he did not announce himself as the bearer of God's word as did the biblical prophets. He says neither "The word of the Lord came to me" (cf. Jer 1:11; Ezek 3:16; Zec 6:9) nor "This is the word of the Lord" (e.g., Is 37:22) nor "Hear the word of the Lord" (e.g., Is 1:10; Jer 2:4; Ezek 6:3; Hos 4:1). He simply spoke as the mouth of God without claiming to do so. In addition, both his entry to Jerusalem and his act in the temple bring to a head the confidence manifest in Galilee. They were not the sort of actions that one given to self-doubt or surges of hesitation would undertake during the Passover season. Such confidence is the symptom of deep conviction, not of sheer arrogance concealing insecurity; it is a mark of empowering trust that what one is about is true and will be vindicated by the One trusted.

Jesus taught his followers to pray to Abba, dared to preface some of his teachings with *Amen*, ventured to embody God's impinging kingship, and taught what life reshaped by that kingship looks like in specific and mundane matters such as oath-taking, divorce, lending money, and settling inheritance disputes, because "the kingdom determines each situation," as Machovec put it.[93] Thereby Jesus evidently sought to engender his hearers' confidence too, because both his and theirs were evoked by the same God's coming reign. The fact that they had to be instructed shows that Jesus' confidence was not simply contagious. This instruction did not take the form of a theory about the kingdom or God's character. Rather, Jesus simply appealed to it as the warrant for his call for moral change that is to reflect God. Right response is not just right doctrine (he assumed that) or esoteric knowledge of God (he rejected that) but rather a righteous life.

93. Machovec, *A Marxist Looks at Jesus*, 94.

Not to be missed in all this is the correlate of Jesus' Abba/Amen confidence in God—the implicit confidence in his hearers. His good news about the impingement of God's kingdom implied that his hearers *can* respond appropriately, though it is not easy to allow God's character to reshape one into a son or daughter of God. Jesus did not talk about sin; he talked with sinners, exposing the heart's illusions about reality, deviousness in obedience, and misplaced security. He went to those at the bottom and at the edges of his society as well as to the scrupulously devout; he welcomed women into his entourage and, no less remarkable, pointed to children as examples of what receiving the kingdom is like, and he took them into his arms as if he were their Abba (Mk 10:13–16). At no point did he encourage those to whom he went, or the sick who came to him, to see themselves as victims whose condition was to be "understood"; rather, he treated them as responsible persons who could choose and act. There is no reason to think that he came to this conclusion after weighing alternatives. That the self is a responsible being was of course part of his religious patrimony, for it is both implicit in the Torah's commandments and explicit in Deuteronomy 30:11–14: "This commandment . . . is not too hard for you. . . . it is in your mouth and in your heart for you to observe." And while the radicality of the requisite response to the kingdom discloses how much must be done to turn to God rightly, Jesus also insisted that the Abba forgives because the primary import of God's reign is not retribution but restoration.

The Embodied Future in Perfect Tense

The foregoing sketch of Jesus the teacher, though far from complete, leads inevitably to the question So what? That is what the perfect tense of Jesus is all about. Since the gospels are written results of asking this question, it is prudent to note first how they responded to it. At the heart of today's question is the pertinence of Jesus' eschatological horizon. This, in turn, implies the relation of Jesus' *theology* to his eschatology, pointing ahead as well to chapter 4.

The gospels as Jesus' perfect tense.   The gospels, and the traditions they use, remain the most important instances of the perfect tense of Jesus, for each in its own way presents Jesus so that his ongoing significance becomes available to the readers' community. This is what careful analysis of the changes made in Mark and Q by the First and Third Evangelists, as well as what they retained, exposes. More difficult to spot are the allegedly nongenuine sayings that may have been added when the tradition was still being transmitted orally or at the point when it was first put on papyrus. However, instead of identifying such sayings so that they can be excluded from the recovery of what Jesus actually taught, examining a block of them here will disclose how they allowed one Evangelist, Mark, to present Jesus in perfect tense for his time.

The sayings in view here are found in Mark 13, which, apart from its introduction (13:1–2), have been regarded widely as nongenuine material added by the Evangelist. Whereas the only other extended discourse in Mark consists of parables and their interpretation (Mk 4:1–34), the sayings in Mark 13 are remarkably diverse: predictions, warnings, assurances, admonitions, and parables—all of which pertain to a dire future depicted in noticeably apocalyptic terms. The authenticity of these sayings has been denied (a) because some of them assume a later historical situation that Jesus allegedly would not have foreseen (e.g., the persecution of Christians [vv. 9–13] and the "desolating sacrilege" [v. 13], often thought to allude to Caligula's order in 40 C.E. to have his statue placed in the temple);[94] (b) because others express ideas found in Jewish apocalyptic texts (e.g., the suffering that must precede the end, vv. 7–8; the tribulation itself, vv. 17–20; changes in the sun, moon and stars, vv. 24–27); and (c) because of what Jesus claims about himself in still others (vv. 23, 31–32). Taken together, these sayings have been deemed to be so inconsistent with the character and content of Jesus' authentic teaching that their nongenuineness has seemed virtually self-evident. The task here, however, is not to adjudicate the arguments or to dispute the general conclusion, but to reflect on the fact that the Evangelist not only included these sayings but also used them to construct a discourse placed in the narrative at a pivotal point: just before the passion story. From whatever angle, this is a remarkable way of portraying the perfect tense of Jesus.

Both the author's intent and the text's import would be easier to detect if one knew where, when, and for whom this gospel was written. That the desolation to be wrought has in view the first revolt against Rome in 66 C.E. is apparent to all students, though they are not agreed on whether the gospel was written just before it began, while it was still raging, or shortly afterward. The Palestinian concerns need not indicate that it was written there, for the prediction that Christians "will stand before governors and kings because of me" could just as

94. The phrase "desolating sacrilege" is taken from Dan 11:31; 12:11, where it refers to the desecration of the temple in the time of Antiochus IV Epiphanes, mentioned also in 1 Mc 1:54. (Mt 24:15 makes the reference to Daniel explicit.) It has been suggested that Mark used an earlier Jewish or Jewish Christian apocalyptic text which saw in Caligula's order a repetition of the same anti-God action. This complex, and not problem-free, theory is discussed in all commentaries and need not be evaluated here.

well refer to circumstances elsewhere (unless it alludes to Palestinian events reported in Acts 12:1–3; 23:33–35; 24:24–26; 25:23–26:32). Moreover, the disastrous events in Palestine, and their effects on the Christians there, were surely known and pondered by fellow believers wherever they were. Besides, the fact that Mark was used heavily in Matthew and Luke, probably written far from Palestine, suggests that this earliest gospel had circulated widely. Because neither Matthew nor Luke omitted this chapter, as they did other parts of Mark, one may infer that the issues posed by the turmoil in Palestine two decades before did not go away and that these later Evangelists deemed it germane to include an "apocalyptic Jesus" in their narratives.

In any case, the likelihood that Mark was written in the time of the first revolt suggests that the Evangelist put this "apocalyptic" event in the context of an apocalyptic understanding of history. Thereby he assured the church that the turmoils of the time do not annul the truth of the gospel because the same Jesus whose deeds and words are reported in chapters 1–12 also said, "I have already told you everything" (v. 23), and had assured the disciples, "Heaven and earth will pass away [surpassing even the darkening of sun and moon, and falling stars] but my words will not pass away" (v. 31). Moreover, although not even he ["the Son"] knows when the present agonies will end, there is one who does know—not God the king but "the Father" (v. 32)—the One who is in charge also cares.

Mark 13 generates an important exegetical question: What did the Evangelist see in Jesus' teaching in chapters 1–12 that allowed him to include the sayings in chapter 13 as an essential part of his story of Jesus? Or is this Jesus wholly out of character with the protagonist in the rest of the gospel?. Actually, what Jesus says here has significant links to what he had said before. Besides, with regard to the apocalyptic horizon of Jesus' mission, the character of both this chapter and of Mark as a whole does not distort the teaching of Jesus himself.

To begin with, Jesus' claim "I have already told you everything" (v. 23) is fully consistent with what Mark, and only Mark, says about Jesus' use of parables: "he did not speak to them [the crowds] except in parables, but he explained everything in private to his disciples" (4:34; see also 4:10–12).[95] So in chapter 13 what Jesus says about the disastrous future is said only to the inner core of the Twelve—Peter, James, John, and Andrew—who "asked him privately, 'Tell us, when will this be [alluding to the destruction of the temple, v. 2], and what will be the sign that all these things are about to be accom-

---

95. Luke and Mark omit Mk 4:33–34; Matthew omits also the reference to private instruction but adds that Jesus' parabolic speech fulfilled prophecy (13:34–35).

plished?'" (v. 3). In both cases, what is ostensibly said to a select few is really said over their heads to the readers, the Evangelist's own church.

Next, although 13:9, 11a, and 12–13a do not actually use the word *persecute* (as does Luke's parallel, 21:12), this is clearly what is in view: legal action against Christians by both Jewish and Roman authorities, betrayal by family members, and being "hated by all because of my name." To Mark's readers this ominous future comes as no surprise, for in the explanation of the parable of the sower and the soils Jesus had already explained that the seed sown on rocky ground, where it has no deep roots, refers to those who, though responding immediately "with joy," fall away "when trouble or persecution arises on account of the word" (4:17).[96] Moreover, in reporting that Jesus promised those who "for my sake and the sake of the good news" had left family and property would receive them back "a hundred fold," only Mark includes the ominous phrase "with persecution" (10:30). In addition, in Mark 13:26–27, 29 Jesus speaks of the coming of the Son of Man: "they will see 'the Son of Man coming in clouds' with great power and glory. Then he will send out the angels and gather his elect."[97] Although Mark understood Jesus to have used the phrase to refer also to his earthly mission (2:10, 28) as well as to his suffering (8:31; 9:31; 10:33, 45), what Jesus says about the future coming of the Son of Man in chapter 13 reminds readers of what he had said in 8:38: "Those who are ashamed of me and of my words in this adulterous and sinful generation, of them the Son of Man will also be ashamed when he comes in the glory of his Father with the holy angels," even though here the role of the Son of Man is that of a witness rather than the administrator of the Judgment.

According to Mark 13:26, the coming of the Son of Man will be seen after the sun is darkened, etc.; there follows the parable of the fig tree: When its leaves appear, "you know that summer is near. So also, when you see these things taking place, you know that he [the Son of Man] is near, at the very gates" (13:28–29; Lk: the kingdom of God is near).[98] Thus Jesus appears to answer the disciples' ques-

96. It is likely that the whole interpretation of the parable (Mk 4:14–20; Mt 13:18–23; Lk 8:11–15) is part of the tradition that the Markan Evangelist received, not created by him, for Matthew and Luke retain the interpretation but ignore the distinctive Markan introduction (4:13).

97. No problem has proved to be more vexing to historical critics than the Son of Man, and no solution has commended itself widely. For a survey of the background and issues of interpretation, see Nickelsburg, "Son of Man."

98. The Greek of Mk 13:29 does not specify the subject of "is near." Since the previous saying refers to the coming of the Son of Man, translators assume that the subject in v. 29 is "he." Wright, however, thinks that Luke saw the point: what "is near" also in Mark is the kingdom of God (*Jesus and the Victory of God*, 364).

tion "What will be the sign that all these things are about to be accomplished?" (v. 4) by speaking of strange events in the heavens—and perhaps of all the other things in verses 5–23 as well. By no means does this understanding of "signs" contradict what Jesus had said in 8:12: "no sign will be given to this generation" (here Q has "no sign except the sign of Jonah"; Lk 11:29; Mt 12:39), for the latter refers to an authenticating sign, whereas the events in chapter 13 are omens.

Especially noteworthy is what Jesus says after speaking of the coming of the Son of Man: "this generation will not pass away until all these things [mentioned from v. 5 onward] have taken place" (13:30). This juxtaposition of a saying about the coming Son of Man and a promise of fulfillment in the hearer's time is clearly anticipated in 8:31–9:1. Here the reference to the coming Son of Man is followed by "Truly I tell you, there are some standing here who will not taste death until they see that the kingdom of God has come with power" (Mt: "the Son of Man coming in his kingdom," 16:28; Lk: "the kingdom of God," 9:27).

When taken with other passages just reviewed, it is apparent that the Jesus of Mark 13 is not incongruent with the Jesus of Mark 1–12, even though he does not mention the kingdom of God as part of his predictions of the future. Because at chapter 13 Jesus shifts from a mission to his contemporaries in light of the future to instructing the disciples about the future, a change in the tone and content of the teaching is understandable; but as Mark tells it, it is the same Jesus, whose words present him in perfect tense—for the Evangelist's time. And these words include warnings against misreading those times (vv. 7, 14) and about "false messiahs" (vv. 6, 21–22).

This conclusion is important from another angle as well. Despite the regrettable habit of mislabeling Mark 13 as a "little [or Markan] apocalypse,"[99] the chapter is *not* an apocalypse, for many of the common traits of an apocalypse are absent: what Jesus says is not derived from a vision; his words are his own, not those of an ancient figure such as Enoch; there is no reference to the overthrow of Israel's enemies, earthly or Satanic, nor mention of the Judgment, resurrection, or symbolized periods of history. Instead, the apocalyptic theme of penultimate woes is made concrete by predicting the persecution of Christians, and the motif of the disturbances in the heavens becomes a sign that the coming of the Son of Man will follow shortly. The function of the whole is disclosed at the end: Just as the man's slaves are to be at work in his absence and not to

99. The label reflects the continuing influence of Colani's theory, proposed in 1864, that Mk 13:5–31 surely interpolates a Jewish Christian apocalypse, since Jesus, having taught that the kingdom is here, could not have had such ideas. For the history, and criticism, of this theory see Beasley-Murray, *Jesus and the Future.*

be caught sleeping at his incalculable return, so the Christian community is to "keep awake"—and at work. In other words, in Mark 13 Jesus does not provide an apocalypse but rather admonition with apocalyptic horizon. That is consistent with Jesus' teaching about God's kingdom in Mark 1–12 and to some degree with Jesus himself. And that, it turns out, poses the central problem that must be addressed if one is to speak of the perfect tense of Jesus the teacher today.

The stumbling block.   Whoever ventures to speak of the ongoing significance of Jesus of Nazareth, the Jesus of Jewish history, must come to terms with what he undertook: to so announce and embody the imminent coming of God's kingdom that those who believed him would already change their lives to reflect the character of God's reign actualized. The scholars' debates about Jesus' understanding of the kingdom is more than a matter of historical correctness; how one reads Jesus' understanding determines what one says about his perfect tense today. The confidence with which he spoke and acted discloses the intensity of his conviction, but that does not show that he was right. Repeatedly, the gospels show that the Evangelists were keenly aware of this, though they were convinced that he was right, for otherwise they would not have reported his conflicts with the Pharisees. But that too does not settle the matter for today's readers—unless one assumes that of course the gospels are right. In addition, this stance does not resolve the issue but only sharpens it when one recalls what has been observed already: according to Mark, Jesus assured his disciples twice that what he expected would be actualized in their lifetimes (Mk 9:1; 13:30). If the saying in Mark 9:1 is genuine (and many deny that it is) it is a stumbling block for those who argue that Jesus did not expect a future coming of the kingdom; those who assert that he did must show that Jesus so redefined the meaning of *kingdom of God* (without pointing this out) that he was not mistaken. Thereby the stumbling block becomes the cornerstone.[100] The issue of whether, or to what extent and in

---

100. This is exactly what occurs in the interpretation advanced by Wright in *Jesus and the Victory of God.* He argues that the whole chapter is Jesus' own coherent prediction of the destruction of the temple (and of the city) as the "literal and physical divine-judgment-through-Roman-judgment" (344), a view espoused later by Josephus. Wright calls attention to the ways in which biblical passages and eschatological themes are used and interpreted, and so rejects efforts to find allusions to the events of 70 C.E. (i.e., "prophecy after the fact"). Wright is scornful of those who think this web of allusions and references, beginning with Mark 11 (Jesus' entry to Jerusalem), is the work of early Christian tradition or of the Evangelist, and he contends that it is the result of the mind of Jesus himself acting out Israel's history and precipitating its crucial hour, because he was "a thinking, reflecting, creative and original theologian" (479), at least as

what way, Jesus was right and wrong in what he expected to happen does not, of course, hang on this one saying alone; broader considerations too must be put into play.

If *kingdom of God* is indeed a tensive symbol, then one aspect of the problem of nonoccurrence evaporates: Since the coming kingdom was neither a matter of the "end of the world" and the events associated with such a catastrophe, nor the arrival of restored paradise, the continuation of the cosmos and history does not flatly invalidate either Mark 9:1 or Jesus' expectation—unless one is prepared to argue that the nonoccurrence of what was not expected annuls also what was expected. The character of *kingdom of God* points in a different direction, not only to the variety of images evoked by Jesus' use of the phrase but especially to the fact that he never *described* what he expected to occur, though he alluded to aspects of it or used them as the warrant for exhortation (e.g., the parable of the judgment in Mt 25:31–46 [M]). One should neither assemble all such references in order to reconstruct the scenario that Jesus allegedly expected nor, like Schweitzer, attribute to his thought a collage of events garnered from diverse Jewish apocalypses. Such an approach would imply that he had the whole future drama in mind but chose to keep it to himself except for those occasions when he deemed it useful to mention a piece of it. There is no reason to think that he was such a teacher.

Jesus did, however, expect God to act soon, though he was even more silent about the "when" than about the "what"; the saying about his not knowing the day or hour (Mk 13:32) simply draws an appropriate conclusion from the fact that the tradition contained nothing about the time of God's expected action or about the length of the time span between Jesus' activity and God's decisive act—probably reflecting the memory that Jesus had said nothing about it. Such considerations probably would not have arisen for one who understood himself to be the "finger" of God's eschatological action, whose vocation it was to embody its impingement and to express what the Godward-turned life now calls for in one situation after another. Running through Jesus' teaching is a sense of urgency because of what has begun to be under way, beginning with the Baptizer. It is the observer who asks When?, not the "finger."

---

bright as his followers. That Jesus was at least as wise and creative as his disciples no one would want to deny, but that does not provide evidence for the genuineness of the discourse in Mark 13. Moreover, the more the sheer complexity and subtlety of the various allusions come into view, the less persuasive is the claim that this kind of material comes from the mouth of Jesus. The allusions reflect the study of texts.

What must not be overlooked, moreover, is the inherent logic of a life built on the kingdom's impingement: Whoever is absorbed by the vocation of expressing and embodying God's impingement but is accused of being Beelzebul's "finger" leans his/her life into the future for God's validation and vindication, for in this case only the Impinger can validate. Remarkably, Jesus is silent about this too. Even if one regards the three passion predictions in Mark (8:31; 9:31; 10:33–34) as genuine, they say not a word about vindication but simply predict what will happen. That the Evangelist regarded Jesus' resurrection as his vindication is probable, but no saying of Jesus has been preserved, or coined, that says he thought so too. Apparently he did not include his own vindication in the content of his teaching. Instead he embodied also that expectation without calling attention to it.

Whatever Jesus expected to happen in connection with his death, we know what did happen: His disciples came to believe that he *was* vindicated by resurrection that transformed him; for them this was a sign that the new age broke in with Jesus, though nothing else had changed visibly (apart from the formation of the community in his name). But believing this changed them! Moreover, all the evidence points to one important fact: Although it was *Jesus* whom God vivified and vindicated by resurrection, and not only his teachings or "cause," the resurrected Jesus is not simply Jesus resumed, as if his death/resurrection had been a mere interruption. (The strange stories of his appearances can be understood as narrative precipitates of the conviction that the same Jesus is now fundamentally "different.") He is for them a Jesus transformed into a mode of existence that *still* assures and presages the future when the new age will be fully actualized. Because it was precisely Jesus, whose vocation was actualizing God's reign not as consummation but as prolepsis, resurrecting *him* validates the tension between the "already" and the "not yet" that he embodied. This tension, so palpable in Paul's letters, was not the apostle's invention in order to rationalize the disparity between salvation experienced and salvation completed, but has its ground in Jesus himself and for believers was ratified by his resurrection. In other words, running through the various stories and conceptualities about the risen Jesus Christ is the (largely unstated) thread: Vindicating impingement and its embodiment by resurrection, an act that signals the coming age, does not invalidate Jesus' own orientation to the future; it confirms it for what it was—a life that embodied the future. Resurrecting Jesus means validating indefinitely the one whose life was lived out of the future, even if what occurred turned out not to be what he expected.

Clearly, this understanding of the matter does not reproduce the thoughts of the earliest believers. But the ongoing significance of Jesus no more depends on repeating their thoughts than it depends on repeating Jesus' own thoughts. Besides, the one is as futile as the other because thoughts have associations, resonances, social rootedness, etc., that simply cannot be recovered and restored. What one can do is understand their thoughts clearly enough that one can penetrate their logic, their inner rationale, in order to know what it is that must be maintained in stating today the significance of what was thought then.

The persistent rectifying power of the kingdom.   There are many reasons why Jesus continues to fascinate and attract persons. Some are drawn to his teachings; others are drawn to his way of life—in our day, especially his concern for the poor or his critical attitude toward the devout guardians of religion. The extent to which this is the result of being grasped by his "already" while ignoring (or denying) his "not yet" is a theme that merits investigation, but not here. The focus is rather on the enduring significance of the "not yet," on its persistent positive power.

One result of the Jesus quest has been a remarkable, and distinctly modern, emphasis on the kingdom of God as a moral task. In nineteenth-century Germany it was especially the Ritschlians who struck this note; in America it was the advocates of the social gospel. They did not hesitate to insist on speaking of the kingdom in a way that never occurred to Jesus and that he probably would have rejected if someone had mentioned it to him—namely, that the kingdom of God is something that Jesus' followers are to "build" or "bring in" as the supreme religiously inspired moral obligation.

Although this interpretation of the kingdom has been faulted at many points, what is striking in this context is its tacit but unmistakable insistence that, while Jesus had the right ideal (the "already"), the "not yet" is so obvious that loyalty to him requires taking up the task of advancing what he began. It was just the nonoccurrence of what Jesus had expected that energized liberal Protestants and others to challenge the harsh results of the industrialized and urbanized world and to work to improve the lot of workers, especially children. The advocates of the social gospel did not, of course, talk much about the "not yet," for as ethical idealists captivated by the idea of social progress they did not see clearly what Weiss and Schweitzer saw in Jesus' central message. Although the bloody twentieth century has invalidated talk of "building" or "bringing" the kingdom, it is still the case that what was expected of God's reign continues to energize many of Jesus' followers, including those who follow at a distance.

It is important to recognize that this energy flows from the subject matter itself—the image of God as sovereign in the face of the world as it is. What is at stake in talk of God's coming kingdom cannot be understood properly as long as one thinks of it as a thing— for example, an airplane whose arrival or delay can be observed and whose distance from the airport calculated. Rather, the kingdom of God is an image for a different sort of reality altogether, one whose relation to time can only be suggested (and inadequately imaged) by tenses and whose relation to space is not properly expressed as distance. The more this is recognized, the more apparent it becomes that the real question posed by Jesus' expectation concerns the nature of that reality, whether its otherness is static (in which case the world remains what is, despite social and economic changes) or whether it is dynamic (in which case the world as it is has a true future through transformation). In short, the real question is not whether Jesus was right or wrong about the time of the kingdom but whether he was right about the God whom he imaged as king and father.

In discussing Jesus' understanding of turning toward the God whose kingdom is coming, it was noted that it was the nature of God that determined the shape of the Godward life because actualizing God's reign, God's "Godhood," entails rectifying what is wrong and vindicating what is presently right. What God's definitive coming in power elicits and effects mirrors the nature of God—not a generic "God" but the Creator, the Chooser and Emancipator of Israel, the Giver of Torah, whose sovereignty is acknowledged by the metaphor "king" and whose enduring care by calling him "Father." The coming of this God's reign is not, therefore, to be imaged as fulfilling the potential of the present—the horrors of this century show what that can be like—but as its rectification, for when this God's "Godness" is truly and decisively actualized, when God is king de facto as well as de jure, all will be made right. In short, the kingdom of God energizes those grasped by Jesus' vision and shaped by his vocation because it refers to God's own rectifying energy that does not rest until God's will is "done on earth as it is in heaven." This is not an inferred deity, the product of astute human reasoning, but one the Bible calls the living God.

But the Jesus who embodied the living God's impingement did not die in bed as a respected, wise old teacher but on a cross as a condemned young criminal. What, then, has the death of Jesus got to do with the living God? That is the animating question of chapter 4.

CHAPTER FOUR

The Fractured Prism
Jesus' Death and the Living God

Jesus was crucified by Roman soldiers. Whoever doubts that must also doubt that Jesus existed. So secure is this historical fact that one cannot think seriously about the ongoing significance of Jesus while ignoring his crucifixion. Indeed, for centuries his death by crucifixion has been the most significant fact about him, especially in Western (i.e., Roman and Protestant) Christianity. Numberless and nameless are the Jews whom Rome put to death by crucifixion,[1] but for nearly two millennia "the cross" has referred to the cross of this one Jew who came from a village so obscure that for centuries only the gospels mentioned its name. In paintings and sculptures of saints and apostles Paul is usually shown with a sword because the Romans beheaded him. But no sword alone represents Paul. Only in the case of Jesus has the means of his execution come to stand for the man himself and for what came to be in his name.

This chapter's focus, however, is not on the cross but on the significance of Jesus' execution for the understanding of God. Jesus makes the explicitly theological character of this chapter inevitable because God's kingship, and the effects of its impingement on the human scene, was what he was all about. For the whole Christian tradition and for those variously influenced by it he has become the prism through which one looks into that Reality called "God."

1. According to Josephus, as many as five hundred (and sometimes more) escapees a day from besieged Jerusalem were caught, tortured, and crucified where the inhabitants could see them. "The soldiers out of rage and hatred amused themselves by nailing their prisoners in different postures; so great was their number that space could not be found for the crosses nor crosses for the bodies" (JW v 449–51, Loeb ed., vol. III). Crucifixion was a widespread and ancient mode of execution, practiced on occasion by the Jewish ruler Alexander Jannaeus, who, according to Josephus, crucified eight hundred Pharisees (JW i, 97, 113, Loeb ed., vol. I). For a discussion of crucifixion in antiquity see Hengel, *Crucifixion*.

Because Jesus' lifework ended on the cross he is the fractured prism, and his "brokenness" remains its essential feature. For Christian theology Jesus' resurrection did not "heal" his brokenness but made it permanently significant.

The understandable desire for accurate knowledge of Jesus' crucifixion and what led up to it is frustrated by both the disparities in the gospels' accounts and the fundamentally divergent ways of reading them. The latter have become especially clear in the recent argument between the late Raymond E. Brown and John Dominic Crossan. Brown, while focused on the passion narratives admittedly deeply dyed by Christian interpretation, also assessed the historical reliability of the traditions.[2] Crossan, however, argues that the gospels provide almost no reliable information because they do not interpret historical facts, what he calls "history remembered," but instead create the appearance of facts out of Old Testament passages, resulting in "prophecy historicized."[3] Crossan's view is far from new, for D. F. Strauss had argued it 150 years before (that precedent does not make it either right or wrong, of course). What is new is disclosed in the subtitle of Crossan's book: *Exposing the Roots of Anti-Semitism in the Gospel Story of the Death of Jesus.*[4] The theme of this chapter does not require solid, detailed, historical knowledge of what happened between Jesus' arrest and execution. Nor does the theological import of his death require knowing whether he was executed because his mission was understood or because it was grossly misunderstood. This chapter's theme does, however, require attending to Jesus' sense of his God-given destiny, to the God he trusted, and to certain aspects of the ongoing significance of the cross.

Galilee and Jerusalem

The disciples were not arrested along with Jesus. Nor is there a hint in the gospels that the authorities made any effort to hunt them down afterward. All the sources indicate that the action was directed at Jesus alone; they also say, in one way or other, that while still in Galilee this is exactly what he expected would happen.

Destiny discerned. Each of the Synoptics emphasizes its passion story, and all of them report that Jesus predicted several times that he (as the Son of

2. Brown, *The Death of the Messiah.*

3. Crossan, *Who Killed Jesus?*

4. Crossan goes out of his way to insist that there is neither anti-Judaism nor anti-Semitism in Brown's volumes; what he faults them for is the absence of "a fair, legitimate and valid criticism of Christianity's passion stories" (*Who Killed Jesus?*, 35)—i.e., for concentrating on the historical exegetical task.

Man) would be put to death; yet none of them says when or in what circumstances this became apparent to him. The placement of the three best-known passion predictions in Mark (8:31; 9:31; 10:33–34), retained but somewhat rephrased in Matthew and Luke, reflects the Evangelist's theological interests, not his desire to explain how it came about that Jesus foreknew his fate beyond a sense of foreboding. Nonetheless, the Synoptics do contain some clues that invite attention precisely because they are not part of the three predictions.

The first clue concerns the possible influence of Herod Antipas's murder of John the Baptist on the way Jesus may have thought of his own task and future. According to Matthew 4:12, it was the news of John's arrest that triggered Jesus' decision to begin his own mission precisely in Antipas's domain, Galilee.[5] Though John's style and message differed sharply from those of Jesus (see Mt 11:16–19; Lk 7:31–35), the two were interlocked because both understood their work to be eschatological events, thereby implying that they were eschatological figures.[6]

Despite their manifest differences, the John-Jesus connection is reported to have been public knowledge. According to Mark, Jesus' disciples report that people were saying that he is John the Baptist (Mk 8:27–28, retained by Matthew and Luke). Mark also reports that when Herod Antipas learned of the disciples' mission, he regarded Jesus as John redivivus: "John, whom I beheaded, has been raised" (Mk 6:14–16).[7] There follows the story of John's fate, abbreviated in Matthew but omitted from Luke. Later Luke rewrote Mark

5. Mark simply says that Jesus came to Galilee "after John was arrested" (Mk 1:14), without indicating that the latter event triggered the former.

6. Boers notes that one should not isolate Jesus from John because "it is in John's activity as the final eschatological figure that Jesus found justification for his behavior, while on the other hand, it was in Jesus' activity that John's proclamation found its fulfillment." Since Boers, following Mt 3:2, thinks John too preached the kingdom of God, he does not hesitate to say that "what is decisive for an understanding of Jesus is not *how* he conceived of the kingdom of God, but *that* he understood the activity of John the Baptist as having inaugurated the time of the kingdom . . . and that one should not live with a sense of doom but with the assurance that God's liberation of a suffering humanity had arrived." In other words, Jesus "took the next step of living out the meaning of the kingdom in word and deed" (*Who Was Jesus?*, 48, 45, 48, resp.). But should not "living out" be given more weight in differentiating Jesus from John?

7. Catchpole regards this as a Markan construction, claiming that Herod's comment would not have been transmitted apart from its present context in which the narrator introduces the same (wrong) popular designations for Jesus that the disciples will report in Mk 8:28. See his "The Triumphal Entry," 327.

6:14–16 to say that Herod "was perplexed" because of what people were saying about Jesus and that he wanted to see Jesus (Lk 9:7–9).[8] This desire was fulfilled in Jerusalem when Pilate sent the Galilean Jesus to Galilee's ruler, Herod (Lk 23:6–12; cf. Acts 4:27–28).[9] The report of Herod's desire conflicts, however, with another story also found only in Luke. Here "some Pharisees" told Jesus to flee because Herod wanted to kill him (Lk 13:31). Crossan says Jesus did not flee because there was so much popular resentment against Herod for getting rid of John, whose influence Herod had feared (according to Josephus, *Antiq.* 18:116–19), that he did not want to risk alienating the peasantry again.[10] This is plausible. It is hard to see how both stories can be true—unless one attributes, without evidence, malice to the Pharisees: they used the threat of Herod to get Jesus to leave. This is implausible. In short, in addition to Jesus' knowledge of John's fate (though only Mt 14:12 reports who told him about it), this fragmentary evidence implies that Jesus knew his mission endangered his life.

That this knowledge prompted him to move from place to place outside Galilee in order to avoid John's fate, as Tyson once proposed,[11] is made unlikely by what Luke 13:32–33 reports Jesus said to the Pharisees who had warned Jesus that Herod was plotting to kill him: "Go and tell that fox, 'Listen: today and tomorrow I shall be driving out demons and working cures; on the third day I reach my goal.'[12] However, I must go on my way today and tomorrow and the next day, because it is unthinkable for a prophet to meet his death anywhere but in Jerusalem." Even if verse 33 ("However . . . Jerusalem") is another saying added here, as is likely, and so is Jesus' comment addressed to the Pharisees but not to "that fox" (see note 12), the point is the same: Jesus clearly sees himself as a prophet whose destiny is that of previous prophets, and this neces-

8. 8. For a discussion of the character and function of these changes, see Fitzmyer, *Luke*, I, 756–60.

9. "When Herod saw Jesus he was glad, for he had been wanting to see him for a long time, because he had heard about him and was hoping to see him perform some sign. He questioned him at length, but Jesus gave him no answer. The chief priests and the scribes stood by, vehemently accusing him. Even Herod with his soldiers treated him with contempt and mocked him; then he put an elegant robe on him, and sent him back to Pilate. That same day Herod and Pilate became friends with each other; before this they had been enemies" (Lk 23:8–12).

10. Crossan, *Who Killed Jesus?*, 49.

11. Tyson, "Jesus and Herod Antipas."

12. The quotation is from NRSV, but the punctuation follows REB, which does not regard the next statement as part of the word to Herod. The problem is discussed in Fitzmyer, *Luke*, II, 1027–33.

sity pertains to Jesus alone, not to his entourage. Since Jerusalem is the place where prophets are killed, in Galilee Jesus is unafraid of Herod.

That John's fate was a factor in Jesus' thinking about his own destiny is disclosed also by his reply to the disciples' question "Why do the scribes say that Elijah must come first?" According to Mark he replies, "Elijah is indeed coming to restore all things. How then is it written about the Son of Man, that he is to go through many sufferings and be treated with contempt? But I tell you that Elijah has come, and they did to him whatever they pleased, as it is written about him" (Mk 9:9–13). Although the logic of the passage is far from clear,[13] this reference to the Baptist's victimization suggests that Jesus surmised that the same fate awaited him.

Jesus' three passion predictions, spoken over the heads of the disciples to the readers, have several functions. (a) They show the reader that Jesus, far from being caught off guard by what happened in Jerusalem, knew exactly what would happen, though only in the Matthean version of the third prediction does Jesus say he will be crucified and not simply "be killed" (Mt 20:19). (b) They also help the reader understand the disciples' behavior in Jerusalem, for the narrators note either that they did not understand what Jesus said (Mk 9:30; Lk 9:46) or were afraid to ask what he meant (only in Mk 9:32) or were simply "greatly distressed" by it (Mt 17:23 [M]). Indeed, Luke even says that "what he said was hidden from them [i.e., by God] and [so] they did not grasp what was said" (Lk 18:34; see also 9:45). Despite the specificity of the predictions, especially the third (Mt 20:18–19; Mk 10:33–34; Lk 18:31–33), only in Luke 18:31 does Jesus see his destiny as the fulfillment of scripture: "See, we are going up to Jerusalem and everything that is written about the Son of Man by the prophets will be accomplished"—a theme to which the risen Jesus returns in Luke 24:25–27 and elaborates in verses 44–50. Otherwise the pre-

---

13. The passage follows the story of the transfiguration in which Jesus told the disciples to keep silent about what they had seen until after the resurrection. Although they wondered what "this rising from the dead could mean," they asked Jesus about something else: the coming of Elijah. Jesus' reply is given above. Matthew rewrote the passage so that Jesus' words about Elijah come first. Then comes the saying about the suffering Son of Man, without referring to what is "written about him"—evidently because the Evangelist knew that no scripture says this about the Son of Man. Matthew, having also omitted the Markan comment that the disciples did not understand "the rising of the dead," concludes the story by saying, "Then the disciples understood that he was speaking to them about John the Baptist," ignoring entirely their response to the predicted suffering of the Son of Man. Luke omits the whole passage.

dictions are just that—they say *what* will happen to Jesus without explaining *why* this is the case or what the purpose is. That is reserved for the ransom saying in Mark 10:45,[14] repeated in Matthew 20:28 but omitted from Luke. And Luke, which emphasizes Jesus' journey to Jerusalem, is content to let the narrator say that Jesus "set his face to go to Jerusalem" (Lk 9:51,53) without explaining why he was so determined. In short, none of the passion predictions changes what is stated in the first: What will happen to Jesus stands under the mysterious "must" (*dei*), a God-given necessity.[15] (c) The combination of foreknowledge and necessity shows the reader that Jesus willingly accepted his destiny—stated theologically, he was obedient even to the point of death (Phil 2:8).

Many, if not most, gospel critics are persuaded that the three passion predictions do not come from Jesus but are Christian formulations in which history after the fact is expressed as prediction before the fact. The various reasons adduced in support of this conclusion need not be rehearsed here; the issues are discussed in an appendix of volume 2 of Brown's *Death of the Messiah*. If, on the other hand, that evidence indicates that Jesus did reckon seriously with the likelihood that he would be put to death violently, then the passion predictions merit another look. That they are not simply precipitates of early Christian belief is indicated by the absence of any interpretation of the significance of Jesus' death. When the details are bracketed out, what remains is the rudimentary sense of destiny.

Particularly intriguing is the fact that nowhere do the Synoptics say, whether through a word of Jesus or through the narrator's comment, how Jesus related his kingdom-centered mission in Galilee to his decision to go to Jerusalem. His reply to Antipas ("today and tomorrow I shall be driving out demons . . . and on the third day I reach my goal") implies that he will go to Jerusalem when his Galilean mission is finished, and that he viewed his task as harbinger and herald of God's kingdom to be preliminary to the goal in Jerusalem. In both phases he apparently saw himself to be the finger of God, though not necessarily in the same way.

---

14. "For the Son of Man came not to be served but to serve, and to give his life as a ransom for many."

15. Bennett points out that *dei* and *gegraptai* (it is written) are synonymous but only in the sense that both are circumlocutions for "God wills it." More important is his observation that *dei* events are generally catastrophic, and that therefore the word does not point to the irruption of God's kingdom but heralds the end of the evil age ("The Son of Man Must . . . ," 128–29).

The public secret.   According to the Synoptics, Jesus made but one, climactic, trip to Jerusalem and said little about the city and its temple during his mission in Galilee. In addition to the reference to Jerusalem already mentioned, Jesus refers to the city only two other times, once affirming its sanctity and once lamenting its history and fate.[16] A reader without prior knowledge of the Jesus story might well be surprised by the sudden focus on Jerusalem.

All four canonical gospels report that Jesus' arrival was marked by acclamation (Mt 21:1–9; Mk 11:1–10; Lk 19:28–38; Jn 12:12–19), but they do not agree on how he obtained the animal he rode, who made the acclamation, what was shouted, or what happened next. Whereas the Synoptics agree that he went directly to the temple, John places Jesus' action there at the beginning of his mission (Jn 2:13–22), thereby separating it from the entry by three years. Clearly, each Evangelist reported Jesus' arrival in the city in a way that expressed the author's understanding of its significance, for which the Book of Zechariah was especially important.[17] Zechariah 9:9 says: "Rejoice greatly, O daughter Zion! / Shout aloud, O daughter Jerusalem! / Lo, your king comes to you; / triumphant and victorious is he, / humble and riding on a donkey, / on a colt, the foal of a donkey." The book ends with the promise that when God will finally triumph, "there shall no longer be traders in the house of the Lord on that day" (Zec 14:21). When Matthew points out that the entry "took place to fulfill what had been spoken through the prophet," quoting Zechariah 9:9, it simply makes explicit what Mark had already assumed; John too quotes Zechariah, though modified: "Fear not, daughter of Zion, / Behold thy king is coming, / Sitting on an ass's colt" (Jn 12:15, RSV). No report of the temple action quotes Zechariah 14:21, however.

16. The former is found only in Mt 5:33–35 ("Do not swear . . . by Jerusalem, for it is the city of the Great King"), the latter in the Q saying (Mt 23:37–39; Lk 13:34–35) in which Jesus speaks as if he were Wisdom's envoy looking back at her frustration: "Jerusalem, Jerusalem, the city that kills the prophets and stones those who are sent to it! How often have I desired to gather your children together as a hen gathers her brood . . . and you are not willing! See, your house [temple] is left to you, desolate [only Matthew has "desolate"]. And I tell you, you will not see me until the time comes when you say, 'Blessed is the one who comes in the name of the Lord.'" Because Matthew has Jesus say this after he had arrived in the city, the prediction appears to refer to the parousia; Luke's earlier placement allows it to be fulfilled when Jesus enters the city (Lk 19:39).

17. Other texts may have been influential as well: Is 62:11—"Say to the daughter of Zion, 'See, your salvation comes'"; Ps 118:26–27—"Blessed is the one who comes in the name of the lord. . . . Bind the festal procession with branches."

If one is not prepared to regard the reports of Jesus' entry to Jerusalem as "prophecy historicized" (Crossan) but as scripture-shaped accounts of an event that probably was simpler,[18] then the crowds of Passover pilgrims probably did not spontaneously see the significance in it that their reported acclamations imply, however important the entry was for Jesus. Somewhat like Luther's nailing ninety-five theses on the church door, its symbolic significance was grasped in retrospect, then reported and written about accordingly.

Since it is highly unlikely that John's report of the entry is derived from any or all of the Synoptics,[19] Jesus' arrival is attested in two independent strands of the Jesus tradition: Mark (used by Matthew and Luke) and John. A key item in both is that Jesus did not enter the city on foot as did other Passover pilgrims but rode into it. Unless one assumes that both strands were spun out of Christian study of Zechariah, this detail must be taken seriously as a symbolic act whose significance probably was clearer to Jesus than to the throngs. The stories, on the other hand, assume that the crowds were sufficiently schooled in the text of Zechariah to understand the symbolic action and so hail Jesus as king. However, no action was taken against Jesus, and the entry was not used as evidence against him at the trial where, according to all the gospels, "king of the Jews" was an issue (Mt 27:11; Mk 15:2; Lk 23:3; Jn 18:33–37). Even if Jesus had Zechariah 9:9 in mind, he evidently did not explain what he was doing. In fact, apart from instructions about finding the colt he was completely silent; only Luke reports that when some Pharisees told him to order his disciples to stop their acclamation Jesus said, "I tell you, if these were silent, the stones would shout out" (Lk 19:39–40). Luke adds that as Jesus neared the city he "wept over it" and predicted its total destruction after a siege (Lk 19:41–44). But neither of these sayings reveals what he thought he was doing by riding into the city. That can only be inferred from the action itself.

Here the reader must be cautioned not to conclude what Jesus "must" have thought or intended to accomplish or that he thought in strategic terms in the first place. There is no evidence that he intended his entry into the city and the subsequent action in the temple to provoke the

18. E. P. Sanders, *Jesus and Judaism*, 308.
19. So too D. M. Smith, "John 12:12ff. and the Question of John's Use of the Synoptics." For a full discussion of the relation of John to the Synoptics, see his *John among the Gospels*.

authorities to move against him in order to set in motion a sequence of events that would fulfill his conviction that as a prophet he must be put to death in the city—i.e., that he engineered his execution. Moreover, although the gospels report that his teaching in Jerusalem repeatedly referred to the kingdom of God, they contain not a word that explicitly connects his arrival in the city or his action in the temple with the coming of the kingdom (see Mt 21:28–32 [M]; 23:13–15 [M]; 24:14 [M]; 25:1–13, 31–46 [M]; Mk 12:34 [only here]; Lk 21:31 [only in Luke's version of Mk 13:29]). Only in the Matthean explanation of the saying about the rejected stone, added to the parable of the wicked tenants (also in Mark), is there a clear connection between the death of the son and the kingdom (Mt 24:43). The likelihood that some of these sayings were spoken on other occasions only underscores the point that there is no evidence that Jesus explicitly connected his arrival and the temple act with the coming of the kingdom—i.e., that he saw these events as hastening its coming. It is just this total absence of evidence that undermines Schweitzer's claim that Jesus came to Jerusalem to throw himself on the wheel of history in order to make it turn. In fact, only at the Supper does Jesus look explicitly beyond his impending death to the kingdom of God (Lk 22:28–30 [L], Mk 14:25 = Mt 26:29, and its variant in Lk 22:18).

Despite these gaps just where one desires clear evidence from Jesus, from the logic of the situation important inferences are valid: (a) Jesus was not executed because he happened to be at the wrong place at the wrong time; (b) since there is no evidence that his disciples or anyone else talked him into going to Jerusalem, he went freely and deliberately, indeed with a sense that his vocation made the trip unavoidable; (c) the events in Jerusalem, though having a distinct character, are of a piece with the Galilean mission, indeed, its climax; (d) in going to Jerusalem he who in Galilee understood himself to be the finger of God put himself and his mission into the hands of God. Is it accidental that he rode in silence?

As the Synoptics tell it, when Jesus arrived in the temple area, God's finger in effect became God's fist, expelling the merchants who sold sacrificial animals and overturning the tables of the money changers (Mt 21:12–13; Mk 11:15–19; Lk 19:45–48); in John, where for theological reasons the action is reported at the beginning of the mission, he made a cord whip and expelled the animals as well, saying, "Take these things out of here! Stop making my Father's house a marketplace." When asked for his right to do such a thing (a "sign"), he replied, "Destroy this temple, and in three days I will raise it up"—an answer dismissed as ridiculous: "This temple has been under construction for forty-six years, and you will raise it up in three days!" Lest the reader miss the point, the narrator explains that Jesus "was speaking of the temple of his body" (Jn 2:13–22).[20] In the Synoptics, however, Jesus' explanation was quite different, a quotation from Isaiah 56:7 ("my house shall be called a house of prayer for all nations"; Matthew and Luke omit "for all nations") coupled with an accusation derived from Jeremiah 7:11, "But you have made it a den of robbers." Although most scholars think that the Synoptics interpret and embellish an event that occurred ("history prophesied"),[21] recently others have insisted that it, like the entry, did not happen but is a Markan creation ("prophecy historicized").[22] One factor in the debate is the gospels' silence about any prompt response by either the temple police or the Romans, who could look down on the temple area from the adjacent Antonia tower. The significance of this silence should not be overemphasized, however. Once one grants that John exaggerates in saying that Jesus "drove *all* of them out of the temple, both the sheep and the cattle," one can reckon with a much more modest action which, given the hustle and bustle in the large temple area, need not have alarmed the authorities.[23] Mark and Luke do, of course, connect the event with the desire to kill Jesus,[24] but neither reports that the action was even mentioned when Jesus was brought before the Sanhedrin and later to Pilate. It is plausible that "the immediate occa-

20. Jesus' response implies that the resurrected Jesus will replace the temple (see also 4:21–24) and that the "temple" that will be destroyed is the currently present Jesus himself. He does not say that he, or anyone else, will destroy the temple building. In the Synoptics, Jesus will later predict its total destruction (Mk 13:1–3, par.), and at his appearance before the Sanhedrin he will be accused (falsely) of having *claimed* that he would destroy it (repeated in the taunts on Golgotha, Mk 15:29–30). In the Synoptic account neither the temple action nor the teaching that follows (except Mk 13:1–3) mentions the destruction of the temple.

21. For example, Mt 21:14–16 amplified the Markan account by reporting that Jesus healed the blind and the lame (who are prohibited from bringing offerings; see Lv 21:17–20) and added the angry response of the chief priests and scribes as well as Jesus' reply, based partly on Ps 8:2.

22. See, e.g., Seeley, "Jesus' Temple Act"; R. J. Miller, "The (A)Historicity of Jesus' Temple Demonstration."

23. So also E. P. Sanders, *Jesus and Judaism*, 308; and Fredriksen, "Jesus and the Temple, Mark and the War," 299.

24. Both say that the chief priests and scribes (Luke adds "leaders of the people") "kept looking for a way to kill him" but the people's response ("spellbound by his teaching") precluded action at the time (Mk 11:18; Lk 19:47–48).

sion of Jesus' death was the temple scene," as Sanders asserts,[25] but this goes beyond what the gospels say.

The purpose of Jesus' action in the temple at Passover coincides with the character of the action. Few, if any, would accept Brandon's views that (a) though Jesus was not actually a Zealot the action was "a truly revolutionary act" that "appears to have coincided with a Zealot uprising" marked by violence and pillage," which the Romans squelched "after bloodshed, and . . . captured some of the insurgents, including one named Barabbas"; (b) two of them were crucified with Jesus; and (c) "Jesus anticipated what the Zealots achieved in A.D. 66."[26] Rather, there is broad agreement that his action was not designed to create change but to symbolize it. The disagreement is over *what* it symbolized, purification ("cleansing") or destruction so that a new temple could replace it.[27] Sanders vigorously rejects the former in order to champion the latter.[28] Yet Evans notes that "there are no texts that predict the appearance of a messianic figure who first destroys (or predicts the destruction of) the temple and then rebuilds it," and he concludes that "the cleansing idea is too firmly entrenched in the tradition to be so easily set aside," adding that this does not imply an attack on the sacrificial system itself.[29]

On the other hand, this is exactly what Neusner sees enacted symbolically. He argues that the money changers made it possible for "all Israelites to participate in the provision of the daily whole-offering, which accomplished atonement for sin on behalf of the holy people as a whole"—something every Jew understood. Therefore "the overturning of the moneychangers' tables represents an act of the rejection of the most important rite of the Israelite cult," implying that this means of atonement "now is null" and that another means is now available—something that was, except to Jesus and his disciples, "simply beyond all comprehension."[30]

Part of the "cleansing" vs. destruction argument depends on what one makes of a detail found only in Mark 11:16: "he would not allow anyone to carry any-

25. E. P. Sanders, *Jesus and Judaism*, 318.

26. Brandon, *Jesus and the Zealots*, 335, 355, 332, 356, 333, 339, 356, resp.

27. Hooker suggests that it was "a prophetic drama signifying God's rejection of the worship" there and points to Jesus' protest about the fruitless fig tree (Mk 11:12–14,20) and the parable of the wicked tenants who refused what is due the owner (Mk 12:1–12, par.); see *The Signs of a Prophet*, 47–48.

28. E. P. Sanders, *Jesus and Judaism*, 61–67.

29. Evans, "Jesus' Action in the Temple," 250, 269, resp.

30. Neusner, "Money-changers in the Temple," 289. Neusner thinks that this other means of atonement is the Eucharist, at another table —fanciful.

thing [literally vessel, *skeuos*] through the temple." Does this mean that he pro-hibited using the temple area as a shortcut, implying concern for its sanctity (and hence part of the "cleansing"), or does it imply that he tried to shut down the whole operation? There appears to be no reason why Mark would have invented this detail; Matthew and Luke may have omitted it because they either did not understand its significance or considered it irrelevant.

The theme of this chapter does not require firm historical conclusions about the nature of the event or about Jesus' precise thinking about it. What matters here is that Jesus' action in the temple was prompted not simply by a villager's disgust at what he saw, though he may well have been angered by it, but was of a piece with prior expressions of his vocation. Put more sharply, here too Jesus acted as God's agent, now claiming the right to dramatize what he verbalized in Mark 13:1–3 as God's judgment on the temple, the implied underside of the kingdom's coming. If Bennett is right in saying that the divine necessity expressed with *dei* (see above, note 15), Paula Fredriksen may have overstated it in writing, "He went up to Jerusalem that Passover because he expected the Kingdom to come that Passover, at or as the climax of his own mission," but she was surely right in saying that "He went to confront no one—not Judean Jews, not the priests, and certainly not Rome."[31] He went to do what he had always done: embody what he knew was coming. In the temple he took the risk of symbolizing it.

Destiny achieved.   For the Roman soldiers, and perhaps for Pilate as well, Jesus' execution was probably just another crucifixion, but for the Evangelists it was the decisive event toward which the whole story had been moving. Although only John has Jesus say at the end, "It is finished!," the Synoptic accounts imply the same point of view. They devote more lines to the circum-stances that accompanied Jesus' death than to his crucifixion and expiration themselves, because the circumstances are to convey the significance of what happened to Jesus at the Skull (place of crucifixion, Golgotha). This crucifix-ion differed from all others because it was accompanied by wonders that sig-naled its apocalyptic significance: starting at high noon darkness for three hours;[32] the curtain of the temple "torn in two, from top to bottom"; and pecu-liar to Matthew, an earthquake and the resuscitation of saints, who waited until after Jesus' resurrection before leaving their tombs (Mt 27:45–56; Mk 15:33–41; Lk 23:44–49; *Gospel of Peter* 5.15–20). None of this is found in John, which keeps the readers' attention fixed on Jesus; nor does John report any

31. Fredriksen, "Jesus and the Temple," 302.
32. In Amos 5:18–20, "the day of the lord" is "darkness, not light"; in 8:9, on that day God "will make the sun go down at noon, and darken the earth in broad daylight."

mockery of Jesus, as do the others (Mt 27:39–44; Mk 15:29–32; Lk 23:35–43; *Gospel of Peter* 4.13).

The crucifixion is not described but stated starkly: "and they crucified him" (Mk 15:24). Neither the shape of the cross nor how Jesus was fastened to it,[33] nor how many soldiers were involved, nor where "the Skull" was located is reported. It is reported that Jesus refused a drink of wine mixed with myrrh (Mk 15:23; Mt 27:34 has "gall"); if this was a sedative (as is often thought) the refusal indicates that Jesus declined something that might have eased the pain. Still, there is no interest in the suffering itself. That his clothing was taken from him (standard procedure) indicates that he died naked, humiliated and exposed. Actually he suffered less than most crucified persons, for according to Mark he was crucified at 9 A.M. and died around 3 P.M. The Evangelists do not comment on his endurance or his faith; Luke, however, shows him continuing his mission of forgiveness by forgiving the soldiers first and then the "penitent thief" (Lk 23:34,[34] 40–43), and John has Jesus make provision for his mother (Jn 19:26–27). Compared with the triumphant "It is finished!" in John, Jesus' last words in Mark and Matthew are brutally shocking: "My God, my God, why have you forsaken me?"[35]—and even this is said to be grossly misunderstood as a call for Elijah (Mk 15:34–36; Mt 27:46–49). With a final inarticulate cry (which Luke turns into "Father, into your hands I commend my spirit") he "breathed his last" (Mt 27:50; Mk 15:37; Lk 23:46). There is nothing heroic here.

Luke and John have Jesus say little,[36] and Mark, followed by Matthew, even less. In these gospels Jesus is totally silent from the time he was crucified until the hour of his death, when his only words were the cry of dereliction.[37] Luke's

33. That nails were used is explicit only in John, and then in retrospect (Jn 20:25).

34. The *Gospel of the Nazarenes* adds, "At this word of the Lord, many thousands of Jews standing around the cross believed."

35. These words begin Psalm 22, some of whose subsequent lines also influenced the crucifixion story: "All who see me mock at me . . . they shake their heads" (cf. Mk 15:29); "my mouth is dried up like a potsherd" (cf. Jn 19:28); "they divide my clothes among themselves, and for my clothing they cast lots" (cf. Mk 15:24, par; the passage is quoted in Jn 19:23–24). Dillon thinks that "the crucifixion sequence in particular (Mk 15:22–29 par.) guarantees that they [the psalms] influenced the tradition at an early, pre-literary stage." See his "The Psalms of the Suffering Just."

36. Only Luke reports that on the way to Golgotha, Jesus turned to the wailing women and said, "Daughters of Jerusalem, do not weep for me but weep for yourselves and for your children," followed by an ominous prediction (Lk 23:27–31).

37. Apart from Jesus' response to the high priest's question "Are you the Messiah, the Son of the Blessed?" and his reply to Pilate's question "Are you the King of the Jews?" (Mk 14:61–62; 15:2), Jesus says nothing throughout.

report of Jesus' last word differs markedly from 4 Mc 6:26–30, in which the aged Eleazar, having been repeatedly tortured in order to get him to eat pork, prayed, "Thou knowest, God, that though I might have saved myself, I die in fiery torment for the sake of the Law. Be merciful to thy people, and let my punishment be sufficient for their salvation. Make my blood an expiation for them, and take my life as a ransom for theirs."

Although it is nearly impossible to learn exactly what happened at Golgotha,[38] the gospels agree that Jesus was not put to death by a mob nor assassinated nor stoned to death but was tried and executed by crucifixion on Pilate's orders; moreover, scholars agree that Jesus was charged with claiming to be, or to become, "King of the Jews"—i.e., a potential challenger of Rome's rule. Though the gospels disagree on the wording, they all report that this charge was put into writing, though only Matthew says it was placed above Jesus' head, and only John says it was written in three languages and that the chief priests demanded that it should be changed to read "This man said, I am the King of the Jews" (Mt 27:37; Mk 15:26; Lk 23:38; Jn 19:19–22; *Gospel of Peter* 4.11). Whatever the exegetical and historical problems may be, the trial narratives not only exonerate Pilate and indict the Jerusalem priesthood, they also show that Jesus was put to death deliberately by persons in power, religious as well as imperial.

The passion story, from Jesus' entry to the city to his expiration outside it, brings into view many other participants: disciples, temple traders, priests, scribes, Sadducees, an unnamed widow, a leper named Simon, a woman with a jar of ointment, a man (!) carrying a jar of water, crowds, the high priest's slave, a young man fleeing naked, the Sanhedrin, the high priest's servant girl, Pilate, Roman soldiers, Simon from Cyrene in North Africa, women at the cross, Joseph of Arimathea—to mention only those that appear in Mark. Not mentioned are Satan or God; God, in fact, is mentioned as having forsaken Jesus. Mark, of course, would not have written this text if he had been convinced that God had indeed abandoned Jesus. Since Jesus had not only called God Abba but had also undertaken to announce and embody the impingement of God's kingdom, yet died as a victim of Caesar's power and Caiaphas's plotting, a theological question becomes inescapable: What is the ongoing import of Jesus' execution for the understanding of God?

38. Mark and Matthew themselves imply the reason for the difficulty: when Jesus was apprehended all the disciples fled (Mt 26:56; Mk 14:50), leaving no one to observe what happened next. In John "another disciple . . . known to the high priest . . . went with Jesus into the courtyard of the high priest"; it was he who persuaded the guard to admit Peter as well (Jn 18:15–16). John does not claim that these two overheard what went on, however.

The Living God Jesus Trusted

Call him what one will—prophet, peasant protester, insurrectionist, patriot, holy man, charismatic healer-teacher, apocalyptic preacher, antiapocalyptic sage, Jewish cynic—Jesus was about God and God's reign in human affairs. Indeed, as did the scripture before him and the rabbis after him, he insisted that the chief commandment (to love God totally, Dt 6:5) cannot be separated from the second (to love the neighbor as oneself, Lv 19:18), and he embodied this fusion in the character of his mission.[39] Even those sayings that do not mention "God" were grounded in his perception of and commitment to that Reality he called "Abba." Moreover, from the earliest days Christians have interpreted him and his significance in light of their understanding of God and reciprocally have interpreted both God and the love of God in light of Jesus.[40] Further, whereas Jesus has had no influence on Judaism's understanding of God, the "Jesus factor" has been pivotal in Christianity, partly because of what he said about God, partly because of who he was believed to be, and especially because of the meanings Christians and others found in his death. It is hard to think of any aspect of human life, from its strivings to its contemplations, across which both the light and the shadow of the cross have not fallen.

Here, however, the focus is on the significance of Jesus' death for Christian gentile understanding of God. Lest it be overlooked, the obvious bears repeating: There would be no such thing as "Christian gentile understanding of God" had not Jesus' earliest followers believed that he had been resurrected and exalted to "God's right hand" and taught others to believe it too. There is no evidence that his first followers developed a Jesus-shaped understanding of God on the basis of

39. Though the double command is found in all the Synoptics, none of them reports it in exactly the same way. Only Luke gives it as Jesus' response to the inquiry about what is necessary for eternal life, and only Mark has Jesus first repeat the Shema' (Dt 6:4); only Mark reports the scribe's positive response to Jesus' reply and in turn Jesus' positive response to him: "You are not far from the kingdom of God." In fact, this is the only time Mark reports such an exchange. Matthew and Luke omit it because they attributed ulterior motives to the questioner (Mt 23:34–40; Mk 12:28–34; Lk 10:25–28). The *Gospel of Thomas* 25 divides what Jesus combined: "Jesus said, 'Love your brother or sister as your soul, and guard them as the apple of your eye.'"

40. Decades later 1 John 4:20–21 shows that Jesus' point was remembered also in the non-Synoptic stream: "Those who say, 'I love God,' and hate their brother or sister, are liars; for those who do not love brother or sister whom they have seen, cannot love God whom they have not seen. The commandment we have from him is this: those who love God must love their brothers and sisters also."

his words alone. Because the theological question that Jesus' death puts on the table does not concern the existence of God but the persistence of God, the discussion first returns to the theme of Jesus' resurrection, which leads to consideration first of "the living God" and then to God's holiness.

Resurrection and the silent abba.   Just as the rabbis expressed their conviction that on occasion God's will was made known decisively by an articulate voice (the Bat Qol[41]) so the Synoptics report that the Voice spoke at Jesus' baptism and later at the transfiguration, both signaling God's commitment to Jesus, God's Son. But no gospel reports that the Voice spoke where one might expect it most of all—at the crucifixion. Neither Jesus' cry of dereliction nor his final inarticulate scream was answered. At Golgotha the silence of God was deafening.

Since the gospels go on to report Jesus' resurrection, the silence of God at Golgotha is not the end of the story but is incorporated into it. For them the resurrection is the tacit standpoint which legitimates—in fact, demands—telling the Jesus story at all. Apart from the belief that Jesus was resurrected, the import of his execution is quite different. What is at issue here can be sorted out by imagining what might have been the case had Jesus' followers not come to believe the resurrection news. For a time some of them might have told others of their deep disappointment (as in Lk 24:21: "we had hoped that he was the one to redeem Israel"); others might have remembered what he had said because they continued to find these sayings perceptive and intriguing, and, revering his memory, they might have told stories about that remarkable brief time—a Jewish Camelot. But in due course, the group—if it had continued—would have disappeared from history, as did the followers of John the Baptist. Others might well have concluded that Jesus was too idealistic to be valid in "the real world" or that he was but the latest instance of what everyone already knew: that repeatedly, good persons are "done in" by the self-preserving structures of power, that there is a stubborn disconnect between the power of goodness and the goodness of power.

Because *resurrection* has accumulated many meanings, as well as misunderstandings—e.g., resuscitation or reanimation—it is useful to recall what those who first claimed Jesus was resurrected probably thought they were saying. The qualifier *probably* is important because no one can reconstruct what they had in mind, since no text comes from those who believed it first. The earliest texts that speak of Jesus' resurrection are Paul's letters, written in the 50s, but they either simply assert it (as in 1 Thes 1:10; Rom 4:24) or interpret it for

41. See Moore, *Judaism,* I, 422.

gentile believers who, from his point of view, misunderstood it.[42] What one can do, however, is rely on Jewish understandings to infer the logic that probably was inherent in the claim that God had raised Jesus from the realm of the dead.

The roots and growth of the belief that there is life after death, replacing shadowy existence in Sheol, has been outlined repeatedly and so need not be rehearsed here.[43] It is enough to recall that some Jews then believed in immortality as God's gift to the souls of the righteous without reference to resurrection (as in Wis Sol 3:1–9) and that those who did look for a resurrection had quite diverse views about it, some seeing it as a reward for faithfulness, especially in times of persecution (as in 2 Baruch 30), others as a necessary prelude to the great judgment (as in Dan 12:1–2; Jn 5:29; the Book of Revelation has both: 20:4–6, 11–15). Either way, resurrection was consistently viewed as involving either a group (the righteous) or all humanity, not single individuals. Exceptionally righteous individuals were thought to have gone directly to heaven, as did Enoch, Moses, and Elijah. Therefore, one must infer that when the earliest believers claimed that Jesus had been resurrected, they not only claimed that God had validated him but also that the general resurrection of the dead was both inevitable and imminent. This is why Paul insisted that if there is no resurrection of the dead, Christ has not been raised either, for they belong together; accordingly, "Christ has been raised from the dead, the first fruits of those who have died" (1 Cor 15:20, 23; see note 42). Moreover, since belief in resurrection was from the start a way of affirming God's faithful response to the righteous who were unjustly treated in this life, resurrection simultaneously vindicates the ultimate justice of God and the earthly righteousness of the faithful. In resurrection the power of God's goodness and the goodness of God's power coincide. Thus on Good Friday the rectitude of both God and Jesus was on the line, and it stayed there until Easter.

The resurrection of the dead and buried Jesus[44] therefore implies the vindication of the whole person, including his execution. The ongoing significance

42. In 1 Corinthians 15 Paul reminds the new Christians that they had accepted the gospel which included Jesus' resurrection. His question "How can some of you say that there is no resurrection of the dead?" (v. 12) therefore suggests that some had restricted the resurrection to Jesus alone, perhaps because they thought this was appropriate for a divine Son of God but not for mortals like themselves. In any case, this is precisely the distinction that Paul rejects.

43. See Nickelsburg, "Resurrection."

44. Crossan thinks the gospels' reports of Jesus' burial are all unhistorical. See *Who Killed Jesus?*, chap. 6.

of this must not be missed. For one thing, since no person's life can be assessed whole until it has ended in death, Jesus' death was part of who he was. This leads to an important point: The resurrection was not the last event in his life, the "happy ending," but God's response to it as a whole, thereby making the cross its permanent capstone. Easter did not displace the cross. To the contrary, it is precisely Easter that forbids Christian theology from so emphasizing the life and teaching of Jesus that the cross becomes a tragedy that broke off a splendid life of love and self-giving; rather, Easter requires Christian theology to keep pondering the meaning of the cross for its understanding of both Jesus and the God he trusted. In short, if God validated and vindicated precisely the Jesus who was executed on Golgotha, then he remains the fractured prism through which one sees into that mysterious Reality called "God."

Here too it is instructive to imagine different scenarios. Had Jesus been primarily a sage surrounded by his pupils or a philosophical thinker like Philo, his teaching would have been the primary thing, perhaps elaborated by his successors as is common in the history of thought. Had he lived to old age, on his deathbed he might have gathered his disciples around him, summed up his legacy, and alerted them to what fidelity to his word and way might well entail.[45] Or suppose there had been a last-minute reprieve because the darkened sky brought a dramatic thunderstorm in which lightning struck the executioner's hammer, nearly killing him. Then perhaps Mark might have reported that the centurion exclaimed, "This is the Son of God" when he saw how Jesus did *not* die, and called off the execution. Then the women at Golgotha would have led Jesus away to wash his lacerated back and nurse him back to full strength. Such a last-minute reprieve would have confirmed Satan's taunt in the wilderness temptation: If Jesus is really the Son of God, he could leap from the temple and not be hurt (Mt 4:5–6). Instead, Jesus—having been abandoned, lashed, taunted, crucified—died with those who, like himself, were deemed criminals.

Neither the resurrection nor the Christian sense of the Risen One's presence makes up for that brutal outcome of Jesus' life. If Christian theology claims to see into the God-Reality through this fractured prism, what or whom does it see if it probes the identity and character of God "within earshot of the dying cry of Jesus," as Moltmann put it?[46] It certainly did not and does not and must not see the dying and rising gods, whose annually repeated story symbol-

---

45. Such "farewell discourses" were a common literary form in antiquity. For a concise overview, see Kurz, *Farewell Addresses in the New Testament*, 19–32. Kurz goes on to analyze the farewell speeches of Paul and Jesus.

46. Moltmann, *The Crucified God*, 201.

izes what is always true[47] and who in the initiation rites of the mysteries create a transitory bonding with the divine (divinization), "meaningful" though the experience surely must have been. What Christian theology sees—that is, should see—is the living God to whom the scriptures of Israel point. Because resurrection by definition is an eschatological event, the nature gods do not resurrect; they simply vivify again and again and again. Only Israel's God resurrects.

The living God.[48]   Israel's God was not the only one who "lives." Indeed, oath formulas from ancient Egypt used the phrase "as Amun lives," as did oaths in Israel (see, e.g., 1 Sam 14:45; 2 Sam 2:27; Job 27:2; misuse of the formula is criticized in Jer 5:1–2). Even the famous line in Job 25:19 "I know that my Redeemer lives" has a parallel in a Ugaritic text about Baal: "And I know that Aleyan Baal lives" (though this may allude to his annual reanimation). When Joshua tells the people that "among you is the living God" who will drive Israel's enemies from Canaan (Josh 3:10, a Deuteronomistic text), his words express what is assumed throughout the Hebrew Bible—it is God's specific actions, not nature's processes, that show Yahweh to be the "living God." This is reflected in the phrases added to the oath such as "As the Lord lives, who has saved my life" (1 Kgs 1:29; see also 2:24; Jer 16:14). Repeatedly God is called "the living God (1 Sam 17:26; Ps 42:3; 84:2; Jer 10:10; 23:36; Hos 1:10). Accordingly, Second Isaiah, speaking for God, has only contempt for gods made of wood or metal, for they can do nothing nor can they answer. Psalm 115 makes the same point: the nations say, "Where is their God?" The answer:

> Our God is in the heavens;
> he does whatever he pleases [REB: wills][49]
> Their idols are silver and gold,
> the work of human hands.
> They have mouths, but do not speak;
> eyes, but do not see.
> They have ears, but do not hear;

47. Here one might well ponder Miskotte's observation: "Paganism is an unquestioning celebration of the given world," whereas "Israel always asked questions where others did not question" (*When the Gods Are Silent*, 309).

48. This discussion draws on Kraus, "Der lebendige Gott."

49. The opening lines of the quotation are easily misunderstood. The Psalmist, however, is not declaring God's sheer willfulness or arbitrariness, for he begins the poem this way: "Not to us, O Lord, not to us, but to your name give glory, / for the sake of your steadfast love and your faithfulness." The Psalmist implies that God's doing "whatever he pleases" is consonant with God's reliable love and fidelity which become actions in due course, or "in God's good time," as the once-common saying puts it.

noses, but do not smell.
They have hands, but do not feel;
feet, but do not walk. . . .
Those who make them are like them,
so are all who trust in them.

The living God of Israel is neither a postulate inferred by cogent reasoning, such as Aristotle's Unmoved Mover, nor Anselm's Being, greater than whom cannot be thought. The living God of Israel is the vital Reality encountered in actions in which faithfulness and love become events in Israel's history and in the lives of individual Israelites. This is the God that Jesus' people had known for centuries because, despite varying forms of repeated forgetfulness and disobedience, they were committed to the God who was committed to them by election and covenant. The "scandal of particularity," usually focused on Jesus (see p. 22) is anchored in the scandalous particularity of the living God of Israel to whom scripture points in one situation after another.[50] This God is not a local Jewish edition of a general "deity" shared by all religions, whether in the "syncretism" of Greco-Roman times or in today's gentile yearnings for a universal generic deity. Rather, Israel's particular God, the Creator, chose Abraham and his descendants to be the means by which the Gentiles are to be blessed (Gn 12:1–3). Understandably, then, Paul interpreted the conversion of Gentiles by saying, "you turned to God from idols, to serve a living and true God, and to wait for his Son from heaven, whom he raised from the dead—Jesus" (1 Thes 1:9–10). Only the living God can bring life out of death.

Moreover, since according to Psalm 115:1 the living God is not capricious but reliable (not to be confused with predictable), one can say that whom God vindicates by resurrection discloses definitively the identity, character, and commitment of God. This, then, implies that the resurrection not only vindicated Jesus but also confirmed the God Jesus trusted and interpreted. And since he trusted the God of whom the law and the prophets speak, "Christians should acknowledge that God's history with Israel and the nations is the permanent and abiding

50. Miskotte notes that Israel's God "cannot be derived from reality as we would derive a truth; what the encounter is, where and how it takes place, must be spoken, shown, called to remembrance." He also observes that the biblical God "is repeatedly reviled, often despised, constantly misunderstood, his Word appears to be no match for paganism; the ark . . . is 'captured' by the Philistines. His priests deceive and are deceived. . . . He is a rover, mighty and unpredictable; he is like a consuming fire. He is described as a man of war . . ., a lion who roars from the forest. . . . And yet this neglected, rejected God remains the Lord; the power of the Lord lies mostly hidden in his patience, his suffering . . . for him power is always the power to judge, that is, to decide, to set things right in his way" (*When the Gods Are Silent*, 161–63).

medium of God's work as the Consummator of human creation, and therefore it is also the permanent and enduring context of the gospel about Jesus."[51]

Characteristically, in liberal gentile Christianity God is remarkably predictable, "always loving" and affirming, having been deprived of the capacity to "do whatever he pleases" in God's own way. Gone too is God's awesomeness and mysteriousness that defies "explanation" and evokes awe as well as bafflement and anger. The often perplexing ways of the biblical living God are expressed in two lines of a Muslim's prayer: "Sometimes He gives while depriving you, / And sometimes He deprives you in giving."[52] Keeping in view the living God of Israel's history and scripture can preserve Christian theology from forgetting that the God-Reality is a mystery whose depth and complexity elude human minds by definition and that the flashlights of reason illumine but a small segment of that Reality and that their beams do not penetrate far. Only the living God who sometimes is perceived to be silent and who sometimes is One with a word, who is sensed as withdrawn and then again as present, and who is experienced as the destroyer as well as the redeemer is really God. When the Old Testament is taken seriously as a whole instead of being perused for usable passages (as if its being the "Old" Testament means that, like an old car, it still has salvageable parts),[53] it becomes evident that the living God-Reality so persists in being itself in its own way against sundry human expectations, illusions, and wickedness that again and again something unexpected occurs portending the time when God's kingdom on earth will be as real as it is "in heaven." Any other God is not the living God but rather a convenient, and perhaps logically necessary, construct which, though shaped by earnest minds, may be no less an "idol" than those made by hand and derided by the composer of Psalm 115 and the unknown "Isaiah" who wrote Isaiah 44:12–30.[54] If the Hebrew Bible's witness is right, not only do

51. Soulen, *The God of Israel and Christian Theology*, 100. Soulen's point is particularly pertinent in light of current efforts to "indigenize" or "enculturate" Christianity in Africa and Asia, for it is an essential criterion for assessing the results of these efforts.

52. Quoted from Westphal, *God, Guilt, and Death*, 30.

53. Seitz observes, rightly, that the Old Testament "resists easy sorting out with some geiger counter set with a Jesus rheostat" (*Word without End*, 6).

54. "He who begins with the love of God without having previously experienced the fear of God, loves an idol which he himself has made, a god whom it is easy enough to love. He does not love the real God who is, to begin with, dreadful and incomprehensible. . . . This is presumably what Whitehead meant when he said that religion is the passage from God the void to God the enemy and from Him to God the companion. . . . [The believing person] endures in the face of God the reality of lived life, dreadful and incomprehensible though it may be. He loves it in the love of God whom he has learned to love." So Buber, *The Eclipse of God*, 36–37.

humans turn away from God but God also turns away from them. At the end of this century so bloodied by illusions and arrogance, only that living God is credible because that One is other. The biblical word for that is *holiness.*

The vitality of God's holiness.   Whoever in the light of the resurrection looks through the prism of Jesus' death into the deep mystery of the God of Israel will see that God is holy, for the holiness of God is the determinative quality that distinguishes God as God. It is a sign of Christian theology's current attenuated link to the Old Testament, and the consequent displacement of this Testament's ways of speaking of God by other modes and categories, that talk of God's holiness has been marginalized if not eclipsed. The historical factors that have collaborated to produce this situation invite investigation, but that task must be left for others. Here it suffices to note that this indifference or uneasiness with the theme of God's holiness goes hand in hand with the variegated rejection of any significant distinction between the sacred and the profane, the result of which is the virtual disappearance of tabus and abominations, now regarded as cultural artifacts from "primitive" societies. At the same time, "the sacred" has not disappeared entirely but has been relocated in the individual, whose worth, potential, and rights must not be violated. In other words, moderns and postmoderns are more concerned to honor the sanctity of the self than the sanctity or holiness of God. That is precisely why pondering the ongoing significance of Jesus' death for the gentile understanding of God cannot neglect God's holiness. The point, of course, is not to rehabilitate ancient tabus but to recover that quality in the God of Israel and its scriptures that is determinative of the living God. Why? Because, as Christopher R. Seitz has written, "the otherness of God for Gentile outsiders [to the covenant relation between God and Israel] has not been erased—it has been disclosed as the holiness of God once known within Israel, now brought near in Christ."[55] What the silence of God on Good Friday discloses, in light of Easter's dawn, is not the indifference of God but the difference of God, God's otherness, which the Bible expresses as God's holiness. What unveils the poignant significance of this theme is P. T. Forsyth's assertion, as valid today as when he said it in 1907, that "all reconstruction of belief must begin with the holiness of God."[56]

Since holiness, at least in the Old Testament sense, has become a strange concept, it is useful to recall that the word renders the Hebrew *qdš*, which can be used to form a noun (the holy one), a verb (to make holy) or an adjective; its

55. Seitz, *Word without End*, 25; "once" does not imply "no longer," of course.
56. Forsyth, *Positive Preaching and the Modern Mind*, 173. The book expands the Lyman Beecher Lectures at Yale in 1906–1907.

basic meaning is "to separate," "mark off from the ordinary" (the profane), and therefore "reserve for," or "dedicate to," God, the Holy One who is inherently holy. Things (e.g., offerings, temple equipment), persons (priests), places (Jerusalem, the temple), times (Sabbath) are not inherently holy (nor is the created order) but become holy by deliberate action, usually ritualized.[57] Von Rad notes that the holy is "the great stranger in the human world," the "wholly other" that in ancient Israel was experienced as power.[58] In fact, it was dangerous for those not authorized to handle holy things, as Uzzah found out when he touched the sacred ark (2 Sam 6:6–11). It was the prophets who saw in God's essential otherness a profound moral meaning. Thus Hosea, having emphasized God's frustration with Israel, has God say, "I will not execute my fierce anger . . . for I am God and no mortal, the Holy One in your midst" (Hos 11:9); so too Isaiah, who calls God "the Holy One of Israel" (e.g., Is 5:29; 10:20; 12:6), declares, "the Lord of hosts is exalted by justice, and the Holy God shows himself holy by righteousness" (Is 5:16). Likewise, the "Holiness Code" (Lv 17– 26) grounds its many commands, both cultic and moral, in God's holiness. Chapter 19 introduces the moral commands by reminding the people, "You shall be holy, for I the Lord your God am holy" (19:2), and later uses its opposite in the command "You shall not swear falsely by my name, profaning the name of your God: I am the Lord" (19:12). The whole point is expressed in Leviticus 20:8: "Keep my statutes, and observe them; I am the Lord; I sanctify you."

The holiness of God is not one of the many "attributes" of God, such as mercy, love, justice, goodness, patience; it is rather that density of God's being that qualifies all attributes into holy mercy, holy love, holy justice, etc. Holiness differentiates the God-Reality from everything else; consequently one encounters God as the Other — indeed, the "wholly other" — the Given, with a self-constituting integrity. Merold Westphal points out that in the presence of the Holy One, one's experience is the opposite of the thinker who follows Descartes's "I think, therefore I am," because the Cartesian can doubt everything but himself or herself and so makes everything relative to one's own existence. But before the Holy we are in the presence of something that is more real than we are, and it is we who are relativized by God.[59]

Rudolf Otto, who characterized the holy as *mysterium tremendum et fascinans* and as "wholly other," also pointed out that the holy is not only "absolute

57. For a survey of usages and ritual acts of sanctifying, see D. P. Wright, "Holiness (Old Testament)."

58. von Rad, *Old Testament Theology*, I, 205.

59. Westphal, *God, Guilt, and Death*, 27.

might, making its claims and compelling their fulfillment, but also a might that has at the same time the supreme *right* to do so, and is thus worthy of praise."[60] In other words, God's otherness is not only ontic but also moral; indeed, God's ontic otherness is the ground of God's moral otherness with which humans are confronted, as Hosea saw. In holiness God's goodness and power are one, giving God the inherent and unqualified right to require the unholy to become holy and to punish the wicked, as well as to elicit wonder and praise for doing so. That is precisely what comes to expression in both the prophets and in Leviticus.

Otto's formulation points to the union of opposites: the *mysterium* repels because the power of its awesome otherness moves against the unholy, the unrighteous, the resistance to the holy;[61] yet the *fascinans* attracts because the same holy that destroys also overcomes the unholy, the unrighteous and the rebellious that provokes the destruction. This duality of the holy is expressed repeatedly in the Old Testament, from the early material to the latest. Thus the ancient Song of Hannah says: "There is no Holy One like the LORD . . . / The LORD kills and brings to life; / he brings down to Sheol and raises up / The LORD makes poor and makes rich, / he brings low, he also exalts" (1 Sam 2:2–7). The Song of Moses, though not mentioning God's holiness, says the same: "There is no god besides me. / I kill and I make alive; / I wound and I heal; / and no one can deliver from my hand. / For I lift up my hand to heaven, / and swear: As I live forever. . . . / I will take vengeance on my adversaries" (Dt 32:39–41). That the same God brings both woe and weal is part of Isaiah's promise of the "day when the LORD binds up the injuries of his people, and heals the wounds inflicted by his blow" (Is 30:26; see also Hos 5:15–6:3). The third- or fourth-century B.C.E. Book of Tobit reports that when Tobit's blindness was healed he said, "May his holy name be blessed . . . though he afflicted me, he has had mercy on me" (Tb 11:14–15); the poetic thanksgiving goes on to say: "Blessed be God who lives forever . . . / for he afflicts and he shows mercy; / he leads

---

60. Quoted from Westphal, 41. Westphal also notes that "the sacred is not worthy because it is in tune with the moral law. Rather, the moral law derives whatever sanctity it has from its ties to the sacred" (42).

61. Westphal's wide-ranging phenomenological analysis led him to observe that the duality of the sacred elicits ambivalence "because the very act of acknowledging its claims reveals a built-in resistance to any moral and spiritual transformation of the self" (ibid., 56). At the same time, acknowledging the Holy also generates a sense of guilt because "*in guilt I approve of the other's disapproval of me*" (ibid., 78, his italics). This guilt can be denied by denying the right of the Other to disapprove; otherwise it must be dealt with.

down to Hades . . . / and he brings up from the great abyss / and there is noth-ing that escapes his hand." This duality implies that God's holiness unites the power of God's goodness and the goodness of God's power into a dense mys-tery. Becoming aware of the former discloses the plight of the unholy, and dis-cerning the latter promises that one can become holy ("sanctified"). At the same time the radical otherness, while self-consistent, precludes one from knowing in advance the means, mode, or time of the Holy One's actions. The Holy One remains a mystery to be acknowledged, not a puzzle to be solved. What *can* be counted on, then, is *that* the living God's holiness is consonant with the purposes of God, namely the actualizing of God's kingship "on earth as it is in heaven." That is why Forsyth could say that "Holiness is the eternal moral power which must do, and do, till it sees itself everywhere."[62] In other words, the living God's holiness is not static but determinedly dynamic, bent on making holy all that has become profane. This is what the postexilic Zechariah expressed when he spoke of that day when ordinary household ves-sels would be as sacred as those in the temple, and when even the bells on horses' harnesses would be inscribed "Holy to the LORD" (Zec 14:20–21). This eschatological horizon does not displace the earlier understanding which accents God's enduring, present demand that Israel be holy because God is holy, but gives voice to the conviction that the holy-making power of God's holiness will, "in God's good time," surely redeem even the most mundane things from their profaneness. Ultimately this is what the vitality of God's holi-ness is all about.

The foregoing sketch of the holiness of God, both in terms of its complex perceptions in the Old Testament and its more formal theological dimension, sets the stage for considering the holiness of God in relation to Jesus' death in light of the Easter faith. God's holiness does not, of course, "explain" Jesus' death, nor does his death "explain" God. Instead, considering each in con-junction with the other can bring otherwise overlooked theological under-standing of both.

To begin with, the death-and-resurrection of Jesus is consonant with the God Jesus trusted, the Holy One of Israel who in his radical otherness mysteri-ously "makes poor and makes rich, brings down to Sheol and raises up, kills and makes alive," the One who Jesus said sends sun and rain on the just and the unjust. The resurrection of the unjustly crucified Jesus does not "explain" this deeply mysterious duality of God's ways; it rather confirms it as a given to be acknowledged and pondered as the signature of the Holy who is One, whose

---

62. Forsyth, *Positive Preaching*, 240.

awesome otherness therefore allows one to recognize also the "dark underside" of the one God instead of attributing the negative in life to a separate malign deity. Not even Satan is that.

Moreover, if the resurrection vindicates Jesus—the Jesus who cried out his sense of abandonment[63]—then this cry and the radical otherness of God must be thought through together. This means that neither the presence nor the absence of the Holy One, who is wholly other, can be inferred from human consciousness or awareness of God; it means rather that God can be "experienced" as absent as well as silent and that Jesus' cry of derelictions puts into words what any sufferer may sense, especially when suffering alone. Indeed, the vindication of the Jesus who expressed his sense of abandonment so forcefully allows one to hear in his cry the agony of all who suffer unjustly, for whom no "explanation" brings solace. For them, as for Jesus, the presence of the wholly Other is sensed as a void. (That some who suffer unjustly do sense the presence of God and, like the Lukan Jesus, die devoutly in no way annuls the stark truth and meaning of the Markan Jesus' death.) But Jesus also addressed the void, not the bystanders. On that darkened day he did not ask *them*, "Why has God forsaken me?" but hurled his question into the unsensed Presence directly, "My God, my God, why have *you* forsaken me?" In those circumstances that was nothing less than the profound cry of faith from the bruised finger of God into the hidden face of God. The common proposal that Jesus silently recited the entire Psalm 22, which ends on an affirmative note, but had strength to utter only the first line, destroys the point—effectively.

The fractured prism on the cross confirms also the positive dimension of God's otherness, its *fascinans*, when that figure is viewed in light of Easter. Apparently it never occurred to those who believed and commended to others the news of Jesus' resurrection that God had acted on the spur of the moment. They assumed that all God's acts are purposeful, even if the otherness of God's ways made them opaque to human understanding at the time. One may infer, then, that since they experienced the living Lord Jesus, particularly at the Table, they concluded that the post-Easter consolidation and expansion of Jesus' community was part of God's purpose not discerned before his execution (reflected in the Synoptics' reports of the disciples' failure to understand the passion predictions). And if that were indeed the case, then the humiliation of Jesus, and the profaning of God that it implied, was the price God purposely

---

63. In reporting the cry of derelictions, Mark lets Jesus express with Psalm 22 what is built into the situation. Theologically, one does not need to know whether Jesus actually said these words or exactly what was going through his mind.

and freely paid for the renewal of their lives and for the new faith community,[64] now itself seen as the harbinger of God's kingly reign. Not surprisingly, Christians have found the audacity to speak of Jesus' execution as an expression of God's love. So far as we can tell, it was Paul who first put it into words: "God proves his love for us in that while we still were sinners Christ died for us" (Rom 5:8; see also Jn 3:16).[65] Thereby he made explicit what was already implied in the tradition he had received two decades before: "Christ died for our sins in accordance with the scriptures" (1 Cor 15:3). It was largely on the foundation of such expressions—"for us" (*hyper hēmōn*) and "for our sins" (*hyper tōn hamartiōn hēmōn*)—that Christian theology, especially in the West, built elaborate doctrines of the atonement and of Christ's sacrifice for everyone's sin.

It is helpful to reflect a bit more on the coinherence of God's holiness and God's love. To begin, theologically the foregoing paragraph implies that the holy God deliberately endured profanation, through the public humiliation of Jesus, in order to unveil the character of sin so that it could be forgiven. This means that the true aim of God's holiness is not self-preservation from contamination but sanctification of the unholy, the transformation of the unrighteous. That becomes visible in the often-overlooked fact that those whose relation to God has been rectified are called "holy ones" (saints) by Paul; they are not the morally or spiritually elite but persons now claimed by the Holy One whose otherness gives what it requires—life transformed by the empowering presence of the crucified and resurrected Jesus experienced as the Holy Spirit. God's radical otherness is neither remoteness nor indifference but the ground of holy love that loves the unlovable into a rectitude that enables the rectified recipient to love the other, be it neighbor or enemy. When God's love is severed from God's holiness, God's love for us and our love for God relentlessly turn into the reciprocal sentiment of the positively disposed. Love that makes itself vulnerable to profanation in order to redeem is passionate but not sentimental. Precisely because such love is grounded in the wholly Other, it can neither be forced nor manipulated.

It is difficult to overemphasize that what Christians discern in the cross— God's holiness activated as love—is not an alternative to God attested in the

---

64. Gunton puts it well: "God is revealed by the cross as one who bears the power of the demonic rather than punishes those who have fallen into its power" (*The Actuality of Atonement*, 84).

65. From a quite different angle Moltmann says much the same: "What Jesus commanded in the Sermon on the Mount as love of one's enemies has taken place on the cross through Jesus' dying and the grief of the Father in the power of the spirit, for the godless and the loveless" (*The Crucified God*, 248).

Old Testament but its confirmation by concreteness at Golgotha. It is therefore understandable that the writers of the New Testament, most of whom were Christian Jews, used biblical language of sacrifice, cleansing from sin, redemption, and forgiveness to understand the significance of Jesus' death for believers, for the same God who had provided the sacrificial system also provided Jesus as the definitive, eschatological sacrifice. Even the Letter to Hebrews, which faults the sacrificial system, sees it as a "shadow of the good things to come" (Heb 10:10) and so produces a theological tour de force in which the author takes up one aspect of the cult after another to show how it is surpassed by Christ's death and its benefits, while also insisting that "it is a fearful thing to fall into the hands of the living God" (Heb 10:31, RSV), especially if one repudiates the Son of God after having benefited from his death.

Finally, since the first century Christians saw in Jesus' death/resurrection an eschatological event and not a local enactment of an annually repeated process, their communities produced only holy people, no holy things. Nor did they venerate as holy the places associated with Jesus. Christian Jews apparently continued to observe the Sabbath, and while Christian Gentiles assembled on "the Lord's day" marking Jesus' resurrection, there is no evidence that they regarded it as a new holy day or that they considered the last days of Jesus as Holy Week. While they designated leaders by the "laying on of hands," thereby consecrating them for special tasks, there were no "holy orders" until later. And since they believed Christ was the once-for-all-time sacrifice, they had no altars or priests to make sacrifices. Indeed, one should not overlook the fact that Christians have never developed a sacrifice-oriented cult; to the contrary, wherever Christianity has taken root, blood sacrifices have ceased, abandoned first by Christians. What could repeated sacrifice of animals possibly add to the sacrifice of Christ? For the early Christians the veil of the temple *was* torn, long before it went up in flames.

The Golgotha Hermeneutic

Jesus' death, isolated from neither the life that preceded it nor from his resurrection that followed it, continues to be the prism through which Christian Gentiles must understand both God and themselves. Thereby the Golgotha event, validated by resurrection and symbolized by the cross, generates and nourishes a distinct hermeneutic, a mode and mentality of interpretation whose range, depth, and impact are not static because various persons and groups discern them afresh in one situation after another. This hermeneutic lies at the heart of the perfect tense of Jesus' death. Three diverse aspects of this hermeneutic invite attention here: the significance of the gospels' reliance on the Old Testament in the passion story, the import of Golgotha for "messianism," and the appropriation of the Golgotha event as paradigm and promise.

Scripture's witness after Golgotha.   Since Golgotha, and what immediately led up to it, is the climax of the Jesus story in each canonical gospel, it is not surprising that here the gospels' reliance on scripture is most manifest. For instance, Kee's analysis of Mark 11–16 located 57 quotations and approximately 160 allusions (not all equally evident) and noted that explicit quotations appear at significant points in the narrative.[66] Recent investigations have increased the sizable corpus of detailed studies concerning the use of the Old Testament throughout the gospels.[67] Especially influential were the psalms, primarily those in which a righteous person laments his unjust suffering yet expects ultimate vindication from God (e.g., Pss 22, 31, 41, 69, 140).[68] That this use of scripture generated details in the Golgotha story is clear to virtually all investigators, though they disagree over the extent to which this occurred, as the argument between Crossan and Brown shows (see above, p. 114). There is no reason to expect that the continuing debate will produce a widely accepted consensus.

More important here in any case is pondering the ongoing significance of the phenomenon itself. On the table is much more than critical historiography's capacity to ferret out "what really happened" (and did not happen), important as that may be. At issue here theologically are the validity and significance of the line in the tradition that Paul received and transmitted: that both Christ's death and his resurrection occurred "in accordance with the scriptures" (1 Cor 15:3–4). Though there is no clear evidence that the gospel writers had read Paul, they manifestly wrote their accounts of Jesus from the same perspective.

At this point it is instructive to observe that the gospels rely on two ways of presenting the Golgotha event as the climax of the Jesus story. On the one hand, each gospel accounts for Golgotha by relying on the narrator's reports of

---

66. Kee, "The Function of Scriptural Quotations."

67. See, e.g., Marcus, *The Way of the Lord*; see also his "The Old Testament and the Death of Jesus"; Brown, "The Old Testament Background of the Passion Narratives," in *The Death of the Messiah*, II, 1445–67. Juel explores the way specific Old Testament passages are used in various texts in his *Messianic Exegesis*.

68. See, e.g., Ruppert, *Jesus als der leidende Gerechte?*

the hostility that Jesus aroused and of the plotting against him that this pro-duced.[69] As the story moves to the crescendo, the narrators report the machi-nations under way and Pilate's odd role. However one may judge the historical reliability of each narrator, all of them present a historical explanation of what happened to Jesus. On the other hand, the Synoptics also report Jesus' passion predictions with their note of divine necessity, expressed also in terms of what "is written" about the Son of Man or the Christ. In John, Jesus speaks of his death in connection with his "I am" sayings (e.g., the bread from heaven for the life of the world "is my flesh," 6:51; the good shepherd lays down his life for the sheep, 10:11) and claims that his death is his God-given task (e.g., 10:17–18; 12:27). Thus the theological explanation of Jesus' destiny is traced to Jesus (in Luke, to the resurrected One especially), not to the narrator. These two explanations do not run on parallel tracks, nor do they compete, for the voice of the narrator and the voice of Jesus support each other. Thereby the nar-rator's intelligible historical story is really the visible actualization of what God had purposed and intimated in scripture. Though present in black and white for all who could read, it was not discernible until the Jesus event happened, and even then only he understood it. Indeed, according to Acts, both Peter and Paul explicitly said that those who had moved against Jesus had "acted in igno-rance" (Acts 3:17; 13:27).

It is not difficult to surmise what animated this bold hermeneutic in which a sequence of events, intelligible in its own right as a historical account, is con-strued as the way in which God's predetermined purpose came to pass: the con-viction that Jesus' resurrection validated him as the inaugurator of the New Age, the time of salvation. Since the Holy One of Israel who had resurrected him is the same One who spoke to and through the psalmists and prophets, their words must be consonant with what occurred in the Jesus event, and some of their words were actualized in it. Moreover, here too Acts has both Peter and Paul insist that certain words of David, the archetypal psalmist, apply only to Jesus (Acts 2:25–35; 13:32–37). Above all, in both these sermons and in the

69. In Mark this appears first at 3:6, where the Pharisees, whose displeasure had been noted before (2:6,16,24), responded to a sabbath healing by consulting with the Herodians "how to destroy him." Subsequently the Pharisees' problem with Jesus is noted repeatedly (Mk 3:22; 7:1–3; 8:11; 10:2) but begins to congeal into action only in Jerusalem (11:18, 12:13), where the story becomes less episodic. On the whole, Matthew and Luke follow the same narrative thread. In John, after a sabbath healing, the narrator comments, "Therefore the Jews started persecuting Jesus because he was doing such things on the sabbath" (5:16); see also the narrator's explanations in 5:18; 7:32, 43–46; 10:31; 11:53.

gospels the focus is *not* on the continuity between biblical ideas and the thoughts of Jesus or his apostolic witnesses but on the relation between word and event. This implies that until the event, the word was essentially promise, waiting to be kept—in New Testament idiom, "fulfilled."

That this way of reading scripture differs fundamentally from reading it historically is obvious. Indeed, historical criticism has insisted that all parts of scripture, like any other literature, must be understood in light of the contexts in which and for which they were written. And the more that insistence was heeded, the more it appeared that the gospel writers used scripture arbitrarily, not only lifting passages out of context but also finding them to say what the original authors had not meant to say and probably would not have said. Inevitably, students of the gospels, themselves historical critics, often have explained the gospels' use of the Old Testament as something readily understandable "back then," especially since the Dead Sea Scrolls also interpreted scripture in much the same way. It would be quite unwise to deem the whole historical enterprise as wrong-headed and to think that one can revert to the gospels' way of reading scripture, as if the historical approach to texts had never happened. The error of the historical approach lies in its arrogant assumption that it is the only legitimate way to read the text, thereby inhibiting serious consideration of what the gospels' way of reading scripture implies theologically, especially for Christian Gentiles.

If one can get beyond disdaining the Evangelists' way of using scripture, then it may be possible to discover why what they did is permanently defining and perhaps more important today than in the first century. Like the earliest believers, the Evangelists were either Christian Jews or Christian Gentiles deeply rooted in scripture; for them it was self-evident that the God who validated Jesus was the Holy One of Israel, not a generic deity or any of the other deities known to be worshiped by their gentile neighbors. One can, of course, regard their assumption as a symptom of their provincialism and their conviction that the Holy One of Israel is the one true living God, the creator of all and the ultimate sovereign of all, as sheer religious imperialism. But in thinking this way one should be aware of the consequences, the chief being that then Christianity inexorably becomes a Jesus religion in which the God that Jesus trusted is replaced by a deity whose character is known apart from Jesus on Golgotha. Then the Old Testament, except for those passages calling for "social justice," becomes either an embarrassment or a semireliable sourcebook for reconstructing the historical background. Theologically it becomes a contributor, along with other texts, to a presumably "higher" concept of God, which then becomes the lens through which one looks at Jesus. Now Jesus, no longer the fractured prism through which one peers into the God-Reality and through which that Reality confirms itself, too becomes a contributor to a nobler, less stringent and offensive, idea of God. This way of thinking is just as imperialist as that alleged of the New Testament.

It is in conjunction with this theme that the reflections about Jesus' Jewishness (chap. 2) must be carried forward and pushed deeper, though this setting permits only a few apodictic assertions that point to the agenda. Since Jesus links Gentiles to Israel and to the Holy One of Israel, it follows that Christian theology cannot first construct a concept of God and then relate Jesus to it but rather must commit itself to the arduous task of thinking "God" and the whole "Jesus event" simultaneously and in ways that require each to inform and illumine the other. This is precisely the import of believing Jesus to be the "Son of God," the one who replicates in time the character of the Eternal, the Holy One of Israel, the wholly other.

Not only is it historically the case that Jesus links Christian Gentiles to Israel and to the God who chose it, but their apprehension and comprehension of this God is shaped by the Jesus event as a whole theologically—i.e., is Christomorphic because for them this God is disclosed by the Jesus event. Moreover, in disclosure by event the disclosing event is inseparable from the disclosing and the disclosed as well. This is one reason the significance of Jesus for the Christian understanding of God led unavoidably to the doctrine of the Trinity which formulates tersely the unity of the Disclosed, the Discloser, and the Disclosing without fusion. This reliance on event precludes Christian theology from becoming preoccupied with reflection on or elaboration of Jesus' ideas of the Holy One. Conversely, it requires theology to attend persistently to the disclosing event in order to find there the clue to the vital center of scripture's diverse and complex witness to the Holy One's ways and will. For Christians convinced that Jesus did not simply "rise from the dead" (as if he were a "pagan" deity) but that the Holy One of Israel resurrected him, Golgotha and what led up to it refocused the inherited understandings of Israel's God and redefined Israel's hope. For Christians, Jesus is not the messiah despite Golgotha but because of it, since after Easter it was Golgotha that redefined *messiah*. In retrospect, this may have been the most important result of the Golgotha hermeneutic.

"Messianism" crucified.   Since there is no known Jewish expectation of a resurrected messiah, much less a crucified one, it is evident that the earliest believers in Jesus would not have regarded him as the messiah simply because

they believed he was resurrected. There is simply no inherent connection between resurrection and messiah. They must, therefore, have had some sense that his work was "messianic" during his lifetime, however confused their understanding may have been. The conviction that God had vindicated him by resurrection would then have validated their previous sense of his significance while at the same time restructuring it.

Whether Jesus regarded himself as messiah remains unclear because the evidence is ambiguous.[70] On the one hand, Mark reports that Jesus responded to Peter's "confession" by insisting that the disciples say nothing about this (Mk 8:30); only in Matthew does Jesus clearly affirm what Peter said (Mt 16:17). On the other hand, only in Mark does Jesus reply "Yes!" to the high priest's question "Are you the messiah, the son of the Blessed? (Mk 14:62); in Matthew and Luke, Jesus avoids a clear answer: "You said this." Both reports in Mark reflect the Evangelist's view of how the Jesus story should be told. There is simply no other saying in which Jesus either announces to the public or shares privately with the disciples his conviction that he is the messiah.

Moreover, unless one could know also what *messiah* meant for Jesus, it is not clear what would be gained by knowing that this is who he thought he was or was destined to be. It is all too often forgotten that in his day being "messiah" could imply various roles, that numerous forms of eschatological hope did not mention a messiah at all, and that there was no inherent connection between the kingdom of God and a messiah. There is, to be sure, no a priori reason why Jesus could not have created his own understanding of messiahship in which he blended his role as herald and harbinger of the kingdom with his own sense of the destined suffering of the Son of Man (itself an idea without precedent), as the gospels imply. The historical question, however, is not what he could have done but whether there is adequate evidence that this is what he did. In any event, no gospel contains a saying in which Jesus either asserted or explained the connection between embodying the impingement of God's reign and messiah or between his impending suffering as the Son of Man and his subsequent role as either witness or judge at the Great Assize.

For the early Christians, Jesus was not the God-sent eschatological figure because he claimed to be the messiah; rather, because the resurrection disclosed him to be the eschatological figure, they saw him as the messiah, as well as other figures such as the prophet promised to Moses (Dt 18:15), because by definition all valid expectations must have pointed to the one whom God vin-

70. See de Jonge, *God's Final Envoy*, chap. 8.

dicated in a definitive way. At the same time, the distinctive traits of Jesus' message and mission, capped by his execution, precluded simply identifying him as the Davidic (royal) messiah and required instead transforming the concept messiah so that it was consistent with the kind of person Jesus was. For Christians, Jesus was the expected messiah, then, but not the sort of messiah that was expected.

Remembering these well-known considerations leads to the main point here: Believing that Jesus is the messiah was from the start distinguished from *messianism* — the belief that through a specific historical person God will actualize the destined future by liberating the people from domination by Gentiles and rule a Zion-centered theocracy. This perspective does, however, surface as the millennial reign of Christ in the late first century anti-Roman Apocalypse of John (Rv 19:11–20:5). It was the restructured understanding of *messiah* and *king* that allowed the Evangelists to report that, ironically, Jesus was mocked and crucified as "king," for they were convinced that what was then a hideously cruel joke would ultimately prove to be true, albeit in a transformed sense. They did not eschew reporting Jesus' entry into Jerusalem, with its tacit royal symbolism, because for them this event was not Jesus' appropriation of first-century messianism but an act that presaged Jesus' eschatological "reign" of a different sort. Luke probably makes explicit what the other Synoptics assumed — that Jesus-inspired messianism was as wrong before the crucifixion (Lk 24:21–27) as it was inappropriate after the resurrection (Acts 1:6–8). In effect, messianism was crucified but — apart from the Johannine apocalypse — not validated by resurrection.

After Golgotha, in other words, it should be clear to Christians that precisely *Jesus'* messiahship disallows fundamentally all messianisms promising to effect or catalyze, by means of human political power, the establishment of God's rule for humanity and that it exposes all messiahs as spurious "pretenders to the throne" even if for a spell they succeed in rectifying intolerable abuses. For Christians and those influenced by the Christian heritage, the Golgotha/Easter Jesus should have ended messianism as effectively as he did animal sacrifice. Logically, the end of both is part of the perfect tense of Golgotha and its hermeneutic.

Golgotha appropriated.   If anything in the Christian tradition epitomizes the distinctive, ongoing significance of Jesus' crucifixion, it is the appropriation of the cross as a protean symbol of a way of life. From the initial years of Christianity until now this symbol has generated multifaceted patterns of living and giving; it has also nurtured remarkable attitudes toward suffering and death, including martyrdom. An adequate history of this moral appropriation of the cross still remains to be written. Here it will suffice simply to call attention to the role of Jesus' cross as both paradigm and promise. The unity of these distinguishable aspects is expressed in the words of Jesus that Mark assembled and appended to the story of the sharp exchange between Jesus and Peter following the first passion prediction: (a) "If any want to become my followers, let them deny themselves and take up their cross [Luke adds "daily"] and follow me. (b) For those who want to save their life will lose it, and those who lose their life for my sake, and for the sake of the gospel, will save it" (Mk 8:34–35).[71]

The paradigmatic role of the cross is manifest in the first saying, where it is used as a vivid symbol of the self-denial that following Jesus requires. The second saying shows that this self-denial is not simply self-deprivation (though that may be the result); it is rather a No! to the persistent primacy of self-preservation as one's leitmotiv. That is why the Revised English Bible translates aptly "renounce self" instead of "lose . . . life." The first saying also assumes that this self-denial was the defining moral characteristic that took Jesus to the cross. The saying does not call on would-be disciples to follow Jesus to *his* cross in order to die with him.[72]

These sayings imply that while Jesus' cross was uniquely his, it was not something that brutally intruded into his life; they imply instead that it disclosed his life's defining quality and that this was not to be uniquely his. To be a follower, then, entails more than appropriating his ideas and heeding his words; it requires also his way of being in the world—a way in which the primary opponent to be overcome is not an external enemy, as in messianism, but a power internal to the self. Jesus' death as a ransom (Mk 10:45) does not free his followers from struggling with the same drive toward self-preservation above all that he too had contended with, but it does assure them that they will indeed "find" exactly what they "lost"—life. In other words, the "ransomed" ones cannot expect a better cost-benefit ratio than can the "ransomer," whether or not

71. Mt 16:25 and Lk 9:25 follow Mark but omit "and for the sake of the gospel." To these sayings Mark added three others as well (8:36–9:1). Varying expressions of the same motifs of cross/discipleship and saving/finding are found also in Mt 10:38–39; Lk 14:27; 17:33; Jn 12:25.

72. In fact, none of the three passion predictions (except for the change made in Mt 20:19) specifies that Jesus will be killed by crucifixion. This suggests that the reference to taking up one's own cross is a Christian addition that correctly brings out the meaning of following Jesus—the self-denial that Jesus talked about and that according to Mk 14:36 he later struggled to maintain in Gethsemane.

they are put to death for following him, because "the disciple is not above the teacher, nor a slave above the master; it is enough for the disciple to be like the teacher, and the slave like the master" (Mt 10:24–25; cf. Lk 6:40; Jn 13:16; 15:20). Following Jesus puts the followers on his path, his way of embodying the coming of God's kingdom; it may take the form of unabridged obedience to God that makes one vulnerable to unjust suffering or of nonreciprocal love for neighbor in accord with the God who sends sun and rain on the just and unjust —not because God is morally indifferent but because God is different. This nonreciprocal love produced Jesus' much-celebrated solidarity with the poor and marginalized for their sake, designed to elicit their Godward turn toward the coming kingdom. Had it been a way of demonstrating his empathy with their plight, it would have been for his sake, not theirs, and he would have "had his reward." In short, seen as a paradigm, Jesus' cross symbolizes a way of life marked by love free of self-regard and the need for approbation for doing good because one relies on the "Father who sees in secret" to give the reward in due course (Mt 6:1–4). As a symbol of embodied love for others, the cross is not a calculable strategy for attaining happiness through good deeds that may cost suffering, though suffering love can bring its own joy that, like peace, "passes understanding."

The second Markan saying begins with "For," signaling that it provides the warrant for the call to follow Jesus by taking up one's own "cross." This warrant is expressed as a paradox whose first part is typically sapiential; it is a general truth whose applicability is not restricted and so functions as an open-ended warning that distills astute observation: "Those who want to save their life will lose it." The second part is more complex, for instead of saying simply "Those who lose their life will find it," it restricts the promise to those who lose life "for my sake and the gospel."[73] (The conclusion of the next chapter will return to the theme of "for Jesus' sake.") The Markan version takes into account what

---

73. The saying has been transmitted in various formulations, Lk 17:33 being the shortest and most rhetorically balanced. It follows the warning "Remember Lot's wife," who was turned to a pillar of salt when she looked back at Sodom and Gomorrah (Gn 19:26). The Lukan version reads: "Whoever seeks to preserve his life will lose it / and whoever loses his life will gain it" (REB). In Mt 10:39 and Lk 9:24 (parallel to Mk 8:35) the saying reads as follows: "Whoever gains his life will lose it; / whoever loses his life for my sake will gain it" (REB). In Mk 8:35 it reads: "Whoever wants to save his life will lose it, / but whoever loses his life for my sake and the gospel's will save it" (REB). Jn 12:25 has it as follows: "Whoever loves himself is lost, / but he who hates himself in this world will be kept safe for eternal life" (REB).

many early Christians experienced because of their faith in Jesus: loss of status, broken family ties, harassment, persecution. Important, then, is what is in view here: "losing" one's life voluntarily, as the price one willingly pays in order to be a Christian. It is this freely assumed suffering for the sake of Jesus, and the promised life that results, that is the warrant for following Jesus, according to this passage. The text implies that just as Jesus voluntarily took up his cross, so the disciples are to take up their "cross"; the text implies also that they, like Jesus, will find "life"—not only life beyond death but true life in the midst of mortal existence and suffering. The ongoing meaning of Jesus' cross for the disciples, its perfect tense, could hardly be expressed more trenchantly.

Understandably, this paradoxical promise of the cross has been extended so that it pertains also to other forms of self-denial and undeserved suffering,[74] especially those that are assumed voluntarily for the benefit of someone else. Such forms of suffering too are forms of "cross bearing."[75] But the promise of the cross pertains also to those situations in which one suffers because someone else has brought it about, whether deliberately (as in torture) or unintentionally (e.g., the result of someone's error or deceit). In such situations one sometimes discovers the paradoxical promise of the cross, which can take many forms. For example, the cross promises that the resentment and rage of the sufferer need not be denied or repressed, since according to Mark, Jesus too shouted his frustration into the face of God. Moreover, if despite Jesus' own sense of abandonment God was present in that horrid void, then one can trust that God is somehow present even when consciousness of God has disappeared. The point is that the cross does not promise explanations but a way of understanding that can release power to persevere and to hope because it is a definitive precedent validated by the God whom Jesus, even in his sense of abandonment, dared to call "My God, my God."

74. Here it is not necessary to discuss how one determines whether or to what extent suffering is undeserved, or who decides it.

75. Christians should ponder Borowitz's trenchant observation: "to Jews, Christians and their churches have not, do not, and are not likely to care as much for others as they care for themselves, their institutions or their fellow Christians, much less to deny themselves for others or, as the Christ did, to sacrifice themselves for them. They surely have not sacrificed themselves for us. The notion of the Christian cross-bearing seems to us to die the death of 'a thousand qualifications.' By the time Christian teachers are done explaining what it means to take up one's cross and suffer with the Christ one seems only to be authorized to consider it a virtue to endure one's bourgeois troubles. Kierkegaard, for all his lacerating attacks on the self-satisfied Christianity of his time, managed to combine being a knight of faith with living as a Copenhagen dandy" ("Gustafson," 134).

There are, tragically, also many situations of mass, not only individual, suffering that mark existence, animal as well as human, and the fact of suffering itself. Some of this is so severe, inescapable, and relentless that it defies all understanding. In the face of suffering of such magnitude, those who nonetheless look to the cross for a clue may well find it epitomizing both humanity's protest against this misery (and what produced it, much of it the consequences of humanity's self-inflicted torture, otherwise called sin) and the moral pressure on God to rectify—to make the kingdom actual. That too is a sign of faith.

CHAPTER FIVE

The Authorizing Judge
Jesus in the Moral Life

Critics of Christianity have seldom faulted Christians for being disciples of Jesus "but rather reproached them with *not* being his disciples, with betraying his cause."[1] Machovec's astute observation points to a remarkable phenomenon—that precisely in the modern era, marked in part by vehement repudiations of Christianity, Jesus has become an essential part of the conscience of Western culture. What he taught and how he lived it elicits acknowledgment that "he was onto something" so perennially true that repeatedly it has been capable of energizing passionate commitments to transform what is into what ought to be, whether the propensity of the human heart or unjust structures of society. Indeed, acknowledging the towering moral stature of Jesus often goes hand in hand with denigrating his Christian followers for domesticating his radical insights, whether because they did not understand him or because they did. Even so, the fact that those who have no intention of becoming part of the Christian community nonetheless expect Christians to live up to the teaching and example of Jesus shows that they regard him as the criterion, the norm, to which his followers are accountable, and in so doing they too acknowledge his moral stature. Jesus remains the focal point of Christian thought, mode of life, and devotion, but in one way or other wherever he is known he looks over everyone's shoulder. This phenomenon deserves far more attention and close analysis, but not here. Though the theme now is the role of Jesus in the moral lives of those in the Christian community, the horizon is also wider than that because his influence is much wider.

The term *moral life* is a convenient though somewhat unsatisfactory way of avoiding less appropriate language for the subject matter of this essay, namely morality and ethics. As used here, the moral life is not a compartment along-

1. Machovec, *A Marxist Looks at Jesus*, 194.

side economic, political, or religious life; it refers rather to what one values deeply enough to live by and, if necessary, suffer and die for because one is convinced that it is both right and true. The moral life is both broader and deeper than morality (patterned behavior) or morals (actions deemed right by a community), for it has to do with the sort of person one is (the doer) as well as with the grounding of what is to be done or not done (the deed). To speak of the moral life is to draw attention to one's responsibility, however circumscribed, for the shape of one's life, including what one allows and refuses to allow to influence it. Also, the moral life is more than decision making, for it has to do with what becomes habitual and so exposes one's character. It refers to life actually lived, whereas the word *morality*, being an abstract noun, signals that the subject matter has been detached from life so that it can be analyzed as a self-consistent whole. To reflect on Jesus' role in the moral life, therefore, is to reflect on his impact on the way life is lived when it is open to his influence.

Reflection on Jesus' role in the moral life is to be distinguished also from *ethics*, though the word has come to be used in so many ways that it is not easy to know what it does not include. In common parlance, *ethics* is used broadly to refer to the content of the good, to right or appropriate behavior (including standards of conduct, as in *professional ethics*), and to the critical disciplined reflection on that content and the reasons adduced as its warrant, including reflection on the reasoning by which one determines or detects that warrant. Obviously, ethics as content and ethics as reflection on it are distinguishable but not separable, and both aspects have deep roots in philosophy and theology. Because *ethics* often refers to behavior that is approved and advocated, it has become common to speak of Jesus' ethics or of his "ethical teachings" (e.g., teachings that pertain to right behavior); strictly speaking, however, he did not teach ethics (critical reflection on right behavior). His teaching did, to be sure, pertain to the moral life in light of the impinging kingdom of God. Even so, what is in view here is not limited to what he said but includes also what he did and the kind of person he was. Since it is that whole complex, and not just his teachings, that forms and informs the moral life of his followers, one can refer to his role in the moral life as a *Jesus ethic* but not as Jesus' ethics.

The impact of Jesus on the moral life can be explored from many directions. For example, a quarter-century ago James M. Gustafson published a major work in Christian theological ethics titled *Christ and the Moral Life*.[2] In it he

2. For a discussion of Gustafson's work, see Borowitz, "Gustafson."

discussed a wide range of Christian thinkers as he explored the following topics: Christ as the Lord who is the Creator and Redeemer, the Sanctifier, the Justifier, the Pattern, and the Teacher. Whereas his rewarding book discussed the role of Christology in shaping the moral life, this chapter's subject matter is more limited, for it concentrates primary attention on the ongoing impact—the perfect tense—of the man from Nazareth. To understand his role in the moral life one must go beyond analyzing his ethics.

It is appropriate to characterize the multidimensional impact of Jesus on the moral life as that of the authorizing judge. Both words are essential. The term *authorizing* points to Jesus' role in legitimating the valuing, affirming, striving, doing, avoiding, and hoping that mark the moral life. The authorizing role fits the subject matter better than the noun *authority*, which carries a good deal of unnecessary freight. The word *judge* is used partly because it invites considering Jesus' role as the norm and partly because it is rarely used in connection with Jesus. In fact, although Sunday after Sunday many congregations say the Apostles' Creed, which includes the line "he shall come to judge the living and the dead," the theme of the Last Judgment has virtually disappeared from much current Christian thought and ethics. This has resulted in a gross impoverishment of discourse about the moral life, as well as a serious abbreviation of the role of Jesus in that life and in the discourse about it. This essay, however, is concerned primarily with Jesus' present role as judge.

Since this discussion focuses on Jesus' role in the moral life and not on his words about it, the first step is to make clear the distinction between talk of Jesus' ethics and reflection on his role in the moral life, here called a Jesus ethic. This will prepare the way for considering Jesus as the authorizing Judge. The chapter will conclude by taking account of a more indirect warrant, one rarely explored: "For the sake of Jesus."

Beyond Jesus' Ethics

For many, ethics is Jesus' most impressive legacy. This is the view of those who respect him but disdain organized Christianity but also of those liberal Christians for whom "Jesus taught us how to live" suffices as a credo. Such a view can be affirmed without, however, accepting it as an adequate way of expressing his significance for the moral life of those who follow him, be it closely or at a distance, because he is more than a teacher of a way of life. That significance takes us beyond what he said and not around it. Nonetheless, it is prudent to examine first Jesus' way of addressing the moral life; that will prompt a consideration of the problems created by speaking of what he said as his ethics, which will then lead to a discussion of a Jesus ethic.

Jesus' stance toward the moral life. Because this discussion builds on what was said about Jesus the Teacher in chapter 3, it is appropriate to recall Sanders's observation that "new ages by definition alter the present."[3] Accordingly, Jesus was convinced that those who accepted his message—that the imminent kingdom of God was already impinging on the present—were both challenged and enabled to live out of the future. Whoever did so was, as Wilder noted, "a self profoundly altered."[4] Living out of the future means living now by what is not yet manifest but impending; as a result one is out of step with those elements in the present that are destined to be abandoned or changed when the kingdom is manifestly here. The eye of the profoundly altered self sees a profoundly altered world not yet visible to those not grasped by the kingdom's coming. Jesus' stance toward the moral life, including his own, is rooted so deeply in such a perception of reality that he cannot be understood apart from it. Conversely, where this overpowering sense of reality is given full weight, the remarkable features of Jesus' posture become more intelligible, though not less demanding—nor less offensive, even for those who are attracted to his way.

The most offensive aspect of Jesus' stance, especially in an era given to emphasizing pluralism's effect of relativizing both conviction and action, is its uncompromising absoluteness, reflecting his unqualified conviction that God's sovereign rule is on the verge of being actualized as never before. For him, the moral life therefore is exposed to the will, character, and power of God in a decisive way that he embodied at the kingdom's dawn. Consequently the will, character, and power of God were more the moral life's immediate warrant than merely its ultimate logical ground. The impingement of God's rectifying rule puts everything on the scale now. Jesus does not empathize with those who, for whatever reason, cannot see the import of his lifework. They know how to look at the sky and predict the weather, but he asks, "Why do you not know how to interpret the present time?" (Lk 12:54–56; Mt 16:2–3). Given Jesus' audacity, it is understandable that the doubters want a "sign" that he really speaks for God, but instead of helping them make the transition from doubt to faith he denounces them: "This generation is an evil generation; it asks for a sign, but no sign will be given it except the sign of Jonah" (Lk 11:29). He condemns Chorazin and Bethsaida for not repenting, despite his wondrous

3. E. P. Sanders, *Jesus and Judaism*, 16.
4. See p. 79.

works there, and even Capernaum (his adopted town) "will be brought down to Hades" (Mt 11:20–24; Lk 10:13–15 [Q]).[5]

What the kingdom's impingement requires is total resolve and unhesitating commitment, comparable to a man who sells everything to buy a field in which he had found a treasure or the pearl merchant who sold everything to buy the one pearl of great value (Mt 13:44–46). Ordinary family obligations are to be ignored (Lk 9:57–62). Jesus did not acknowledge the need to find a middle way between conflicting values; to the contrary, "No one can serve two masters; for a slave will either hate the one and love the other, or be devoted to the one and despise the other. You cannot serve God and wealth [mammon]" (Mt 6:24; Lk 16:13; [Q]). He rejects divorce without any allowance for mitigating circumstances (Mk 10:1–12; Mt 19:9 allows it if "unchastity" is involved). Jesus appears to assume that any appeal to exceptional circumstances is an attempt to evade a completely unambiguous resolve to do the absolute will of God, whose reign is at hand. Never did he reason, "If this is the case, then . . . ; but should that be the case, then. . . ." Nor is there any room for a sense of moral achievement. To the contrary, "when you have done all that you were ordered to do, say, 'We are worthless slaves; we have done only what we ought to have done'" (Lk 17:7–10).

Moreover, Jesus assumed that his hearers could do what he required in the name of the kingdom. Paul wrestled with the contradiction between willing to do the good and not being able to (Rom 7:13–25), but in the teaching of Jesus there is not even a hint of such a dilemma. For Jesus, the inherited structures and patterns of life were not the givens to which the kingdom's import must be adjusted in order to be "workable," because by definition the kingdom so re-creates reality for those grasped by it that what was not possible before is now within reach and mandatory. The Godward-turned life attuned to the kingly rule of God is no longer governed by the extant habits of reciprocity (loving those who love you) but by the character of the God who sends sun and rain on the unrighteous as well as on the righteous. New wine must have new containers (Mk 2:22). The conclusion is now unavoidable: "Be perfect, therefore, as your heavenly Father is perfect" (Mt 5:48; Lk 6:36 has "merciful").[6] Even if

---

5. Allison observes that what offended people was not Jesus' inclusiveness but his exclusiveness, for he linked salvation to himself and his mission ("Jesus and the Covenant," 72).

6. "Perfect" (*teleios*) probably means whole, complete, uncompromised, not the perfection of an ideal. See Davies and Allison, *Matthew*, I, 561–66. Betz suggests that "be" (*esesthe*) is deliberately ambiguous, combining the various possible meanings: imperative, prediction, and eschatological promise (*The Sermon on the Mount*, 321).

this is Matthew's own formulation, it expresses the point aptly: the unqualified, complete, goodness of God mandates corresponding unqualified goodness because the kingly rule of the "perfect" God is at hand. There is no room here for the *Didache's* concession: "For if you can bear the whole yoke of the Lord, you shall be perfect; but if you cannot, do what you can" (*Did.* 6.2).[7]

At the same time, what the kingdom's impingement demands and makes possible is neither inevitable nor natural, for Jesus is quite aware that the self does not abandon its old ways easily. He rebukes the disciples for resenting the parents for bringing their children to be touched by Jesus; he not only pointed out that "it is to such as these that the kingdom of God belongs" but "took them up in his arms, laid his hands on them, and blessed them" (Mk 10:13–16). When two of his closest followers ask for places of honor, they show their need to be told that "whoever wishes to become great among you must be your servant, and whoever wishes to be first among you must be slave of all" (Mk 10:35–44). He encourages his hearers to believe that God will indeed answer their prayers by pointing out, "If you, then, who are evil, know how to give good gifts to your children, how much more will your Father in heaven give good things [Lk: the Holy Spirit] to those who ask him?" (Mt 7:9–11; Lk 11:11–13). He warns against seeing the speck in the neighbor's eye while ignoring the log in one's own (Mt 7:3–5; Lk 6:41–42). If one peruses the sayings of Jesus, one sees his spotlight shine on one aspect of village life after another, revealing the kingdom's alternatives to entrenched customs and habits of mind with regard to religious practices, lending money, hospitality, personal insult, oath taking, and charity—to name but a few. He reminds people that the deed expresses the self (the heart) and warns that an evil heart can no more produce good deeds than a thorn bush can produce figs (Lk 6:43–45). Given this realism about the human heart, it is understandable that Jesus insists not only that forgiveness is essential but also that those forgiven by God must forgive each other.

Jesus had a purpose, but he did not have a program, an agenda for reform, for improving the life of the villagers. Nor did he, as did the Old Testament prophets, address those in power, calling on them to ameliorate the lot of the impoverished or advocating changes in the land tenure system. In fact, the more one examines what he said and did not say (or assume) about the moral life, the clearer it becomes that what he taught should not be called ethics.

7. *Didachē* (Greek for teaching) abbreviates the full title, "Teaching of the Twelve Apostles," found in 1883. Probably written at the end of the first or beginning of the second century, it contains various admonitions, an early church order, and a brief apocalyptic section.

On talking of Jesus' ethics.   Before considering some reasons why talking of Jesus' ethics is inadequate, it is important to emphasize that many of
Jesus' teachings *can* be analyzed and interpreted by relying on some modes
of discourse used in the discipline of ethics. For example, a saying that com-
mends or commands a given action can be analyzed in terms of its warrant
and, if included, its sanction (as noted on p. 79, n. 44). Likewise, one can
inquire about the extent to which what Jesus calls for is closer to a deonto-
logical ethic, emphasizing what must be done, or a prudential ethic, accenting the wiser course of action in light of the result. Such categories are useful
heuristic tools for exposing the reasoning built into Jesus' teaching about
behavior. Likewise, it is often instructive to use modes of analysis derived
from sociology and anthropology to discern the social location of both Jesus'
words and the (assumed) attitudes of those addressed, particularly what they
took for granted.[8] Fruitful as the results of such work may be, however, it
would be illusory to think that what they bring into view is Jesus' ethics. That
is because the subject matter itself resists being called ethics.

This resistance is evident in what is absent from Jesus' teachings as well as
what is present (the content). They contain no disciplined reflection on the
nature and ground of the good or the just and their opposites; this is hardly
surprising since such analyses are rooted in the abstract reasoning developed
in the Greek philosophical tradition, from which Jesus' mentality was far
removed. Jesus did not analyze; he addressed. In this regard he was indeed
more like a Cynic-Stoic than a philosopher such as Plato or Aristotle. Since
the content of his teaching about good and bad behavior was not derived
from a general, universal principle as was the ethics of Kant, for example, he
did not explain how his various admonitions and imperatives are related to
each other or how they flow from a root principle—both of which are called
for as soon as one speaks of someone's ethics (and not simply of one's morality or morals). Students interested in Jesus' teachings have, nonetheless, not
hesitated to identify just such a root principle, often said to be love, doubtless
prompted to do so by the double command to love God and neighbor.
Because Jesus actually said little about love, and nothing at all about God's
love for humans,[9] locating love as the principle from which Jesus' ethics are
derived shows clearly enough that it is the ethics-minded interpreter who
makes this move in order to give coherence to the diverse and often divergent

8. In *Biblical Social Values* Pilch and Malina make available succinct and nontechni-
cal discussions of, for example, compassion, honor and shame, parenting, pity.

9. Noted by Knox, *The Ethic of Jesus*, 19.

sayings. In effect, one thereby creates Jesus' ethics for him, as if compensating for what he had overlooked.

That *ethics* is a mischievous word for Jesus' teaching about behavior is shown also by the consequences of dissolving the concreteness and particularity into a principle. On the one hand, the portrayal of Jesus is distorted. For instance, by ignoring the fact that according to the gospels, Jesus articulated the double love command as a specific reply to a question,[10] one can treat it as a fundamental theme or principle that governs all his sayings, even though there is no evidence that he ever brought up the subject voluntarily or made it the theme of his public preaching. (Positing a unifying principle or perspective in Jesus' teachings is not wrong, of course. Indeed, as chapter 3 indicated, that is precisely what occurs when one sees the kingdom of God as the overarching theme of Jesus' mission. But one must never lose sight of the fact that it is the interpreter who is doing the unifying.) More important, regarding Jesus' teachings as ethics based on a root principle makes it all the easier to downplay or ignore his thorough Jewishness, including the apocalyptic character of his thinking. On the other hand, the more his teachings are regarded as ethics, the easier it is to treat them as a generally valid code of conduct, or as rules that can then be "applied" by astute reason. Thereby a corpus of discrete individuated glimpses into what responding to the new reality of the kingdom requires is transformed into a new law, one purged of the intense eschatological horizon in light of which Jesus' specific commands made concrete the appropriate responses to God's gracious gift in bringing the kingdom into the distorted present.

Another undesirable consequence of speaking about Jesus' teachings as ethics is that it so concentrates attention on the deed that it neglects unduly the doer, thereby distorting Jesus' own emphasis on the latter. Did not Jesus shift the focus from the deed to the doer when he suggested that adultery occurs in the lustful heart before it occurs in the bed (Mt 5:28)? Moreover, the saying appears to be "unethical" in one of two ways: it either falls below ethics (teaching the right thing to do) by ignoring the difference between a desire not realized and one that is, or it rises above it by tacitly requiring the doer to be so thoroughly transformed that the question of adultery does not even arise.

Another point is that a good deal of ethics concentrates attention on making difficult choices—sometimes between conflicting goods and sometimes

10. According to Mark, a scribe asks, "Which commandment is the first of all?" (Mk 12:28). In Matthew a lawyer asks the question in order to test Jesus (Mt 22:35). In Luke a lawyer with the same motive asks what he must do to inherit eternal life (Lk 10:25).

between unavoidable evils, and usually between shades of gray. Therefore ethics accents the reasoning by which one arrives at an intelligible, justifiable course of action that takes account of circumstances as well as foreseeable consequences. It also accepts as given that often one value must be compromised in order to adhere to another. Some ethicists also claim that "middle axioms"[11] are needed if one is to avoid either fanaticism or despair. None of this—the very stuff of ethics as commonly taught—comports with Jesus' teachings, characterized by a relentless either/or, leaving no room to negotiate and offering no guidance whatever for paddling through the white water of difficult choices. The result of insisting nonetheless on talking of Jesus' ethics is not hard to comprehend: They are turned swiftly into ideals to be borne in mind or are regarded as emergency measures required for, and valid in, the brief interval before the kingdom's arrival (Schweitzer's "interim ethics") or are put in escrow until the kingdom has actually arrived. It is as ironic as it is inevitable that each of these views generates its own "interim ethics" for life in the meantime "in the real world."[12]

Finally, speaking of Jesus' ethics tends to separate the message from the man. The more this occurs, the more his role as the "bearer of the word" (Bultmann's phrase) overshadows his role as its embodiment in his life as a particular, distinct, Galilean Jewish person. Consequently it discourages serious attention to the fact that the bearer of the word also made himself the model for those who responded positively to him. But Jesus' role in the moral life of the disciple cannot be understood apart from loyalty to him as a person.

The moral power of the person.   Shifting the discourse from Jesus' ethics to the figure of Jesus is neither a way of avoiding the difficulties of speaking about the coherence of his ad hoc teachings nor a way of resolving them; it does, however, provide a different way of thinking about them because it gives due weight to the role of Jesus, the herald and harbinger of the kingdom, in shaping the life of those committed to him.

11. It was John C. Bennett who argued for "middle axioms" as a way of moving from the absolute principle, like love, to specific programs that included legislation and political strategy. They are said to provide guidance for judging decision making by appealing to common moral convictions that Christians share with non-Christians. For a brief summary, see Gustafson, *Christ and the Moral Life*, 231; a somewhat fuller, though less lucid, account is offered by Lehman, *Ethics in a Christian Context*, 148.

12. Hiers, reflecting on the results of his analysis of the treatment of Jesus' ethics by Harnack, Schweitzer, Bultmann, and Dodd, notes that actually "all ethics are interim ethics" (*Jesus and Ethics*, 166).

Although the distinction between emphasizing Jesus' teaching about the moral life and accenting the role of the figure of Jesus is important, it is not absolute. He did, after all, have a good deal to say about the kingdom's impingement on the moral life. Being alert to the problems generated by talking about his ethics does not lead to downplaying what he said in order to play up his style of life. The ethics of Jesus and the Jesus ethic have similar formal features: both create and shape those who look to Jesus; both can energize his adherents; both elicit loyalty as well as risk disloyalty. Materially, however, they shape the moral life differently. Unfortunately, a thorough phenomenological analysis remains to be done. In this context, however, three elemental considerations must suffice.

First of all, the nature of the moral life calls for more than attending to Jesus' teachings about what is and is not to be done, important though they are. The moral life is more than choosing and more than knowing what to choose and how to choose it, for neither the quality, shape, or direction of the self is determined decisively by deciding, even though Bultmann thought it was. The moral life is also, if not chiefly, the result of one's responses to what is not chosen at all but occurs nonetheless, sometimes making choice a luxury. In any case, the moral life pertains to the doer before it pertains to the deed, and the doer has a history that he or she brings to every deed, the neglected and rejected deed no less than the chosen one. Moreover, the moral life is forged by the interactions (and often by lack of interaction) between persons more than by resolute application of carefully considered teachings, principles, or ideals; indeed, characteristically it is from persons that one learns these things, and it is from wise persons that one learns how they actually function in one circumstance after another. In this light, it is not only Jesus' teachings about right behavior that shape the follower's moral life but especially Jesus' demeanor, his way of responding to situations, his way of being engaged, that determines the kind of influence he has. The Evangelists often provided the settings for Jesus' sayings, not simply because they wanted to create a more vivid narrative but also because they sensed that the sayings' impact is enhanced if one encounters them as Jesus' particular response in a particular situation rather than as disembodied teaching. Even in Matthew the five discourses, created by assembling the words of Jesus pertaining to a particular theme, are given narrative settings (4:23–25; 10:1–4; 13:1–2; 18:1–4; 24:1–2).[13] In short, it is Jesus' life, captivated by the kingdom, that endows his teaching with moral power.

13. If the last discourse includes chapter 23, then the setting for the whole is provided briefly in 22:46.

What Klausner said about the secret of Jesus' influence merits attention still, however one may assess his views that Jesus' ideals, surpassing those of Hillel, were beyond reach of ordinary mortals and that unlike Judaism ("an all-embracing, all-inclusive political-national social culture") Jesus had no interest in such matters.[14] For Klausner, the key is in the combination of Jesus' methods of teaching (especially parables and epigrams) and his complex personality, marked by "many and amazing contradictions": Though tender and tolerant, he was also "utterly unbending . . . and reproving"; he understood life as it really was yet was "a most unworldly visionary in his belief in the supernatural." Indeed, "the contradictory traits in his character, its positive and negative aspects, his harshness and his gentleness, his clear vision combined with his cloudy visionariness—all these united to make him a force and an influence, for which history has never yet afforded a parallel."[15] Though few today would agree with all of this, Klausner saw something important: It is Jesus himself—a real person whose passionate commitment to God's impending reign did not make him a one-dimensional figure but released logically contradictory traits in response to specific situations—who suffused his teachings with enduring power in the moral life of those attracted to him.[16] Indeed, it is precisely his teachings' rootedness in this thoroughly human, many-sided life that still makes him credible even when difficult to understand, and that draws the fascinated into his orbit. It is the evocative power of a lived life, not only of pungent sayings or alleged principles, that elicits a loyalty sufficiently persistent to put one's life under his aegis.

This leads to a second, related, reason why Jesus, and not his teachings alone, is the shaper of the moral life: Jesus is not a construct but a historical event. This is as important for the moral life as his true humanity is for Christology, and for two reasons at least: The integrity of the past must be respected because its pastness makes it different, and it is precisely the different that has the capacity to shape the present. These rather abstract dicta must now be made concrete with regard to Jesus. The integrity of the past that is different refers in this context to a major achievement of the historical study of Jesus: He was a pre-70 Galilean Jew deeply rooted in the religion-shaped culture of his people—a culture that, whatever its legacy to subsequent generations, is now alien and irretrievable. When all the limits of the historical critical method, the conditionedness of the historian, and the ambiguities of "history" have been

14. Klausner, *Jesus of Nazareth*, 392–97.

15. Ibid., 408–11.

16. See also J. T. Sanders's similar comments, p. 17 above.

duly acknowledged, it remains the case that Jesus was who he was, did what he did, and said what he said, which are not what moderns and postmoderns wish he had been, done, or said. That otherness of Jesus, whether it be his attitude toward Gentiles (noted in chapter 2) or the "contradictions" noted by Klausner, must be respected.

To respect the past in its otherness is to sit patiently before it, to be open to its own vision of reality, instead of rushing to say what it really was by marshaling data that document what theory decrees must surely have been the case. In recent years that segment of the past called the Jesus event has become as much the victim of theory, especially about the peasant class to which he has been assigned, as he formerly was of church dogma which decreed what he must have been. While theory can indeed be a useful resource for interpreting data, all too often it gains control over the past instead of exposing its otherness. And absent this otherness there is little sense of wonder or bafflement. To respect the Jesus who was, fragmentary though knowledge of his history may be, is to acknowledge the mystery of his strangeness and the resistance of his complex lived life to "explanation." True as it is that no two people have exactly the same image of the Jesus who was, it is equally true that because he was an event in history he is a "fact" that must be reckoned with and whose very otherness repeatedly asserts itself if one allows it to.[17] Only the Jesus who is other, different, intriguing, frustrating, fascinating can change what one already is. A Jesus who is like the self only reinforces what is already in place. And changing the self is precisely what his role in the moral life is all about.

The third consideration is of a somewhat different kind—namely, the shaping role of Jesus is consonant with the biographical character of the canonical gospels, including John. That they are like ancient biographies of community or tradition founders,[18] not like modern biographies, does not affect significantly the important point here: They do narrate the story of Jesus' mission and execution, thereby anchoring the sayings of Jesus in the portrayal of his life and character. This distinguishes them decisively from all those gospels that consist of Jesus' teachings alone, such as the *Gospel of Thomas*, and from Q as well, even though it included the story of Jesus' temp-

17. What C. S. Lewis said about art applies also to history: "The first demand any work of art makes upon us is surrender. Look. Listen. Receive. Get yourself out of the way" (quoted by Westphal, *God, Guilt, and Death*, 133).

18. For a recent, thorough analysis of the canonical gospels in light of ancient "lives" (*bioi*), see Burridge, *What Are the Gospels?*

tations.[19] Such collections of Jesus' teachings did, of course, imply a certain devotion to Jesus, but it was to him as an astute teacher of truths; following him was concentrated on living out his insights (or revealed gnosis) rather than following the precedent of a lived life, even if it is assumed that he had lived as he taught. In any case, when the creators of Matthew and Luke incorporated Q into their revisions of Mark, they tacitly insisted that the teachings can be understood rightly only when they are the words of one whose way led to the cross, that is, when they are part of a story portraying a person. As Stanley Hauerwas, commenting on Augustine's *Confessions*, notes, "the only form which can exhibit an action without pretending to explain it is . . . narrative."[20]

The Judge Who Authorizes

The roles of Jesus as the authorizer and as judge are distinguishable but not divisible into opposites; the one is the obverse of the other. True, building on the New Testament, the creeds speak of Jesus Christ's coming "to judge the quick and the dead," not of Jesus of Nazareth as the Judge. But here too the latter cannot be isolated from the former because it is the Jesus who "was crucified under Pontius Pilate" who by resurrection was exalted to the place of power at God's "right hand." It is this continuity between the crucified Nazarene and the exalted Christ that provides the theological basis for letting this discussion focus primarily on the perfect tense of Jesus in the present moral life, while not ignoring his future tense.

Jesus' authorizing role.   As already stated, *authorizing* refers to Jesus' role in determining the various dimensions of the moral life. He is the warrant for any moral life that deliberately takes its cue from who he was and what he said. He has this role wherever the concept disciple appears (as well as elsewhere). Those whose moral lives he governs are his apprentices. Because he authorizes the disciples' moral lives, he is the authority to whom one defers and the one

19. Crossan has distinguished four types of gospels: (a) sayings gospels, without narrative (Q and *Thomas*); (b) biographical gospels (the canonical texts); (c) discourse gospels devoted to Jesus' postresurrection teachings (e.g., *Apocryphon of James, Sophia of Jesus Christ*); and (d) biographical-discourse texts with rudimentary narrative (second-century *Epistle of the Apostles*). In this diversity he sees, rightly, a theological conflict between the canonical biographical gospels and those that sunder Jesus from his earthly, historical life; he also insists that it is the canonical gospel type that is normative, not just because of the content but also because of their form (*The Birth of Christianity*, 31–40).

20. Hauerwas, "From System to Story," 32. See also "Story and Theology" in the same volume.

whose approbation one desires. *Authorizing*, then, is authority exercised, not as coercion but as generating, energizing, legitimizing influence.

Unfortunately, when the word *authority* is associated with persons, it often suggests that the person is authoritarian rather than authoritative; this makes it difficult to speak of Jesus as an authority and doubly so in an era when authority implies infringement of freedom, especially from "hierarchy," and when egalitarianism is nearly the summum bonum. Ironically, even those who advocate egalitarianism become authorities for those who heed them. It is hard to imagine any society or community, however, without some sort of authority, be it structured, seized, or supposed. In any case, despite the rhetoric of defiance, current American society is highly deferential to all sorts of authorities, be they experts quoted, precedents honored, or persons imitated. Indeed, one's identity, style, and goals to a large extent bear the imprint of those to whom one looks up (itself an interesting phrase!) and also of those often unrecognized. Non-personal realities such as habits of thought and speech, animosities and anxieties—especially when absolutized—also function as authorities in the moral life. Modern life is plagued not so much by lack of authority or even by rebellion against authority as by a multiplicity of authorities. The notion of an autonomous self is a conceit with which moderns delude themselves. If so, then the supreme task is to identify that authority, or cluster of authorities, to which one opens the moral life. P. T. Forsyth got it right in saying that "the first duty of every soul is not to find its freedom but its Master."[21]

When Jesus had the audacity to invite people to become his disciples he tacitly asserted his right to be the authority in their moral lives, to authorize their character and direction. After his ignominious death their conviction that God had vindicated him solidified the community, which now traced its increasingly distinct ethos to what he had said and done. Indeed, it is likely that the Evangelists wrote the Jesus story and wrote it as they did partly to stabilize the Jesus traditions and partly to show how the community's unusual ethos was warranted by Jesus. Consequently the gospels ignore what Jesus and the subsequent community shared with non-Christian Jews (e.g., dietary practices, observance of holy times such as Passover) and concentrate on what was different enough to require justification. Nowhere is this more explicit than in Mt 5:21–48, usually mislabeled as the "antitheses" because of the sixfold formulaic introduction, "You have heard that it was said . . . but I say to you." The same standpoint underlies the Jesus tradition as a whole.   At this point there emerges a question whose character is both historical and hermeneutical: How shall we understand the relation

21. Forsyth, *Positive Preaching*, 28.

between the exhortations and commands of Jesus in the gospels and the communities in which and for which they were written? All too often historians of early Christianity use Jesus' words about what is to be done as evidence of what early Christians did, instead of using it as evidence for the norm from which they were deviating but needed to be brought back into alignment. It is more likely that the gospels had both functions: on the one hand, their portrayal of Jesus legitimated their emerging ethos; on the other, their portrayal of Jesus judged it. In other words, the gospels present Jesus as the authorizing judge—and they should be read that way today as well.

The gospels show Jesus authorizing the disciples' behavior in various ways. (a) Most common are his explicit commands, such as "Give to everyone who begs from you; and if anyone takes away your goods, do not ask for them again" (Lk 6:30; Mt 5:42 has the first demand but changes the second to read "and do not refuse anyone who wants to borrow from you"). Frequently he relied on parables to drive his point home. Thus the story of the unforgiving slave who had been forgiven a huge debt (Mt 18:23–35) is a negative example that reinforces the importance of forgiveness. So too Jesus' words about new wine in new wineskins authorizes the distinct lifestyle of the community (Mk 2:22).

(b) For the gospels, Jesus authorizes also by his tart responses in specific situations. For instance, according to Mark 3:31–35, Jesus' mother and brothers came to see him but, being unable to get to him because of the crowd in the house, sent word that they were waiting for him. His reply was startling: "Here are my mother and my brothers. Whoever does the will of God is my brother and sister and mother." Thereby he authorized his followers to forego their natural kinship ties in order to find a new "family" in the communities centered in Jesus. Matthew uses this story (Mt 12:46–50; Lk 8:19–21) to reinforce with Jesus' example what he had said previously (and Luke to warrant what he will say later), that he had not come to bring peace but contention and to divide families (Mt 10:34–37; Lk 12:51–53; 14:26; see also *Gospel of Thomas* 55, 101).[22] Likewise,

---

22. There is considerable variation in the words of Jesus reported in these texts, but the same theme is expressed in all of them. According to *Thomas* 55, Jesus said, "Whoever does not hate father and mother will not be able to be my disciple; and whoever does not hate brothers and sisters and does not take up the cross in my way will not be worthy of me." In Logion 101 he said, "Whoever does not hate father and mother in my way will not be able to be my disciple, for my mother (gave me falsehood?) but (my true mother?) gave me life." (The words in parentheses are conjectural because the manuscript is damaged.) The animosity between generations that Jesus foresees, especially in the Synoptics, actualizes what Micah 7:5–6 describes as the corrupted state of society.

when the Synoptics report that Jesus defended his disciples' Sabbath behavior in the grainfield (Mk 2:18–19, par.) they have him authorize Christian Sabbath observance. Especially interesting is the way they report his defense of the disciples' decision not to fast: "The wedding guests cannot fast while the bridegroom is with them, can they?" This retort implies that the time of Jesus is celebratory rather than penitential. Apparently the early Christians did not reject fasting altogether, however. Didache 8 says, "Let not your fasts be with the hypocrites, for they fast on Mondays and Fridays, but do your fast on Wednesdays and Fridays." So the tradition drew out the implications of "while the bridegroom is with them" by having Jesus authorize subsequent Christian fasting: "the days will come when the bridegroom is taken away from them, and then they will fast on that day" (Mk 2:18–20).

(c) Jesus also authorizes by example, shown by the sayings about taking up one's own cross and following him and his taking children into his arms, mentioned earlier (Mk 10:13–16, par.). The peculiarly Johannine story of Jesus' washing the disciples' feet (Jn 13:1–15) emphasizes the exemplary character of Jesus' mission. After pointing to the symbolic meaning of this act as a "cleansing" of the disciples, Jesus adds another interpretation: "if I, your Lord and Teacher, have washed your feet, you also ought to wash one another's feet. For I have set you an example" (*hypodeigma*). The story, especially when taken together with sayings such as "Whoever wishes to be first among you must be slave of all" (Mk 10:44) and "I am among you as one who serves" (Lk 22:27), has long been regarded as an apt expression of the sort of person Jesus was and therefore as an appropriate image of the moral life that bears his imprint.

The otherness of Jesus points to the fact that the authorizer is external to the self. Not only did the Jesus event occur far away and long ago, but knowledge of that event relies on texts that are external objects, printed and bound into books. This externality can become a problem, for it leaves one vulnerable to construing obedience as mere compliance. When one's "heart" (the self) is not in it, the deed does not express the doer rightly.

This situation changes significantly, however, if the external authorizer is internalized, but *not* in the sentimental sense of "He walks with me, and talks with me, and tells me I am his own." In view here is something much more demanding than devout sentiments. It is the deliberate, persistent appropriation of Jesus into the moral life so that he becomes its internal compass and criterion of the doer and the deed. When Jesus' word and way are assimilated, he becomes "habit forming." Then he is not simply cited as an external authority the way one quotes a rule book or and eminent expert; instead his words and precedent come readily and naturally to mind because he has already shaped one's disposition, will, and way of being in the world. Perhaps some analogies will suggest the sort of phenomenon envisaged. In times past some persons prayed in biblical language because the King James Bible, that they had internalized and to a remarkable extent memorized as well, naturally gave them a way of thinking because it had become part of them. Emily Dickinson has become so much a part of a friend's outlook that in one situation after another the poet's words come naturally to mind, not as the expert's oracle but as a perceptive resource that is simply there, a companion on the way. Jesus too can be such a "text." It is the internalized authorizing that creates character, develops identity, grows virtue, and forms one's disposition—that "somewhat stable readiness to speak and act [and think] in a certain way," as Gustafson put it.[23] Here too Forsyth saw clearly when he wrote, "if within us we find nothing over us, we succumb to what is around us."[24]

It is not Jesus himself who is internalized, of course, but an image of him, formed by configuring and construing the various elements whose weighting varies from person to person and from time to time even in the same person's understanding. But Jesus cannot be internalized if externally he is a stranger or a casual acquaintance about whom one knows a few stories and sayings. What such knowledge is more likely to produce is a caricature instead of a trustworthy image. Not only must one acquire true familiarity with the gospels, but one must also be left alone with them in order to ponder the figure they portray. Internalizing Jesus requires steady exposure; a sudden impulse to "look it up" in the gospels will not suffice. It is just at this point that the historical study of Jesus becomes important—though not all important—for his authorizing role. Even though the historical enterprise can produce neither many indubitable "facts" about Jesus beyond his crucifixion and baptism nor portrayals of Jesus that are wholly free of the historian's perspectives, it remains the only means by which one can answer the question, To what extent is it Jesus or an imagined Jesus who is being assimilated? It is the otherness of Jesus that sound historical study should exhibit, that resists the powerful drive to remake him to fit easily into the moral life one already has. When this occurs, the tide of influence changes, and one subtly and unwittingly authorizes him. But the more it is his different way and often distressing word that are internalized, the more likely it is that his absolutism, noted above, exposes the true quality of one's moral life

23. Gustafson, *Christ and the Moral Life*, 248.
24. Forsyth, *Positive Preaching*, 32.

so that it can be reconformed, comparable to the way the holiness of God reveals what needs to be hallowed. The internalized Jesus does not only settle questions; repeatedly he also unsettles answers.

The saying about fasting shows that what Jesus authorizes is not a slavish effort to replicate him but the freedom, as well as the responsibility, to discern what his word and way call for in situations he could not have imagined. For instance, from Jesus' saying that what defiles is not what enters a person but what comes out, Mark inferred that "he declared all foods clean" (Mk 7:17–23). This had not been Jesus' point, but the Evangelist believed that the implication of what Jesus had said did authorize this inference, which was important for Christian Gentiles. The same responsible freedom was claimed when an ex-Pharisee found it necessary to counsel new Christian Gentiles about marriage and divorce. In 1 Corinthians 7:8–16 Paul, without actually quoting Jesus' prohibition of divorce (as found in Mk 10:2–12), says, "I give this command—not I but the Lord—that the wife should not separate [i.e., divorce] from her husband" and vice versa. Yet he also says, "but if she does separate, let her remain unmarried or else be reconciled to her husband"; thereby he shows that he sees himself authorized to make a provision for disobedience. Turning to the situation where only one spouse is a believing member of the community, he continues: "I say—I and not the Lord" that so long as the unbelieving spouse does not insist on divorce, the believer should not seek it either. In the same letter he found it necessary to justify the fact that he worked for a living instead of being supported by those he won to the faith. Although he notes that "the Lord commanded that those who proclaim the gospel should get their living by the gospel" (perhaps an allusion to Mt 10:10), he goes on to say that he does not make use of this "right" (1 Cor 9:3–15). Paul surely did not see himself asserting his right to disobey Jesus. Rather, as did Mark, he too saw that obedience to Jesus sometimes requires going beyond what Jesus had actually said.

Repeatedly since then Jesus' followers have claimed to be authorized by him to express their apprenticeship in ways they deemed appropriate to their own situation. In doing so they have erred often enough, sometimes egregiously. But in antiquity they also felt authorized to rescue infants exposed to the elements, emancipate slaves, care for the sick and dying, and translate the gospels; in modern times they have taught the illiterate to read, founded schools, and engaged in nonviolent action to gain civil rights for others as well as for themselves. Jesus might well have been surprised by all this. But then again he might not.

Finally, in authorizing the moral life Jesus evokes a commitment to what he was committed to himself—the kingdom of God and the rectifying import of its impingement. Otherwise one can end up believing *in* Jesus without believing *him*. The authorized follower is committed also to the community that is energized by him. It is, after all, this community that hands on the Jesus story and relies on it both to nourish and to correct its understanding of what Jesus authorizes. As Hauerwas also noted, how the story should be told is "basically a moral issue, since it is also a question about what kind of people we ought to be"[25]—and, one might add, are enabled to be.

Jesus the judge.   *Judge* is not a welcome image for Jesus. Nonetheless, he is the judge both in and of the moral life. This role does not depend on the historian's success in demonstrating that Jesus expected to be the Judge. The coming eschatological judgment was an essential part of his message, even if there is reason to conclude that some sayings about it were fed into the Jesus tradition from the reservoir of Jewish apocalyptic thought. Those who deny to Jesus an apocalyptic outlook altogether must therefore reject approximately that one-fourth of the Jesus sayings that manifest the judgment theme, according to Reiser's estimate.[26] Besides, they must also insist that either Jesus broke completely from the Baptizer or that John was not as Judgment-oriented as the Synoptics portray him to have been. Denying that Jesus spoke repeatedly of the coming judgment creates far more problems than it solves. Since chapter 3 discussed these topics, there is no need to rehearse the evidence again, especially since the validity of what is advanced here does not depend on what Jesus said about the subject but on who he actually is in the moral lives of those attracted to him. Those whose moral lives he authorizes are accountable to him even if he had never mentioned the Last Judgment.

To begin with, when Jesus is the internalized authorizer, the flow of interpretation is dialectical. He is no longer the primary one being explained, discerned, and interpreted; now the character and quality of the follower's moral life are disclosed and interpreted as well. Since the disclosure pertains to both doer and deed, exposing the degree of disparity between what Jesus authorizes and what is actualized, it is no longer only Jesus who needs interpretation and justification but also the doer. For example, Jesus commands that one turn the other cheek, to give to every beggar, and to love the enemy (Mt 5:38–44). When one explains and interprets Jesus, one can link these sayings to the

---

25. Hauerwas, A *Community of Character,* 67.

26. Reiser, *Jesus and Judgment,* 303–4.

nature of the kingdom and to Galilean village life. But when Jesus is the internalized authorizer, one discovers that Jesus ignores the consequences of the deed and concentrates all attention on changing the doer by changing his or her attitude toward the other. This calls for a reinterpretation of the self as a self and not simply as a moral agent. Jesus' words now reveal the doer as a person whose reluctance to obey probably manifests an inability, or unwillingness, to heed Jesus' way of actualizing the kingdom's impingement on the urge toward self-preservation and self-aggrandizement. Moreover, insofar as Jesus is the acknowledged authorizing judge, the discerned disparity between what is authorized and what is achieved is not simply a diagnostic datum that can be noted as a piece of information about the self and filed; it is rather a datum that accuses the doer of failure for which one is responsible. Indeed, it is precisely being authorized that makes one a responsible self, a self accountable *for* oneself but *to* the authorizer and not primarily to oneself. Here the old adage "Unto thine own self be true" is replaced by "Unto thine authorizer be true."

One can, of course, insist on interpreting Jesus instead, explaining that the horizon of these demands is that of personal relations in a Galilean village and so they do not really fit in an urban and suburban, postindustrial society, that they are evoked by an unshakable conviction of the kingdom's imminence, and so forth. The more one proceeds in this way, the less Jesus remains the authorizing judge and turns instead into a resource, if that, whose usability is determined by the user.

To a large extent the foregoing observations are valid in any situation in which a person is the defining authorizer of the disciple's mode of life and/or thought, because those dynamics are structured into the model-apprentice relationship. This makes it all the more important to bear in mind that it is Jesus, more precisely the image of Jesus, who is the authorizing judge and not some other figure. Here it is what characterizes Jesus that matters most. Four characteristics of Jesus invite attention, for it is these traits, especially when taken together, that continue to make Jesus a person who evokes a positive response, the faltering as well as the firm.

First, people sense that Jesus has the moral right to be the authorizing judge. The adjective *moral* differentiates this right from a legal one (e.g., the right of the community's head) or a metaphysical one (Jesus as the incarnate Son of God). A moral right cannot be conferred; it can only be achieved. Such an achievement, moreover, is an integrity that comes from rightly choosing, rarely without struggle, and appropriate action afterward. No one knows the inner life of Jesus, and speculation about his choices is the stuff of novels (though sometimes disguised as history). The Synoptics do, of course, frame their accounts of his mission with stories about a profound struggle, the temptations at the outset and the Gethsemane agony at the point where he ceases to act and instead becomes acted upon. In John when the shadow of impending death darkened the horizon, even the Johannine Jesus, who is master of every situation, said, "Now my soul is troubled. And what should I say—'Father, save me from this hour?' No, it is for this reason that I have come to this hour" (Jn 12:27). One reason people acknowledge Jesus to be a compelling moral figure is that these stories, by their sophisticated simplicity, indicate that Jesus achieved his integrity in the choosings that they recognize as defining their own existence as well. It is not surprising, then, that they acknowledge his right to be the authorizing judge, for in him word, deed, and person are one event. Although each gospel sometimes distinguishes Jesus' public teaching from private instruction and explanation, they give no hint of a public persona who differs from the private self. The Synoptics portray a Jesus who had a moral right to be a judge in the moral life because he made no demands on others that he did not make on himself, and carried out.

A second trait, mentioned previously but in passing, now merits more comment—namely, it is the choosings' and the doings' consequences for the doer that are the focus of Jesus' concern. Apparently he simply assumed that the right deed will benefit the recipient, be it the beggar to whom one gives or the victim of robbery for whom the "good Samaritan" cared. At no point does Jesus say that before choosing one should calculate the effects of one's choices on the other person (e.g., Does giving to every beggar encourage panhandling?), group, or social patterns—an essential dimension of ethics. What he does urge is that one calculate the doer's cost: the tower builder, for example, should compute the cost before starting to build, and the king should determine whether he can win a war with but half the troops of the enemy (Lk 14:28–32). Jesus does not explain why he has no interest in making choices that will have the best, or least problematic, consequences under the circumstances. The decision-making process, the shibboleth of our time, is nowhere an evident concern of his; consequently, today this lack is a significant part of his otherness. Whether one regards this trait as a sign of naïveté (one that self-aware sophisticates are prepared to forgive him) or as a mark of wisdom, it is the effect that is not to be missed: Jesus does not hold the doer responsible for the consequences of his or her actions on others; he concentrates attention on the deed's consequences on the doer. This judge makes the doer judge oneself. Jesus apparently realizes that one cannot follow him without a change of heart and mind-set; apart from this change—the Godward turn in response to the kingdom's impingement—the doer can comply yet not be obedient. It is this insistence on integrity that drives Jesus' polemic against its opposite, hypocrisy. Here is a profound expression of Jesus' real egalitarianism, for he assumes that everyone—no matter what socioeconomic status, gender, or mental prowess—can and must take responsibility for the effect of one's choosing on oneself.

In short, Jesus is the sort of judge who, by holding the self responsible for the self, for the doer rather than the deed's consequences, does not allow one to play either victim or manager of situations. When Jesus' teachings are regarded as his "ethics," this concentration on the integrity of the doer either embarrasses those determined to change the world in Jesus' name or induces them to overcome the imbalance in his perspective by inferring his principles, which can then be "applied." That the world needs change is not in dispute; what is disputed is whether one can convert a doer-focused authorizer into a calculating consequence-oriented one.

The third trait that characterizes Jesus is grounded in the second—namely, his total indifference to his own power, either to advance it or to preserve it. Nothing in the gospels suggests or implies that he calculated what course of action would produce results that accrued to his benefit. The temptation stories express this succinctly. The gospels show Jesus simply responding to human need, not merely on impulse but because the kingdom's coming constrained him to do so regardless of the consequences for him. His reported silence when standing before Pilate reflected neither fear nor awe of Pilate's power but his refusal to manipulate it for his own benefit. No protest of innocence, no plea for mercy crossed his lips. Even if one infers that he knew that neither recourse would make any difference,[27] the essential point is the same: Jesus refused to play the power game precisely when it might have spared him death. Here, as in Galilee, Jesus did not manage his image or his future, this time by coming to an "understanding" with Pilate. He neither sought death nor fled it but left his life in the hands of God as he had always done. He would not put it into Pilate's hands, for once he lost it there was nothing he could do to

---

27. Rivkin insists that from a strictly historical view, "it mattered not who said what, or what sparked who, or who sparked what, or what the political motivation of the sparker happened to be. Even if Jesus had pleaded for measured calm by calling out, 'This is not what I meant at all, not at all,' it would have made no difference to the authorities. What mattered were the consequences for the high priest and procurator if the crowds had gone wild shouting, 'The kingdom of God is at hand, and Jesus is our king'" (*What Crucified Jesus?*, 100–101).

get it back. He heeded his own warning: "What will anyone gain by winning the whole world [what Satan promised in the wilderness!] at the cost of his own life? Or [having lost it] what can he give to buy his life back?" (Mt 16:26, REB).

The fourth trait is the coherence of Jesus' compassionate concern for the "sinners," the downtrodden poor, and the diseased and demon-possessed, on the one hand, and, on the other hand, his uncompromising criticism of any use of the law that would lead one away from genuine obedience to the will and character of the Lawgiver whose actualized kingship was imminent. His criticism was not that of a jaded observer but that of a Jew profoundly grounded in the Bible, which taught him that the powerful God tilts toward the weak, that the Righteous One stands by the faithful and destroys the impenitent wicked. That Bible also taught him that obedience to the God of Abraham and Moses was both an obligation and an opportunity to respond rightly to the One who can be counted on to make all things, and all persons, right at the right time. Both Jesus' criticism and his compassion express his passionate commitment to this biblical-Jewish heritage that formed him. When Christian Gentiles acknowledge him to be the authorizing judge, they submit their moral lives to the Authorizer who authorized Jesus, to the Holy One of Israel who has a "history" of contending with his covenanted people in order to "make the crooked straight." Jesus did not reach out to the downtrodden because he idealized them; he no more thought that poverty made the destitute virtuous than he thought being possessed made one holy. He went to the despised and impoverished because he saw that they most of all needed the gracious rectifying power of God's kingdom which alone could restore them to the community with which God keeps faith.

The accountability of the authorized self.[28]   Whoever is authorized is accountable, and whoever is accountable acknowledges that he/she lives in an authority structure in which one is vulnerable to the verdict of someone authorized to render it. A discussion of Jesus the authorizing judge would be incomplete, therefore, if it did not look at the matter from the standpoint of the authorized, and hence accountable, self. Accountability to God or Christ is commonly associated with Christ's "second coming" and/or the Last Judgment. The marginalization that these beliefs have undergone in certain strands of Christianity may be one reason that there is little discussion of accountability. Be that as it may, the focus here is not one's accountability at the Great Assize that lies beyond history but rather on the accountable self in the present.

---

28. The observations in this section carry forward my discussion in "The Accountable Self."

Focusing on the present, however, does not banish the transhistorical judgment from view. It is impossible to do so for two reasons: (a) the Christ who is to come "to judge the living and the dead" is not someone other than the Jesus who presently is the authorizing judge and who once lived in Galilee and died in Jerusalem; (b) a major purpose of the various images of the Great Judgment is not so much to impart information to satisfy curiosity as it is to put the present in the perspective of ultimate significance, so that the moral life is taken with utmost seriousness. (This is true also of the biblical-Jewish apocalyptic tradition in which Christian views of the Judgment are formed.) Accordingly, there is no dichotomy between one's accountability then and one's accountability now, though they must be differentiated because one's life is not yet finished; the present may be decisive, but by definition it is not final. So too concentrating here on one's accountability to the perfect tense of Jesus as the authorizer of the moral life in no way replaces accountability to the exalted Christ at the Judgment beyond time; rather it indicates what is at stake.

Being vulnerable to the verdict of the authorizing judge is what makes the self accountable. This vulnerability may, in fact, have played an unacknowledged role in the decline of attention given to the whole theme of accountability, for one's vulnerability is not a welcome theme in a culture that prizes the *ageric* self (the self as agent) who sets goals and strives successfully to reach them. The account giving in the commonplace "annual reports," while a symptom of accountability, emphasizes achievement and obscures failure as much as possible because the reporter is aware of his or her vulnerability: If what is reported is deemed unsatisfactory, one can be reprimanded, demoted, or fired ("given the opportunity to resign," thereby maintaining the appearance of the ageric self even when the recipient of another's action). In other words, by definition the status of the accountable self is contingent on the judgment of the authorizer. This is why the identity and character of the authorizing judge are pivotal for the one authorized. These general, rather formal, observations must now be elaborated and made concrete by asking What, then, does it mean to know oneself accountable to Jesus?

To begin, insofar as Jesus has been internalized as the authorizer of one's moral life, one is not accountable to a stranger, as to a previously unknown inspector who arrives from the main office, but to one whom one is already committed to and who already functions as the conscience. Conscience, at least here, is not understood to be an entity such as an invisible listening device implanted in one's body at birth; rather, as a noun it reifies an act, the act in which the self views itself (there is no verb *to conscience*). Just as the capacity and the criteria for this self-viewing are socially conditioned into "conscience," so the internalization of Jesus occurs in the community that looks to Jesus and in which the Jesus story is told and retold. In such a community one learns to accept the story "as normative by allowing it to shape one's own story," as Hauerwas put it.[29] This is why a community that talks only of Jesus' principles and ideals understands itself to be accountable to inferred abstractions, not to a lived life. The accountable self knows itself "monitored" by Jesus the internalized authorizer, not by an alien criterion, for even Jesus' otherness is internalized

The result is what some people used to call a "Christ-like life." Such a life is not formed by asking, What would Jesus do?, for the moral life in view here does not result from astute second guessing; it comes from asking, rather, What is the appropriate thing to do and be in light of the kind of person Jesus was? For the person who asks this, being accountable to Jesus may be difficult, but it is not onerous. The disciple who has internalized Jesus does not experience accountability as a burden but as an opportunity to give a discernible Jesus form to the moral life. He or she knows that Jesus leaves his mark on those who trust him—and are grateful this is the case.

Moreover, the authorized follower of Jesus does not experience giving an account as something to be dreaded but as the occasion for discipline and the basis for hope. Although the Beatitudes and other expressions of God's grace are as hard to assimilate as the stern sayings that point to the utter seriousness of the present, both summon the follower to keep reshaping one's moral life until it reflects more clearly and deeply the Jesus event and its vision. The future horizon of the present experience of being accountable points to the ultimate, transhistorical moment when present faithfulness is vindicated. No good deed will have been ignored—not even a cup of water (Mt 10:42).

In the Synoptics the disciples' vindication is often expressed as promised reward, which is normally understood to be in the future, either at the coming Judgment or at death. Both are beyond history in any case. Still, the idea of reward is often regarded as a sign of an inferior, if not outright objectionable, ethic on the premise that virtue is its own reward. In this light, promises of reward can readily suggest that Jesus authorized his hearers to become disciples with an eye on the reward, to do the good because it would be rewarded and to avoid evildoing because it too would be repaid, but with retribution. When reward is the motive, does not doing good use the plight of others for one's own

---

29. Hauerwas, "From System to Story," 34; see also his *A Community of Character*, 49.

enhancement? And to what extent is one accountable for one's motives anyway, even if one could identify them? The role of reward in the moral life is obviously a theme far too complex to be ventilated here, but a few observations about the way it appears in Jesus' teaching can be noted.

To begin with, in Matthew 6:1–18 Jesus addressed the question of motive in the sayings about almsgiving, prayer, and fasting even if the "hypocrites" are parodied: they "sound a trumpet . . . so that they may be praised by others"; "they love to stand and pray in the synagogues and at the street corners, so that they may be seen by others"; they "disfigure their faces to show others that they are fasting." These exaggerations reflect a culture in which honor and shame are powerful forces in motivating behavior, for one's reputation reflects on the family as well. In such a setting, to be seen as generous and devout adds to one's stature in a village community. Jesus tartly observes, however, that "they have their reward." He therefore urges that the disciples do these same things in secret and promises that "your Father who sees in secret will reward you." He specifies neither the nature of the reward nor when it will be given. Thereby he achieves several things at once: by transforming the reward he virtually removes it as a motivating factor; he implies that these things are to be done because they are right, not because they secure one's "image"; by insisting that the doer should rely on the all-seeing God (who sees also the motives in the heart), he tacitly requires one to decide whether to trust God not to overlook any good thing. Whoever grasps Jesus' point is indeed made accountable for one's motives.

In addition, in the hierarchically structured society governed by patron-client relationships (master-slave, landowner-tenant, father-household) reward expressed justice, the right response of the superior to the right behavior of the inferior. Giving no reward would show indifference as well as gross injustice for service rendered and loyalty maintained. A sense of this value system is especially important for understanding Jesus' words about God's reward for those who now experience various forms of alienation and harassment because they are Jesus' followers: "Rejoice and be glad, for your reward is great in heaven [with God], for in the same way they persecuted the prophets who were before you" (Mt 5:11–12). One is not motivated to endure (presumably) unjust suffering by a promise of reward. Rather, reward is personalized justice from the God who is not imperiously indifferent to what people endure because of their fidelity. Nor does Jesus imply that one is to seek persecution in order to be rewarded; instead, the assurance of reward motivates them to be faithful in spite of persecution, for they know that though they may suffer in isolation where no friend can see their endurance, God does see and does not forget.

While the fact of reward expresses God's just response and so is "deserved" as a matter of justice, its "content" cannot be earned, as if one could increase it by doing more and doing better. That is precisely the point of Jesus' offensive parable of the vineyard workers, all of whom got the same pay even though some had worked all day while others had worked only for an hour (Mt 20:1–15). With this should be considered the conclusion Jesus draws from the example of the slave who, after a day's work outside, obeyed the master's order to prepare and serve dinner: "Do you thank the slave for doing what was commanded? So you also, when you have done all that you were ordered to do, say, 'We are worthless slaves; we have done only what we ought to have done!'" (Lk 17:7–10).

Above all, Jesus' treatment of rewards occurs in a totally different conceptual, as well as cultural, context from that of ethics, in which reward is presumed to be a factor in one's moral calculus and therefore disdained. Moreover, insisting that virtue is its own reward, that the good must be done for its own sake and not be motivated by extrinsic considerations such as reward, simply does not characterize those whose lives are on the line; for them, the whole theme of reward is transposed into another key: because Jesus was vindicated beyond death, they carry their crosses with the confident hope that they, and what they may have to die for, too will be vindicated as he was—on the yonder side of history and by the One whose holiness unites goodness and power.

"For Jesus' Sake": The Power of the Perfect Tense

The Jesus ethic is characterized by its focus on the figure of Jesus more than on his teachings, though they are not ignored. This attention to the person is signaled by a characteristic vocabulary which expresses the relation of Jesus to the self in terms of learning or copying. Most common are *teacher* and *disciple*; close to this is the idiom derived from crafts: *master* and *apprentice*. In one way or other, the *imitatio Christi* motif runs through such expressions of the follower's relation to Jesus, a relation which the follower regards as personal. As Gustafson observed, "The fact that Jesus Christ was a person enables us to have a personal relation to him; this is for many a more meaningful way to live than a life devoted to intellectual and moral principles."[30] It is true, of course, that for believers this personal relation is with the living Lord Jesus, but it is the image of Jesus of Nazareth that provides his defining traits. Further, what characterizes this personal relation is commitment, whose enduring quality is expressed as loyalty.

30. Gustafson, *Christ and the Moral Life*, 159.

Moreover, loyalty to a person is a significant factor in motivation, sometimes prompting one to do extraordinary things for the sake of the one to whom one is loyally committed. Such loyalty, and what it generates, is best expressed in the phrase "for Jesus' sake." In fact, it is a useful way to think of Jesus' role in the moral life as a whole because it refers to Jesus holistically, on the one hand, and, on the other, it points to his role in motivating and activating the moral life. Since "for Jesus' sake" has generally eluded examination, it deserves brief discussion here. Analyzing the phrase and its rationale will show that it has both a backward reference and a future reference, making it an apt way of understanding the perfect tense of Jesus in the moral life.

"For the sake of" and its rationale.   "For Jesus' sake" is not to be confused with "For Christ's sake," an epithet that expresses exasperation, as do its nontheological surrogates "for heaven's sake" and "for goodness's sake." The noun *sake* is no longer used apart from such phrases. The word itself is of old Germanic origin and still is related to the common German word *Sache* (thing, matter, or cause), though the modern German adds the suffix *willen* to *Gott* to form *um Gotteswillen* as the equivalent of "for God's sake." The English phrase is used in various ways, such as "for old time's sake" = in memory of old times; "for the sake of her birthday" = out of respect for the day; "for the sake of the company" = for its well-being or benefit; "for the sake of appearances" = in order to preserve or improve one's public image; "for the sake of Grandpa's diet" = in deference to his regimen. Each of these expressions uses the phrase as a warrant for an action (or nonaction), yet the warrant is characteristically indirect and allusive. Each discloses at least as much about the doer's motivation as it does about the person or consideration mentioned. What the expression reveals is not obedience or compliance with a rule, requirement, or an authority figure's command but an attitude of respect and deference, a commitment that is strong enough to affect and motivate behavior. Grandpa's diet could have been ignored, perhaps to his detriment, but instead the speaker expressed her willingness to adjust the menu to avoid offense or risk. So too appearances are important enough to commend overriding a more convenient or pleasurable course of action. Likewise, the company benefits when its well-being is the deciding factor in a policy-making decision even though profits will decline in the short run. To do something "for old times' sake" is to honor the past, whether by doing something special or by continuing a tradition which would otherwise be abandoned. The point is that none of the beneficiaries mandates the action, but each nonetheless elicits it because the doer acts out of consideration for the other person or group.

Since "for the sake of" has various, not always neatly separable, meanings, it is not surprising that New Revised Standard Version uses it to translate three differ-

Abbreviations

ABD	*Anchor Bible Dictionary* (ed. D. N. Freedman; New York: Doubleday, 1992)
AMNTSU	Arbeiten und Mitteilungen aus dem Neutestamentlichen Seminar zu Uppsala
BA	*Biblical Archaeologist*
BAGD	*Greek-English Lexicon of the New Testament* (ed. W. Bauer, W. F. Arndt, F. W. Gingrich, and F. W. Danker; Chicago: University of Chicago Press, 1979)
Bib	*Biblica*
BTB	*Biblical Theology Bulletin*
CBQ	*Catholic Biblical Quarterly*
EvTheol	*Evangelische Theologie*
FRLANT	Forschungen zur Religion und Literatur des Alten und Neuen Testaments
HTR	*Harvard Theological Review*
JBL	*Journal of Biblical Literature*
JES	*Journal of Ecumenical Studies*
JR	*Journal of Religion*
JSNT	*Journal for the Study of the New Testament*
JSOT	*Journal for the Study of the Old Testament*
JTS	*Journal of Theological Studies*
NovTest	*Novum Testamentum*
NTS	*New Testament Studies*
SBLSP	Society of Biblical Literature Seminar Papers
SBS	Stuttgarter Bibelstudien
SBT	Studies in Biblical Theology
SNTSMS	Society of New Testament Studies Monograph Series
TynBul	*Tyndale Bulletin*

Works Cited

Allen, Charlotte. *The Human Christ: The Search for the Historical Jesus.* New York: Free Press, 1998.

Allison, Dale C. "Jesus and the Covenant: A Response to E. P. Sanders." *JSNT* 29 (1987): 57–78.

Baeck, Leo. "The Gospel as a Document of the Jewish Faith." In *Judaism and Christianity.* Translated by Walter Kauffman, 41–136. Philadelphia: Jewish Publication Society, 1958. German ed. *Das Evangelium als Urkunde der Jüdischen Glaubengeschichte* (Berlin: Schocken, 1938).

——. "Harnacks Vorlesungen über das Wesen des Christentums." *Monatsheft für Geschichte und Wissenschaft des Judentums* 45 (1901): 97–120.

Bammel, Ernst. "The Revolution Theory from Reimarus to Brandon." In *Jesus and the Politics of His Day*, edited by E. Bammel and C. F. D. Moule, 11–68. Cambridge: Cambridge University Press, 1984.

Bammel, Ernst, and C. F. D. Moule, eds. *Jesus and the Politics of His Day.* Cambridge: Cambridge University Press, 1984.

Barr, James. "'Abba' Isn't 'Daddy.'" *JTS* 39 (1988): 28–47.

Batey, Richard A. *Jesus and the Forgotten City: A New Light on Sepphoris and the Urban World of Jesus.* Grand Rapids, Mich.: Baker, 1991.

——. "Jesus and the Theatre." *NTS* 30 (1984): 563–74.

Beasley-Murray, George R. *Jesus and the Future: An Examination of the Criticism of the Eschatological Discourse, Mark 13, with Special Reference to the Little Apocalypse Theory.* New York: St. Martin's Press, 1954.

Ben-Chorin, Shalom. "The Image of Jesus in Modern Judaism." *JES* 11 (1974): 401–30.

Bennett, William. J., Jr. "The Son of Man Must. . . ." *NovTest* 17 (1975): 9–14.

Berlin, George L. *Defending the Faith: Nineteenth Century American Jewish Writings on Christianity and Jesus.* Albany: State University of New York Press, 1989.

Betz, Hans Dieter. "Jesus and the Cynics: Survey and Analysis of a Hypothesis." *JR* 74 (1994): 453–75.

——. *The Sermon on the Mount.* Hermeneia. Minneapolis: Fortress Press, 1995.

Boers, Hendrikus. *Who Was Jesus? The Historical Jesus and the Synoptic Gospels.* San Francisco: Harper & Row, 1989.

Borg, Marcus. *Jesus: A New Vision*. San Francisco: Harper & Row, 1987.

———. *Jesus in Contemporary Scholarship*. Valley Forge, Pa.: Trinity Press International, 1994.

Boring, Eugene M. "The Kingdom of God in Mark." In *The Kingdom of God in 20th Century Interpretation*, edited by Wendell Willis, 131–45. Peabody, Mass.: Hendrickson, 1987.

Bornkamm, Gunther. *Jesus of Nazareth*. Translated by Irene McLuskey and Fraser McLuskey with James Robinson. New York: Harper and Bros., 1960. German ed., *Jesus von Nazareth*, 3rd ed. (Stuttgart: Kohlhammer, 1956).

Borowitz, Eugene B. "Gustafson: The Christ and Ethics." In *Contemporary Christologies: A Jewish Response*, edited by E. Borowitz, 99–147. New York: Paulist Press, 1980.

Bousset, Wilhelm. *Jesu Predigt in ihrem Gegensatz zum Judentum, ein religions-geschichtlicher Versuch*. Göttingen: Vandenhoeck und Ruprecht, 1892.

———. *Jesus*. Translated by Janet Penrose Trevelyan. Crown Theological Library 14. Reprint. London: Wm. Norgate and Sons/New York: G. P. Putnam's Sons, 1911. German ed., *Jesus*. Religionsgeschichtliche Volksbücher für den deutschen christlichen Gegenwart (Halle: Gebauer-Schwetske, 1904).

———. *Die Religion des Judentums im späthellenistischen Zeitalter*. Handbuch zum Neuen Testament 21. Tübingen: J. C. B. Mohr [Paul Siebeck], 1903.

Brandon, S. G. F. *Jesus and the Zealots: A Study of the Political Factor in Primitive Christianity*. Manchester: Manchester University Press, 1967.

Brazill, William J. *The Young Hegelians*. New Haven: Yale University Press, 1970.

Breech, James. *The Silence of Jesus: The Authentic Voice of the Historical Man*. Philadelphia: Fortress Press, 1983.

Brown, Raymond E. *The Birth of the Messiah*. Garden City, N.Y.: Doubleday, 1977.

———. *The Death of the Messiah: From Gethsemane to the Grave*. 2 vols. New York: Doubleday, 1994.

Buber, Martin. *The Eclipse of God: Studies in the Relation between Religion and Philosophy*. New York: Harper, 1952.

Bultmann, Rudolf. *The History of the Synoptic Tradition*. Translated by John Marsh. Oxford: Basil Blackwell/New York: Harper & Row, 1963. German ed., *Die Geschichte der synoptischen Tradition*. FRLANT 12, 3rd ed. (Göttingen: Vandenhoeck und Ruprecht, 1958).

———. *Jesus and the Word*. Translated by Louise Pettibone Smith and Erminie Huntress Lantero. Reprint. New York: Charles Scribner's Sons, 1958. First English ed., 1934.

Burridge, Richard A. *What Are the Gospels? A Comparison with Graeco-Roman Biography*. SNTS 70. Cambridge: Cambridge University Press, 1992.

Cadbury, Henry J. *The Peril of Modernizing Jesus*. New York: Macmillan, 1937.

Case, Shirley Jackson. "Jesus and Sepphoris." *JBL* 45 (1926): 14–22.

Catchpole, David R. "The Triumphal Entry." In *Jesus and the Politics of His Day*, edited by E. Bammel and C. F. D. Moule, 319–34. Cambridge: Cambridge University Press, 1984.

Charlesworth, James H. "The Dead Sea Scrolls and the Historical Jesus." In *Jesus and the Dead Sea Scrolls*, edited by J. H. Charlesworth, Anchor Bible Reference Library, 1–74. New York: Doubleday, 1992.

——. "Hillel and Jesus: Why Comparisons Are Important." In *Hillel and Jesus: Comparative Studies of Two Major Religious Leaders*, edited by J. H. Charlesworth and L. L. Johns, 3–30. Minneapolis: Fortress Press, 1997.

——. "Jesus Research Expands with Chaotic Creativity." In *Images of Jesus Today*, edited by J. H. Charlesworth and W. P. Weaver, Faith and Scholarship Colloquies 3. 1–41. Valley Forge, Pa.: Trinity Press International, 1994.

——. *Jesus within Judaism: New Light from Exciting Archaeological Discoveries*. Anchor Bible Reference Library. New York: Doubleday, 1988.

Charlesworth, James H., and Loren L. Johns, eds. *Hillel and Jesus: Comparative Studies of Two Major Religious Leaders*. Minneapolis: Fortress Press, 1997.

Chilton, Bruce. *A Galilean Rabbi and His Bible: Jesus' Use of the Interpreted Scripture of His Time*. Wilmington, Del.: Michael Glazer, 1984.

——. *God in Strength*. JSOT. Reprint. Sheffield, England: Sheffield Academic Press, 1987.

——. "Jesus and the Repentance of E. P. Sanders." *TynBul* 39 (1988): 1–18.

——. "Jesus Within Judaism." In *Jesus in Context: Temple, Purity and Restoration*, edited by B. Chilton and C. A. Evans, 179–201. Leiden: E. J. Brill, 1997.

——. *Pure Kingdom: Jesus' Vision of God*. Grand Rapids, Mich.: Eerdmans/London: SPCK, 1996.

——. *The Temple of Jesus: His Sacrificial Program within a Cultural History of Sacrifice*. University Park: Pennsylvania State University Press, 1992.

The Complete Gospels: Annotated Scholars Version. Edited by Robert J. Miller. Sonoma, Calif.: Polebridge Press, 1994.

Crawford, Barry S. "Near Expectation in the Sayings of Jesus." *JBL* 101 (1982): 225–44.

Crossan, John Dominic. *The Birth of Christianity*. San Francisco: HarperSanFrancisco, 1998.

——. *The Cross that Spoke: The Origins of the Passion Narrative*. San Francisco: Harper & Row, 1988.

——. *The Historical Jesus: The Life of a Mediterranean Jewish Peasant*. San Francisco: HarperSanFrancisco, 1991.

——. *Who Killed Jesus? Exposing the Roots of Anti-Semitism in the Gospel Story of the Death of Jesus*. San Francisco: HarperSanFrancisco, 1995.

Dahl, Nils. "The Early Church and Jesus." In *Jesus in the Memory of the Early Church*, edited by Nils Dahl, 166–75. Minneapolis: Augsburg, 1976.

Davies, Stevan L. *Jesus the Healer: Possession, Trance, and the Origins of Christianity*. New York: Continuum, 1995.

Davies, W. D., and Dale Allison. *A Critical and Exegetical Commentary on the Gospel According to Saint Matthew*. 3 vols. Edinburgh: T. & T. Clark, 1988–1997.

Deutsch, Celia. *Hidden Wisdom and the Easy Yoke: Wisdom, Torah, and Discipleship in Matthew 11:25–30*. JSNT Supp. 18. Sheffield, England: Sheffield Academic Press, 1987.

Dillon, Richard. "The Psalms of the Suffering Just in the Accounts of the Passion." *Worship* 6 (1987): 430–40.

Documenta Q: Reconstructions of Q through Two Centuries of Gospel Research Excerpted, Sorted, and Evaluated. Edited by J. M. Robinson, P. Hoffman, and J. S. Kloppenborg. Louvain, Belgium: Peeters, 1994– .

Dodd, C. H. *The Parables of the Kingdom.* London: Nisbet and Co., 1961.

Drews, Arthur. *Die Christusmythe.* 2 vols. Jena: Eugen Diederichs, 1910–1911.

Duling, Dennis C. "Kingdom of God, Kingdom of Heaven." *ABD* 4 (1992), 49–56.

Dunn, James D. G. *Christology in the Making.* Second ed. Grand Rapids, Mich.: Eerdmans, 1989.

——. *The Evidence for Jesus.* Philadelphia: Westminster, 1985.

Eddy, Paul Rhodes. "Jesus as Diogenes? Reflections on the Cynic Jesus Thesis." *JBL* 115 (1996): 446–69.

Evans, Craig A. "Jesus' Action in the Temple: Cleansing or Portent of Destruction?" *CBQ* 51 (1989): 237–70.

Falk, Harvey. *Jesus the Pharisee: A New Look at the Jewishness of Jesus.* New York: Paulist Press, 1958.

Fitzmyer, Joseph A. *The Gospel According to Luke.* 2 vols. Anchor Bible 28. Garden City, N.Y.: Doubleday, 1981.

Flusser, David. "Hillel and Jesus: Two Ways of Self-Awareness." In *Hillel and Jesus: Comparative Studies of Two Major Religious Leaders,* edited by J. H. Charlesworth and L. L. Johns, 71–107. Minneapolis: Fortress Press, 1997.

——. *Jesus.* Rev. ed. Jerusalem: Magnes Press, 1997.

Forsyth, P. T. *Positive Preaching and the Modern Mind.* London: Independent Press, 1907.

Fredriksen, Paula. "Jesus and the Temple, Mark and the War." In *Society of Biblical Literature 1990 Seminar Papers,* edited by D. Lull, 293–310. Atlanta: Scholars Press, 1990.

Freyne, Sean. *Galilee, Jesus, and the Gospels: Literary Approaches and Historical Investigations.* Philadelphia: Fortress Press, 1988.

——. "The Geography, Politics and Economics of Galilee and the Quest for the Historical Jesus." In *Studying the Historical Jesus,* edited by B. Chilton and C. A. Evans, 75–122. Leiden: E. J. Brill, 1994.

Goguel, Maurice. *Jesus the Nazarene: Myth or History?* New York: D. Appleton, 1926.

Gottstein, A. Goshen. "Hillel and Jesus: Are Comparisons Possible?" In *Hillel and Jesus: Comparative Studies of Two Major Religious Leaders,* edited by J. H. Charlesworth and L. L. Johns, 31–55. Minneapolis: Fortress Press, 1997.

Grundmann, Walter. *Die Geschichte Jesu Christi.* Berlin: Evangelische Verlagsanstalt, 1956.

——. *Jesus der Galiläer und das Judentum.* Leipzig: Georg Wigand, 1940.

Gunton, Colin. *The Actuality of Atonement: A Study of Metaphor, Rationality and Christian Tradition.* Grand Rapids, Mich.: Eerdmans, 1989.

Gustafson, James M. *Christ and the Moral Life.* New York: Harper & Row, 1968.

Hagner, Donald A. *The Jewish Reclamation of Jesus. An Analysis and Critique of the Modern Jewish Study of Jesus.* Grand Rapids, Mich.: Zondervan, 1984.

Hamerton-Kelly, Robert. *God the Father: Theology and Patriarchy in the Teaching of Jesus.* Philadelphia: Fortress Press, 1979.

Harnack, Adolf von. *The Sayings of Jesus.* Translated by J. R. Wilkinson. Crown Theological Library. London: Williams and Norgate/New York: G. P. Putnam's Sons, 1908.

——. *What Is Christianity?* Translated by Thomas Bailey Saunders. Library of Religion and Culture. New York: Harper and Bros., 1957.

Hauerwas, Stanley. *A Community of Character: Toward a Constructive Christian Social Ethic.* Notre Dame, Ind.: University of Notre Dame Press, 1981.

——. "From System to Story: An Alternative Pattern for Rationality in Ethics." In *Truthfulness and Tragedy*, edited by Stanley Hauerwas, 15–39. Notre Dame, Ind.: University of Notre Dame Press, 1977.

Hengel, Martin. *The Charismatic Leader and His Followers.* Translated by James Greig. Reprint. New York: Crossroad, 1981.

——. *Crucifixion.* Translated by John Bowden. Philadelphia: Fortress Press, 1977.

Hiers, Richard J. *Jesus and Ethics: Four Interpretations.* Philadelphia: Westminster Press, 1968.

——. "Pivotal Reactions to Eschatological Interpretations: Rudolf Bultmann and C. H. Dodd." In *The Kingdom of God in 20th Century Interpretation*, edited by W. Willis, 15–34. Peabody, Mass.: Hendrickson, 1987.

Hock, Ronald F. "Cynics." *ABD* 1 (1992): 1221–26.

Hollenbach, Paul. "The Historical Jesus Question in North America Today." *BTB* 19 (1989): 11–22.

Hooker, Morna D. *The Signs of a Prophet: The Prophetic Actions of Jesus.* Harrisburg, Pa.: Trinity Press International, 1997.

Horbury, W. "The Twelve and the Phylarchs." *NTS* 32 (1986): 503–27.

Horsley, Richard A. *Galilee. History, Politics, People.* Valley Forge, Pa.: Trinity Press International, 1995.

——. *Jesus and the Spiral of Violence: Popular Jewish Resistance in Roman Palestine.* San Francisco: Harper & Row, 1987.

——. "Jesus, Itinerant Cynic or Israelite Prophet?" In *Images of Jesus Today*, edited by J. H. Charlesworth and W. P. Weaver, 68–97. Faith and Scholarship Colloquies, 3. Valley Forge, Pa.: Trinity Press International, 1994.

——. "Q and Jesus: Assumptions, Approaches and Analysis." *Semeia* 55 (1991): 175–209.

Jeremias, Joachim. *Jesus' Promise to the Nations.* Translated by S. H. Hooke. Reprint. London: SCM Press, 1958; Philadelphia: Fortress Press, 1982.

——. *The Proclamation of Jesus. New Testament Theology: Vol 1.* Translated by John Bowden. New York: Scribner's, 1971.

——. *The Parables of Jesus.* Translated by S. H. Hooke. New York: Charles Scribner's Sons/London: SCM Press, 1963.

Jonge, Marinus de. *God's Final Envoy: Early Christology and Jesus' Own View of His Mission.* Grand Rapids, Mich.: Eerdmans, 1998.

Juel, Donald. *Messianic Exegesis: Christological Interpretation of the Old Testament in Early Christianity.* Philadelphia: Fortress Press, 1988.

Keck, Leander E. "The Accountable Self." In *Theology and Ethics in Paul and His Interpreters: Essays in Honor of Victor Paul Furnish,* edited by E. H. Lovering and J. L. Sumney, 1–13. Nashville: Abingdon Press, 1996.

———. "Bornkamm's *Jesus of Nazareth* Revisited." *JR* 49 (1969): 1–17.

———. *A Future for the Historical Jesus.* Nashville: Abingdon Press, 1971; Philadelphia: Fortress Press, 1981.

———. "Rethinking 'New Testament Ethics.'" *JBL* 115 (1996): 3–16.

Kee, Howard Clark. "The Function of Scriptural Quotations and Allusions in Mark 11–16." In *Jesus und Paulus: Festschrift für Werner Georg Kümmel zum 70 Geburtstag,* edited by E. E. Ellis and E. Grässer,165–88. Göttingen: Vandenhoeck und Ruprecht, 1975.

———. "Membership in the Covenant People at Qumran and in the Teaching of Jesus." In *Jesus and the Dead Sea Scrolls,* edited by J. H. Charlesworth, 104–22. New York: Doubleday, 1992.

Kittel, Gerhard. "The Jesus of History." In *Mysterium Christi: Christological Studies by British and German Theologians,* edited by G. K. A. Bell and A. Deissmann, 31–49. London: Longmans, Green and Co., 1930.

Klausner, Joseph. *Jesus of Nazareth: His Life, Times and Teaching.* Translated by Herbert Danby. London: George Allen and Unwin, 1928.

Kloppenborg, John S. *The Formation of Q: Trajectories in Ancient Wisdom Collections.* Philadelphia: Fortress Press, 1987.

Knox, John. *The Ethic of Jesus in the Teaching of the Church: Its Authenticity and its Relevance.* New York: Abingdon Press, 1961.

Koester, Helmut. *Ancient Christian Gospels: Their History and Development.* Philadelphia: Trinity Press International, 1990.

Kohler, Kaufmann. *The Origins of the Synagogue and the Church.* New York: Macmillan, 1929.

Kraus, Hans-Joachim. "Der lebendige Gott." *EvTheol* 27 (1967):169–200.

Kümmel, Werner G. *Promise and Fulfillment.* Translated by Dorothea M. Barton. SBT 23. Naperville, Ill.: Allenson, 1957. German ed., *Verheissung und Erfüllung.* Rev. ed. (Zurich: Zwingli-Verlag, 1956).

Kurz, William S., S.J. *Farewell Addresses in the New Testament.* Collegeville, Minn.: Liturgical Press, 1990.

Lapide, Pinchas. *Israelis, Jews, and Jesus.* Translated by Peter Heinegg. Garden City, N.Y.: Doubleday, 1979. German ed., *Ist das nicht Josephs Sohn? Jesus im heutigen Judentum* (Stuttgart: Calwer/Munich: Koesel, 1976).

———. *Der Rabbi von Nazaret: Wandlungen des jüdischen Jesusbildes.* Trier: Spee, 1974.

Lehman, Paul. *Ethics in a Christian Context.* New York: Harper & Row, 1963.

Lemcio, Eugene E. *The Past of Jesus in the Gospels.* SNTSMS 68. Cambridge: Cambridge University Press, 1991.

Lindeskog, Gösta. *Die Jesusfrage im neuzeitlichen Judentum: Ein Beitrag zur Geschichte der Leben-Jesu-Forschung.* AMNTSU 8. Uppsala: A.-B. Lundequistska/Leipzig: Alf. Lorenz, 1938.

Lowe, Malcolm. "From the Parable of the Vineyard to a Pre-Synoptic Source." *NTS* 28 (1982): 257–63.

Lührmann, Dieter. "Bornkamm's Response to Keck Revisited." In *The Future of Christology: Essays in Honor of Leander E. Keck,* edited by A. J. Malherbe and W. A. Meeks, 66–78. Minneapolis: Fortress Press, 1993.

Machovec, Milan. *A Marxist Looks at Jesus.* Philadelphia: Fortress Press, 1976. German ed., *Jesus für Atheisten* (Stuttgart: Kreuz, 1972).

Mack, Burton L. *The Lost Gospel: The Book of Q and Christian Origins.* San Francisco: HarperSanFrancisco, 1993.

Marcus, Joel. "The Old Testament and the Death of Jesus: The Role of Scripture in the Gospel Passion Narratives." In *The Death of Jesus in Early Christianity,* edited by J. T. Carroll and J. B. Green, 205–33. Peabody, Mass.: Hendrickson, 1995.

———. *The Way of the Lord: Christological Exegesis of the Old Testament in the Gospel of Mark.* Louisville, Ky.: Westminster John Knox, 1992.

Martyn, J. Louis. 1997. *Galatians.* Anchor Bible 33A. Garden City, N.Y.: Doubleday, 1997.

———. Introduction. In *Jewish Perspectives on Christianity,* edited by F. A. Rothschild, 21–41. New York: Continuum, 1996. Reprinted as "Leo Baeck's Reading of Paul" in *Theological Issues in the Letters of Paul,* by J. L. Martyn, 47–69 (Nashville: Abingdon Press/Edinburgh: T. & T. Clark, 1997).

Massey, Marilyn C. *Christ Unmasked: The Meaning of 'The Life of Jesus' in German Politics.* Chapel Hill: University of North Carolina Press, 1983.

Meier, John P. *A Marginal Jew: Rethinking the Historical Jesus.* 2 vols. Anchor Bible Reference Library. New York: Doubleday, 1991–1994.

———. "The Circle of the Twelve: Did It Exist during Jesus' Public Ministry?" *JBL* 116 (1997): 635–72.

Meyers, Eric M. "The Challenge of Hellenism for Early Judaism and Christianity." *BA* 55 (1992): 84–91.

Miller, Robert J. "The (A)Historicity of Jesus' Temple Demonstration: A Test Case in Methodology." In *Society of Biblical Literature 1991 Seminar Papers,* edited by E. H. Lovering, Jr., 235–52. Atlanta: Scholars Press, 1991.

Miller, Stuart S. "Sepphoris, the Well Remembered City." *BA* 55 (1992): 74–83.

Miskotte, Kornelis H. *When the Gods Are Silent.* Translated by John W. Doberstein. New York: Harper, 1967. German ed., *Wenn die Götter Schweigen* (Munich: Christian Kaiser, 1963). Dutch ed., 1956.

Moltmann, Jürgen. *The Crucified God: The Cross of Christ as the Foundation and Criticism of Christian Theology.* Translated by R. A. Wilson. New York: Harper & Row, 1974.

Moore, George Foote. "Christian Writers on Judaism." *HTR* 14 (1921): 197–254.

———. *Judaism in the First Centuries of the Christian Era: The Age of the Tannaim.* 3 vols. Cambridge, Mass.: Harvard University Press, 1954.

Neusner, Jacob. "Money-changers in the Temple: The Mishnah's Explanation." *NTS* 35 (1989): 287–90.

———. "The Use of the Later Rabbinic Evidence for the Study of First-Century Pharisaism." In *Approaches to Ancient Judaism: Theory and Practice,* edited by W. S. Green, 215–28. Brown Judaic Studies 1. Missoula, Mont.: Scholars Press, 1967.

Nickelsburg, George W. E. "Resurrection: Early Judaism and Christianity." *ABD* 5 (1992), 684–91.

———. "Son of Man." *ABD* 6 (1992): 137–50.

Otto, Rudolf. *The Kingdom of God and the Son of Man.* Translated by F. V. Filson and B. L. Woolf. London: Lutterworth, 1938.

Pals, Daniel L. *The Victorian "Lives" of Jesus.* San Antonio, Tex.: Trinity University Press, 1982.

Pelikan, Jaroslav. *Jesus through the Centuries: His Place in the History of Culture.* New Haven: Yale University Press, 1985.

Perrin, Norman. *Jesus and the Language of the Kingdom.* Philadelphia: Fortress Press, 1976.

———. *Rediscovering the Teaching of Jesus.* New York: Harper & Row, 1967.

Pilch, John J., and Bruce J. Malina, eds. *Biblical Social Values and Their Meaning: A Handbook.* Peabody, Mass.: Hendrickson, 1993.

Pixner, B. "Jesus and His Community: Between Essenes and Pharisees." In *Hillel and Jesus: Comparative Studies of Two Major Religious Leaders,* edited by J. H. Charlesworth and L. L. Johns, 193–224. Minneapolis: Fortress Press, 1997.

Powell, Mark Alan. *Jesus As a Figure in History: How Modern Historians View the Man from Galilee.* Louisville, Ky.: Westminster John Knox, 1998.

Pui-lan, Kwok. *Discovering the Bible in the Non-Biblical World.* Maryknoll, N.Y.: Orbis, 1995.

Rad, Gerhard von. *Old Testament Theology.* Translated by D. G. M. Stalker. 2 vols. New York: Harper & Row, 1962.

Reiser, Marius. *Jesus and Judgment: The Eschatological Proclamation in Its Jewish Context.* Translated by Linda M. Maloney. Minneapolis: Fortress Press, 1997. German ed., *Die Gerichtspredigt Jesu: Eine Untersuchung zur eschatologischen Verkündigung Jesu und ihrem frühjüdischen Hintergrund* (Münster: Aschendorff, 1990).

Renan, Ernst. *The Life of Jesus.* Modern Library. New York: Random House, 1927.

Riches, John. *Jesus and the Transformation of Judaism.* New York. Seabury, 1982.

Riesner, Rainer. "Jesus, the Primitive Community, and the Essene Quarter of Jerusalem." In *Jesus and the Dead Sea Scrolls,* edited by J. H. Charlesworth, 198–234. New York: Doubleday, 1992.

Rivkin, Ellis. *What Crucified Jesus?* Nashville: Abingdon Press, 1994.

Robinson, James M., ed. *The Nag Hammadi Library.* San Francisco: Harper & Row, 1977.

———. "The Real Jesus of the Sayings Gospel Q." *Princeton Seminary Bulletin* 18 (1997): 135–51.

Rothschild, F. A., ed. *Jewish Perspectives on Christianity.* New York: Continuum, 1996.

Ruppert, Lothar. *Jesus als der leidende Gerechte? Der Weg Jesu im Lichte eines alt- und zwischentestamentlichen Motivs.* SBS 59. Stuttgart: Katholisches Bibel Werk, 1972.

Saldarini, Anthony J. "Pharisees." *ABD* 5 (1992): 289–303.

Sanders, E. P. *The Historical Figure of Jesus.* London: Allen Lane/Penguin Books, 1993.

———. *Jesus and Judaism.* Philadelphia: Fortress Press, 1985.

Sanders, Jack T. "The Criterion of Coherence and the Randomness of Charisma: Poring through Some Aporias in the Jesus Tradition." *NTS* 44 (1998): 1–25.

Schweitzer, Albert. *The Mystery of the Kingdom of God.* Translated by Walter Lowrie. London: Adam and Charles Black, 1956. First English ed., 1914.

———. *The Quest of the Historical Jesus.* Translated by W. Montgomery. London: Adam and Charles Black, 1952. Second English ed., 1910.

Scott, Bernard. "Jesus as Sage: An Innovative Voice in Common Wisdom." In *The Sage in Israel and the Ancient Near East,* edited by J. G. Gammie and L. G. Perdue, 399–415. Winona Lake, Ind.: Eisenbrauns, 1990.

Seeley, David. "Jesus and the Cynics Revisited." *JBL* 116 (1997): 704–12.

———. "Jesus' Temple Act." *CBQ* 55 (1993): 263–83.

Segal, Alan F. "Conversion and Messianism: Outline for a New Approach." In *Messiah: Development in Early Judaism and Christianity,* edited by J. H. Charlesworth, 296–340. Minneapolis: Fortress Press, 1997.

Seitz, Christopher. *Word without End: The Old Testament as Abiding Theological Witness.* Grand Rapids, Mich.: Eerdmans, 1998.

Sievers, J. "Who Were the Pharisees?" In *Hillel and Jesus; Comparative Studies of Two Major Religious Leaders,* edited by J. H. Charlesworth and L. L. Johns, 137–55. Minneapolis: Fortress Press, 1997.

Smith, D. Moody. *John among the Gospels: The Relationship in Twentieth-Century Scholarship.* Minneapolis: Fortress Press, 1992.

———. "John 12:12ff. and the Question of John's Use of the Synoptics." *JBL* 82 (1963): 58–64.

Smith, Morton. *Jesus the Magician.* San Francisco: Harper & Row, 1981.

Smith, William Benjamin. *The Birth of the Gospel.* New York: Philosophical Library, 1957. German ed., *Der vorchristliche Jesus* (Jena: Eugen Diederichs, 1906).

Soulen, R. Kendall. *The God of Israel and Christian Theology.* Minneapolis: Fortress Press, 1996.

Strange, James F. "Sepphoris." *ABD* 5 (1992): 1090–93.

Strauss, David Friedrich. *The Christ of Faith and the Jesus of History.* Lives of Jesus Series. Translation and introduction by Leander E. Keck. Philadelphia: Fortress Press, 1972.

———. *The Life of Jesus Critically Examined.* Lives of Jesus Series. Translated by George Eliot. Reprint. Intro. by Peter C. Hodgson. Philadelphia: Fortress Press, 1972.

Talbert, Charles H., ed. *Reimarus: Fragments.* Translated by Ralph S. Fraser. Lives of Jesus Series. Philadelphia: Fortress Press, 1970.

Telford, William R. "Major Trends and Interpretive Issues in the Study of Jesus." In *Studying the Historical Jesus: Evaluations of the State of Current Research*, edited by B. Chilton and C. A. Evans, 33–74. New Testament Tools and Studies 19. Leiden: E. J. Brill, 1994.

Tuckett, Christopher M. "A Cynic Q?" *Bib* 70 (1989): 349–76.

———. *Q and the History of Early Christianity*. Edinburgh: T. & T. Clark, 1996.

Twelftree, Graham. *Jesus the Exorcist: A Contribution to the Study of the Historical Jesus*. Peabody, Mass.: Hendrickson/Tübingen: J. C. B. Mohr [Paul Siebeck], 1993.

Tyson, Joseph B. "Jesus and Herod Antipas." *JBL* 79 (1960): 239–46.

Vaage, Leif E. *Galilean Upstarts*. Valley Forge, Pa.: Trinity Press International, 1994.

Verheule, Anthonie F. *Wilhelm Bousset: Leben und Werk*. Amsterdam: Ton Bolland, 1973.

Vermes, Geza. *The Dead Sea Scrolls in English*. Fourth ed. New York: Penguin, 1995.

———. "Jesus the Jew." In *Jesus' Jewishness: Exploring the Place of Jesus within Early Judaism*, edited by J. H. Charlesworth, 108–22. New York: Crossroad, 1991.

———. *Jesus the Jew: A Historian's Reading of the Gospels*. New York: Macmillan, 1973.

———. *The Religion of Jesus the Jew*. Minneapolis: Fortress Press, 1993.

Watson, Francis. *Text and Truth: Redefining Biblical Theology*. Grand Rapids, Mich.: Eerdmans, 1997.

Westphal, Merold. *God, Guilt, and Death: An Existential Phenomenology of Religion*. Bloomington: Indiana University Press, 1984.

Whitelam, Keith W. "King and Kingship." *ABD* 4 (1992): 40–48.

Wilder, Amos. *Eschatology and Ethics in the Teachings of Jesus*. Rev. ed. New York: Harper and Bros., 1950.

Willis, Wendell. "The Discovery of the Eschatological Kingdom." In *The Kingdom of God in the 20th Century*, edited by W. Willis, 1–14. Peabody, Mass.: Hendrickson, 1987.

Windisch, Hans. *The Meaning of the Sermon on the Mount*. Translated by S. M. Gilmour. Philadelphia: Westminster Press, 1951. German ed., *Der Sinn der Bergpredigt*. Rev. ed. (Leipzig: J. C. Hinrichs, 1937).

Winter, Paul. *On the Trial of Jesus*. Studia Judaica 1. Berlin: de Gruyter, 1961.

Witherington, Ben, III. *The Christology of Jesus*. Minneapolis: Fortress Press, 1990.

———. *The Jesus Quest: The Third Search for the Jew of Nazareth*. San Francisco: InterVarsity Press, 1995.

———. *Jesus the Sage: The Pilgrimage of Wisdom*. Minneapolis: Fortress Press, 1994.

———. *Women in the Ministry of Jesus: A Study of Jesus' Attitudes to Women and Their Roles As Reflected in His Earthly Life*. Cambridge: Cambridge University Press, 1984.

Wright, David P. "Holiness (Old Testament)." *ABD* 3 (1992): 237–48.

Wright, N. T. *Jesus and the Victory of God: Christian Origins and the Question of God*. Vol. 2. Minneapolis: Fortress Press, 1996.

———. *The New Testament and the People of God: Christian Origins and the Question of God*. Vol.1. Minneapolis: Fortress Press, 1992.

———. *Who Was Jesus?* Grand Rapids, Mich.: Eerdmans, 1992.

Yoder, John Howard. *The Politics of Jesus*. Grand Rapids, Mich.: Eerdmans, 1972.

Index of Passages

Index of Modern Authors

Hiers, R., 71, 159
Hock, R., 48
Hodgson, P., 12
Hollenbach, P., 11
Holmes, J., 27
Hooker, M., 99, 123
Horbury, W., 51
Horsley, R., 36, 40, 44, 46, 53, 67

Jeremias, J., 58, 71
Johns, L., 33
Jonge, M. de, 90, 145
Juel, D., 141

Keck, L., 14, 29, 72, 79, 173
Kee, H., 53, 141
Kittel, G., 22
Klausner, J., 38, 39, 161–62
Kloppenborg, J., 67
Knox, J., 157
Koester, H., 14
Kohler, K., 39
Kraus, H.-J., 131
Kümmel, W., 71
Kurz, W., 130
Kwok, P., 58

Lapide, P., 32, 40
Lehman, P., 159
Lemcio, E., 3
Lewis, C. S., 162
Lindeskog, G., 32
Lowe, M., 100
Lührmann, D., 29

Machovec, M., 79, 102, 151
Mack, B., 67
Malina, B., 157
Marcus, J., 141
Martyn, J. L., 37, 62
Massey, M., 12
Meier, J., 6, 47, 50, 54, 74, 75, 82
Meyers, E., 56
Miller, R. J., 122
Miller, S., 56
Miskotte, K., 131, 132
Moltmann, J., 130, 139

Moore, G., 24, 25, 92, 128
Moule, C., 40

Neusner, J., 39, 123
Nickelsburg, G., 106, 129

Otto, R., 78, 136

Pals, D., 27
Pelikan, J., 2
Perrin, N., 14, 65, 69
Pilch, J., 157
Pixner, B., 35
Powell, M., 2

Reimarus, H., 23
Reiser, M., 169
Renan, E., 27, 36, 55
Riches, J., 70
Riesner, R., 35
Rivkin, E., 172
Robinson, J., 66, 67
Rothschild, F., 37
Ruppert, L., 141

Saldarini, A., 34
Sanders, E. P., 17, 31, 45, 49, 50, 70, 72,
    82, 87–88, 120, 122, 123, 154
Sanders, J., 17, 161
Schleiermacher, F., 12
Schweitzer, A., 5, 12, 13, 23, 28, 45, 46,
    66, 71, 89, 109, 111, 121, 159
Scott, B., 90
Segal, A., 34, 35
Seeley, D., 48, 122
Seitz, C., 133, 134
Sievers, J., 34
Smith, D. M., 120
Smith, M., 82
Smith, W., 13
Soulen, K., 133
Strange, J., 56
Strauss, D., 12

Talbert, C., 23, 72
Telford, W., 2
Thiering, B., 12